.NET Development for Java Programmers

PAUL GIBBONS

.NET Development for Java Programmers
Copyright ©2002 by Paul Gibbons

ISBN (pbk): 1-59059-038-4

Printed and bound in the United States of America 1 2 3 4 5 6 7 8 9 10

Trademarked names may appear in this book. Rather than use a trademark symbol with every occurrence of a trademarked name, we use the names only in an editorial fashion and to the benefit of the trademark owner, with no intention of infringement of the trademark.

Technical Reviewer: David Pollak
Editorial Directors: Dan Appleman, Peter Blackburn, Gary Cornell, Jason Gilmore, Simon Hayes, Karen Watterson, John Zukowski
Managing Editor: Grace Wong
Project Manager: Alexa Stuart
Copy Editor: Kim Wimpsett
Production Editor: Janet Vail
Composition: Impressions Book and Journal Services, Inc.
Indexer: Shane-Armstrong Information Services
Cover Designer: Kurt Krames
Manufacturing Manager: Tom Debolski
Marketing Manager: Stephanie Rodriguez

Distributed to the book trade in the United States by Springer-Verlag New York, Inc., 175 Fifth Avenue, New York, NY, 10010 and outside the United States by Springer-Verlag GmbH & Co. KG, Tiergartenstr. 17, 69112 Heidelberg, Germany.
In the United States, phone 1-800-SPRINGER, email orders@springer-ny.com, or visit http://www.springer-ny.com.
Outside the United States, fax +49 6221 345229, email orders@springer.de, or visit http://www.springer.de.

For information on translations, please contact Apress directly at 2560 9th Street, Suite 219, Berkeley, CA 94710.Phone 510-549-5930, fax: 510-549-5939, email info@apress.com, or visit http://www.apress.com.

The information in this book is distributed on an "as is" basis, without warranty. Although every precaution has been taken in the preparation of this work, neither the author nor Apress shall have any liability to any person or entity with respect to any loss or damage caused or alleged to be caused directly or indirectly by the information contained in this work.

The source code for this book is available to readers at http://www.apress.com in the Downloads section. You will need to answer questions pertaining to this book in order to successfully download the code.

To my family, for all the things you continue to teach me.

Contents at a Glance

Contents

Foreword

REALISTICALLY SPEAKING, MOST enterprise development in the near future will use either .NET or J2EE. This book tells Java programmers what they need to understand about C# and the .NET platform to get started. Chapters give about the same level of detail as in *Core Java*—that is, they give you enough information to start writing real code for real applications. (Of course, just as with *Core Java*, for full details of the extraordinary power of the .NET APIs, you will need to turn to books that cover each topic in full depth. I obviously hope you will turn to the ones Apress publishes!)

That having been said, this book seemed to supply exactly what I needed now. For example, how do servlets and JSP map to their equivalents in ASP.NET? How do you develop for databases via ADO.NET if you are used to JDBC? How do you build client-side applications using Windows Forms instead of Swing? What are the Message-Oriented Middleware features that one would expect to be hosted by the EJB application server? What about threading issues? (By the way, double-checked locking for the singleton pattern works fine in .NET.) These topics (and more) are all in this book, presented in a concise but thorough fashion. In addition, the XML basis of much of .NET (which is much more fundamental in .NET than it is in Java) is also covered succinctly but in enough detail so that I could learn what I needed to know.

Of course, the book starts with a brief introduction to C#, the language in which most of .NET is written. C# is obviously close enough to Java so that an experienced Java programmer can learn the C# language in a few hours; however, C# is sufficiently different from Java to need some coverage, and Gibbons spends the right amount of time doing this. That is, he focuses on the differences (such as the existence of value types, operator overloading, and events and delegates) but not the obvious similarities. (Java programmers hardly need a course in how to design classes to use a single-inheritance, multiple-interface language.)

It is ironic in a way: In late 1995 when Cay Horstmann and I sat down to write the first edition of *Core Java*, Java was a rather nice, small language, with lots of potential. The APIs supplied were quite small, and even simple database connectivity was nonexistent. Over the years, the Java APIs have grown to the point that the fifth edition of *Core Java* has more than quadrupled in size to two very fat volumes. And for Java developers, the Enterprise APIs rather than client-side Java have become all-important. But where does that leave the Java language? Well, as we said way back in 1996, it was difficult for designers of a language as acclaimed as Java to admit that maybe, just maybe, they had made some mistakes that needed fixing.

Thus, the famous quote about "standing on the shoulders of giants" applies here: As good as Anders Hejlsberg (designer of Turbo Pascal and Delphi, by the way) and Scott Wiltamuth are, when they sat down to design the C# language, they obviously knew about both the good and bad points of the Java *language* (forget the APIs for the moment). By building on the six years of experience of the good and the bad of the Java language, they were able to create a language that is *today* a better language for software development. For example, having events and properties as first class parts of the language is a definite plus! Having value types that automatically convert to object types when you need to stick them in a data structure is great—heck, having the ability to create value types is also a big plus. Building XML comments into the language was wonderful. (Java's HTML comments were a great improvement on previous attempts to write self-documenting code, but XML is so much richer.)

In sum, I may be naïve, but I believe that competition is good, and we can hope that the competition from C# will force improvements to the Java language until it can reclaim its crown and then C# will need to get better and so on and so forth! But, in the end, languages do not matter; getting the job done does. And whether you need to move from a Java-based enterprise environment to a .NET-based one, or you just want to add another line to your résumé in these hard times, *.NET Development for Java Programmers* is the book that will do the job for you!

—Gary Cornell
Publisher, Apress
Co-author, *Core Java*

About the Author

PAUL GIBBONS WORKS AS A consultant for Volt Technical Resources. He jumped into computer science early on, entering his first programs on paper tape while in high school. Paul earned his bachelor's of science degree in data processing from Loughborough University in England. In more than 25 years of software development he has worked with many languages on many different platforms. Paul has worked at both large corporations (AT&T, Amazon.com, and Microsoft) and several small startups. He enjoys developing distributed systems using object-oriented techniques. Originally from Yorkshire, England, Paul has lived in the United States for the past 15 years and currently resides in the Seattle area with his wife and three children.

About the Technical Reviewer

 DAVID POLLAK IS CEO OF Govedo, a Java and .NET tools vendor. David graduated cum laude from Boston University School of Law. You may be asking what a CEO lawyer thinks he is doing as technical editor of a .NET book. David has written nearly a dozen commercial shrink-wrapped applications including the best-selling Mesa spreadsheet for NextStep and OS/2. He also wrote the world's fastest spreadsheet, Integer, in Java. David enjoys cooking for his wife, coding with cats on his lap, rescuing failing technology projects, and driving way too fast. He lives in San Francisco, and he does not miss New England, where he grew up, too much.

Acknowledgments

First and foremost I must say thank you to my wife Madeleine, for encouraging and helping me when I needed it most. I could not have finished this book without you. Thanks also to my children Anna, Megan, and John. You may be too young to read this book, but your unfailing confidence in my ability to write it was a source of inspiration at the most frustrating moments.

I owe a huge debt of gratitude to the fantastic team at Apress. Specifically, thanks to Gary Cornell for getting me started and Alexa Stuart for keeping everything running smoothly no matter what curve balls were pitched her way. Thanks also to my editors David Pollak, Kim Wimpsett, and Janet Vail for keeping me honest and turning my words into what you see before you. And thanks to all the other great folks I did not deal with directly.

Thanks also to my friends Karen Klamm, Barry and Juanita Hansen, and Bryan Sera who helped out on a moment's notice when I needed their talents most.

Last, but not least, thanks to the .NET, C#, and Java development teams without whom I would have had nothing to write about in the first place!

Introduction

"C# IS JUST MICROSOFT'S NEW JAVA. They changed the name of Visual J++ because they lost the lawsuit with Sun." I heard these words more and more often as 2000 became 2001. You might think that by living in a town next to Redmond, the facts would be less diluted by the time they reached me. However, working in a heavily Java and Unix environment, the views I heard originated far from Redmond.

The twists and turns of life in a small dot-com company gave me occasion to take a closer look at Microsoft's new baby, and the more I looked, the more interested I became.

Being a Java and C++ programmer, I was naturally drawn to the new C# language. I soon found out it is not just a renamed Visual J++. That said, much of what I learned moving from C++ to Java was also relevant to this new language.

As I continued my investigations I noticed that many other pieces of the .NET Framework have counterparts in Java 2 Enterprise Edition (J2EE). The analogies are not as straightforward as they are between the Java and C# languages, but leveraging the knowledge I already had made it easier to pick up this new platform.

It occurred to me that others would be undertaking the same journey I was. So much of what you already know from Java gives you a frame of reference for this new world. So here they are—my trail notes of sorts for the journey you are about to undertake.

Who Should Read This Book

This book is for experienced Java programmers. I draw on your existing knowledge to help you understand the elements of C# and the .NET platform. The more Java you know, the better.

I assume you are familiar with the core Java language. If an aspect of C# is the same as in Java, I will say so and leave it at that, relying on your knowledge of Java to cover that aspect of the language. Our time will be spent on the differences.

I do not expect you to know C++, though. Only Java knowledge is assumed. However, where an analogy to C++ will help readers who are familiar with that language, I will use it. But I will not rely on that analogy alone to explain the concept.

I also assume you are familiar with the J2EE platform. I do not expect a thorough knowledge of all the components, but you should be familiar with the more commonly used ones, such as Java Server Pages (JSP) and Java Database Connectivity (JDBC).

What You Will Need

Microsoft .NET development is only fully supported on Windows 2000 and Windows XP at the time of writing. You can develop on Windows NT 4, but certain features, notably ASP.NET, are not supported. Your programs will run on Windows 98 and Windows ME, but the Software Development Kit (SDK) will not install there.

The Microsoft .NET SDK is the minimum needed to run the examples in this book or develop your own programs. The Microsoft Visual Studio .NET Integrated Development Environment (IDE) is a far more productive option that I will assume you have available when I walk you through the examples. For professional software development, you will rely on the IDE far more heavily than you might in the Java world, especially for non–user interface (non-UI) development. You want at least the Professional Edition, as the Standard Edition has far too many limitations.

ASP.NET WebForms and Web Services (covered in Chapter 5, "Building Web Sites with ASP.NET," and Chapter 8, "Understanding Networking," respectively) require the Internet Information Services (IIS) component be present in your Windows installation. You can add this from the Control Panel if it is not already present. Go to Start ➤ Control Panel ➤ Add or Remove Programs. When this comes up, click the Add/Remove Windows Components button, which will enable you to see which optional components you have installed. You can then install IIS and any other components you need.

 **CAUTION** *Add IIS to your system before installing the .NET Framework SDK or Visual Studio .NET. If you do not, ASP.NET will not be installed. Running repair from the Control Panel will not suffice; you will need to uninstall and then reinstall the .NET Framework SDK.*

The ADO.NET examples in Chapter 6, "Exploring ADO.NET," require SQL Server or Microsoft Desktop Engine (MSDE). You can modify them to use another supported database such as MS Access, but you will have to do that yourself. MSDE is packaged with both the .NET Framework SDK and Visual Studio .NET.

The Message Queuing (also known as MSMQ) examples in Chapter 12, "Communicating via Message Queuing," require that the message-queuing components of the operating system be installed. As with IIS, you can add these from the Control Panel if they are not already present. An Active Directory server is not required because the examples in this book use only private queues.

You must have Internet Explorer 6 (IE 6) or higher for examples involving a Web browser. Earlier versions of IE or other browsers may work in some cases, but you are on your own if you use them. The .NET SDK and Visual Studio .NET both require IE 6, so this is probably a moot point.

Finally, all the source code for the examples in this book is available at `www.apress.com` in the Downloads section.

Introducing C#

C# IS NOT THE ONLY LANGUAGE available for the .NET platform. It is, however, the natural choice for programmers moving from Java. The first Java program you wrote probably resembled the classic HelloWorld program even if it was not actually called HelloWorld.java. In this chapter you will develop HelloWorld in C#—first using only the tools available in the .NET Framework Software Development Kit (SDK) and then once again using Visual Studio .NET. Although HelloWorld.cs is not exactly earth shattering, it will convince you that C# is not Java and provides an opportunity to familiarize yourself with the tools you will use to develop C# programs.

Creating HelloWorld in C# Using the SDK Tools

You will first create the HelloWorld program without using Visual Studio .NET. Open Notepad or your favorite trusty editor and enter the following program:

```
public class HelloWorld
{
    public static void Main( string[] args )
    {
        System.Console.WriteLine("Hello world from C#" );
    }
}
```

This looks pretty familiar, doesn't it? `System.Console.WriteLine` replaces `System.out.println`, `Main` replaces `main`, and `string` replaces `String`, but otherwise it could be Java.

The standard suffix for C# source files is .cs, so save the program you just entered as HelloWorld.cs.

Before you can compile the program, you must set your path to include the .NET Framework tools. The .NET Framework is typically installed into `C:\Windows\Microsoft.NET\Framework\v1.0.3705` where 3705 is the build number for the RTM release of Version 1 (it was 2204 for Beta 1 and 2914 for Beta 2). Open a command window by selecting Start ➢ All Programs ➢ Accessories ➢ Command Prompt. Now add this location to your PATH as follows:

```
path %SystemRoot%\Microsoft.NET\Framework\v1.0.3705\;%PATH%
```

Use the `cd` command to navigate to the directory where you saved
HelloWorld.cs and then compile it by entering this:

```
csc HelloWorld.cs
```

Unless you mistyped something, it should have compiled cleanly and you
can now run it by entering:

```
.\HelloWorld
```

You should see the familiar message shown in Figure 1-1.

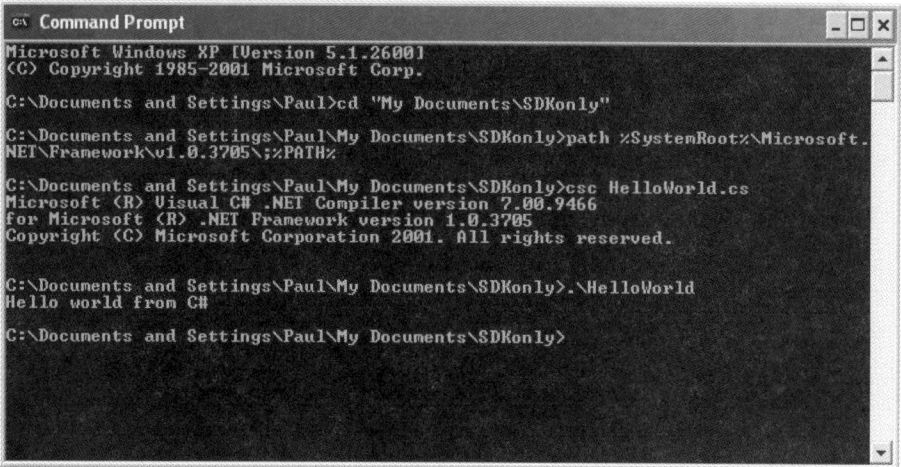

Figure 1-1. The output from HelloWorld

Hold on a minute! Now you have a significant difference from Java. Take
a look at the contents of the directory where you built this program. Yes, you
compiled the code to an executable and ran it just like any other executable.
There is nothing that corresponds to Java's .class file, and C# programs do not
require you to run a separate launcher program to invoke them.

Creating HelloWorld in C# Using Visual Studio .NET

Now let's create the HelloWorld program the way you would in the real world—using the IDE, Visual Studio .NET.

If you do not already have a shortcut to Visual Studio .NET set up, you can run it from Start ➤ All Programs ➤ Microsoft Visual Studio .NET ➤ Microsoft Visual Studio .NET.

When Visual Studio .NET comes up, you will see the Start page. If this is the first time you have run Visual Studio .NET, it will default to the My Profile tab, as shown in Figure 1-2.

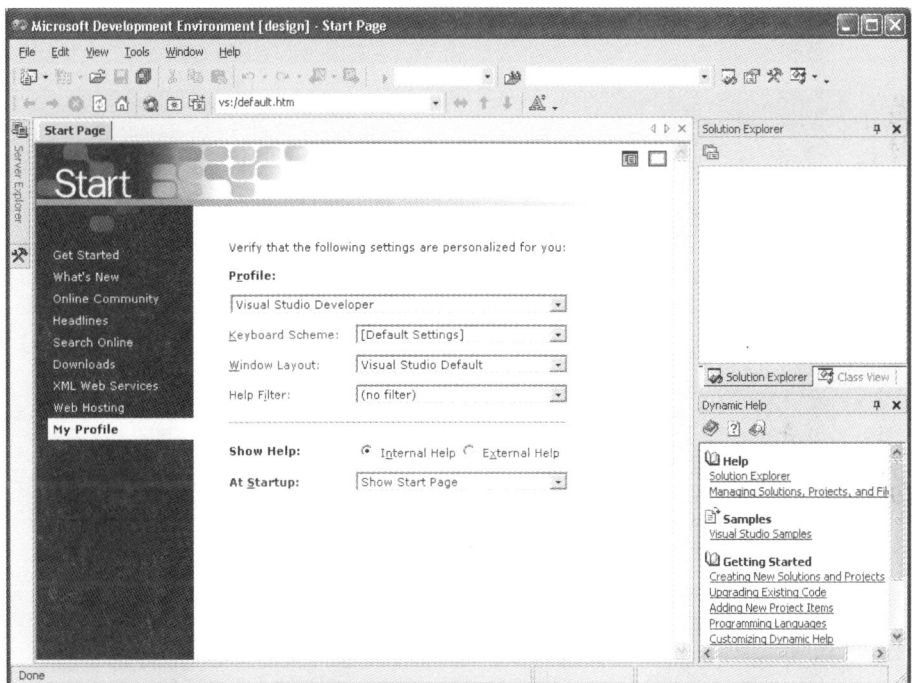

Figure 1-2. Visual Studio .NET as it opens the first time

This tab allows you to customize some of the behavior of the Integrated Development Environment (IDE). For now leave it set to the default values and select the Get Started tab. This will be the default tab when you open Visual Studio .NET on future occasions (see Figure 1-3).

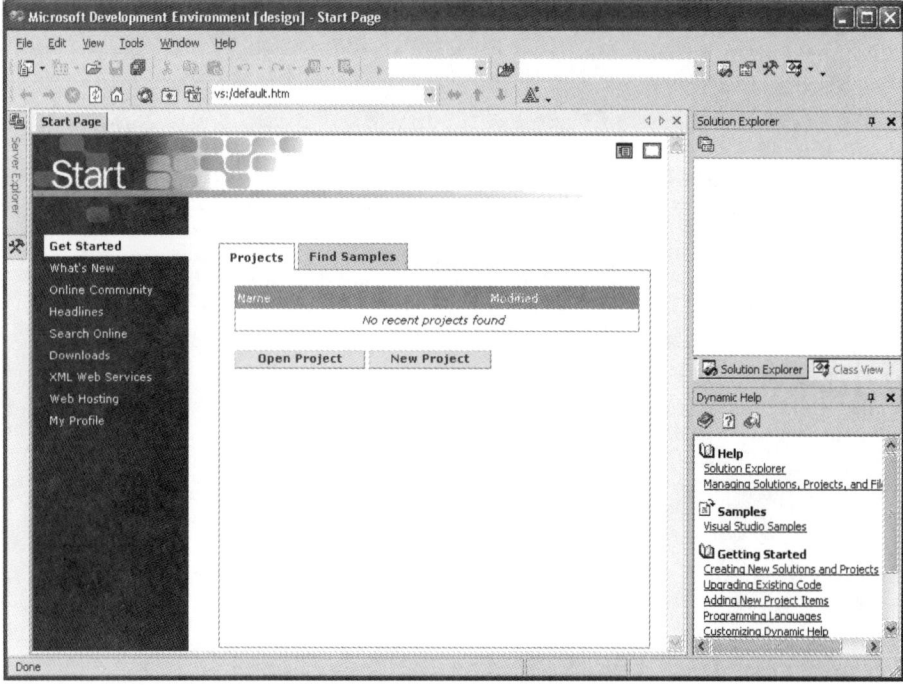

Figure 1-3. The Get Started tab of the Visual Studio .NET Start page

Your recently used projects will be listed here for easy access. Click the New Project button. Next select Console Application from Visual C# Projects and change the name from the default suggestion of ConsoleApplication1 to **HelloWorld,** as shown in Figure 1-4. Then click OK.

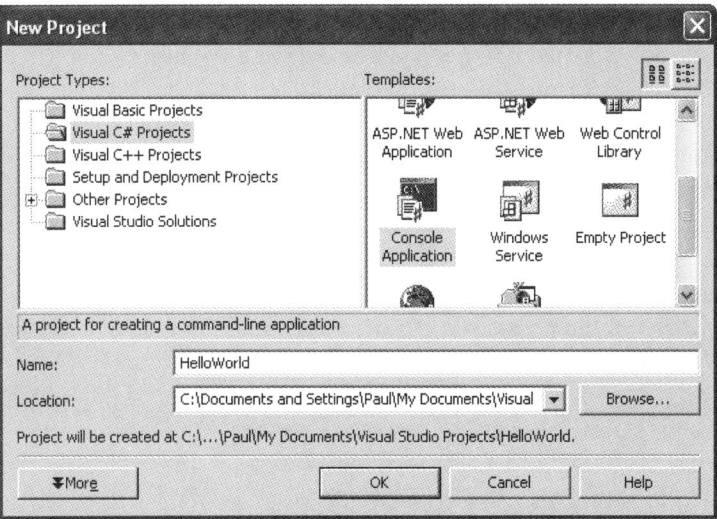

Figure 1-4. Creating a project in Visual Studio .NET

Visual Studio .NET will generate the following code in HelloWorld.cs:

```csharp
using System;

namespace HelloWorld
{
    /// <summary>
    /// Summary description for Class1.
    /// </summary>
    class Class1
    {
        static void Main(string[] args)
        {
            //
            // TODO: Add code to start application here
            //
        }
    }
}
```

This definitely is not Java! Having said that, there are Java equivalents for each of the new things you see in this program.

Anyone with a C++ background will recognize using System as importing names from a namespace and namespace HelloWorld as introducing a namespace. So think of a namespace as analogous to a package, and you can relate these statements to import System.* and package HelloWorld, respectively.

The other differences are the triple slash comments with XML in them. These are C# *doc comments,* which are used to document the source code in a similar manner to Javadoc comments. Instead of extending /* . . . */ into /** . . . */ with @ keywords, the C# designers chose to extend // into /// and use XML keywords.

Back to the task at hand—let's finish writing the program. Replace the TODO comment lines with this:

```
System.Console.WriteLine( "Hello world from C#" );
```

Now compile the program by selecting Build ➢ Build HelloWorld and then run it by selecting Debug ➢ Start. A command window briefly displays the message and then exits. If you want a chance to see the contents of the command window, right-click the closing curly brace (}) of the Main method and select Insert Breakpoint from the context menu, as shown in Figure 1-5.

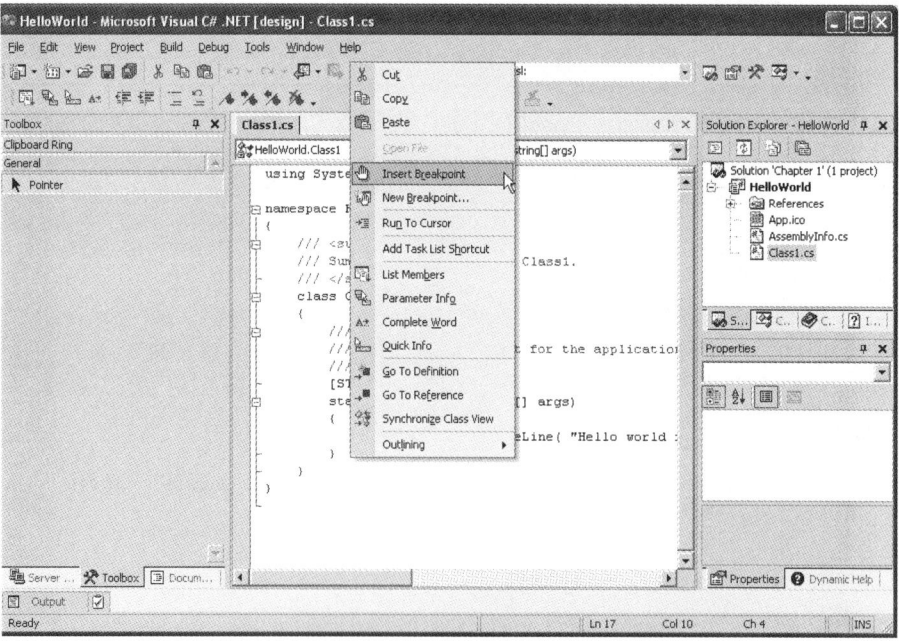

Figure 1-5. Setting a breakpoint so you can see the output

This time when you run the application execution will stop and enable you to view the output. Select Debug ➤ Continue to resume execution.

Take a look at the Solution Explorer window (if you cannot find it, select View ➤ Solution Explorer). In addition to the Class1.cs file you just edited, there is another .cs file listed, AssemblyInfo.cs. Double-click it so that the source is displayed (see Listing 1-1 for the first part of the file).

Listing 1-1. Part of the Assembly.cs File Created by Visual Studio .NET

```
using System.Reflection;
using System.Runtime.CompilerServices;

//
// General Information about an assembly is controlled through the following
// set of attributes. Change these attribute values to modify the information
// associated with an assembly.
//
[assembly: AssemblyTitle("")]
[assembly: AssemblyDescription("")]
[assembly: AssemblyConfiguration("")]
[assembly: AssemblyCompany("")]
[assembly: AssemblyProduct("")]
[assembly: AssemblyCopyright("")]
[assembly: AssemblyTrademark("")]
[assembly: AssemblyCulture("")]

//
// Version information for an assembly consists of the following four values:
//
//      Major Version
//      Minor Version
//      Build Number
//      Revision
//
// You can specify all the values or default the Revision and Build Numbers
// by using the '*' as shown below:

[assembly: AssemblyVersion("1.0.*")]
```

The square brackets ([ ]) enclose attributes that in this case provide information about an *assembly*. You could consider the information specified in Assembly.cs analogous to that placed in the manifest of a .jar file, but attributes are not limited to providing data like this. The simple addition of an attribute can turn your class into a Web Service or a COM object, freeing you from writing a lot of stock plumbing code. Attributes are an important part of .NET programming, as you will learn in later chapters.

So what is an assembly? The HelloWorld.exe files you created from the command line and through Visual Studio .NET are both assemblies. It is reasonable to consider an assembly as analogous to a .jar file, but an assembly is not required to be a self-contained .exe or .dll file. An assembly may consist of multiple files that should be thought of as a single unit.

Summary

In this chapter you learned how to compile and run your C# programs using both the command line and Visual Studio .NET. You also know that this is not just Java with a new library. Chapter 2, "Introducing the C# Language," takes things to the next level with a thorough comparison of Java and C#. Chapter 3, "Introducing the .NET Platform," introduces the .NET Framework and its virtual machine, the Common Language Runtime (CLR). You should read these to ensure you understand the basic differences from Java before moving on to the later chapters, which examine specific technologies.

Let's get started, shall we?

Introducing the C# Language

THIS CHAPTER EXAMINES THE C# language in detail, focusing on where it differs from Java.

The History of Java and C#

In March of 1995, Sun released an alpha version of Java on the Internet. That release was a huge hit with software developers, especially C++ developers. In October 1996, Microsoft released Visual J++, their Java development environment. The Visual J++ compiler and virtual machine included Windows-specific enhancements. A year later, in October 1997, Sun sued Microsoft over those enhancements. Although the enhancements made programming Java on Windows easier, Java programs that used those enhancements were not portable to other platforms.

In March 1998, a Microsoft team led by Anders Hejlsberg of Turbo Pascal and Delphi fame, released Windows Foundation Classes (WFC). This Java class library, which further facilitated Windows development, was not portable either. By December, Sun released Java 2, but under the shadow of Sun's lawsuit, Microsoft's J++ remained frozen at Java 1.1.4. The two companies eventually settled the lawsuit, and Microsoft issued a patch to the J++ compiler, which disabled the Windows-specific enhancements by default.

In June of 2000, Microsoft announced .NET and the new C# language. The chief designer of this new language was none other than Anders Hejlsberg. Hejlsberg's team had created a language that leveraged experience with both Java and C++ to give programmers the strengths of both languages.

Microsoft announced in July 2001 that it would not ship its Java Virtual Machine (JVM) as part of the upcoming Windows XP operating system. Because Microsoft had submitted the .NET runtime and the C# language for standardization, a number of independent vendors initiated efforts to create .NET runtime environments for non-Windows platforms.

Microsoft finally released version 1 of the .NET platform, including C#, in January 2002.

Understanding Simple Types

What Java terms *primitive types* are known as *simple types* in C#. On the surface, the C# simple types look like the basic building blocks from Java, but there are subtle differences; the names int, bool, and so on are aliases for the classes System.Int32, System.Boolean, and so forth. C# cannot exist without a class library to provide implementations of the simple types. These simple types provide many utility methods directly, avoiding the need for the utility classes you know from Java.

Table 2-1 details each of the simple types, including the Java equivalent where applicable.

Table 2-1. C# Simple Types

C# TYPE	DESCRIPTION	ALIAS OF	JAVA EQUIVALENT
sbyte	8-bit signed integer	System.SByte	byte
byte	8-bit unsigned integer	System.Byte	
short	16-bit signed integer	System.Int16	short
ushort	16-bit unsigned integer	System.UInt16	
int	32-bit signed integer	System.Int32	int
uint	32-bit unsigned integer	System.UInt32	
long	64-bit signed integer	System.Int64	long
ulong	64-bit unsigned integer	System.UInt64	
char	16-bit Unicode character	System.Char	char
float	32-bit IEEE 754 floating point	System.Single	float
double	64-bit IEEE 754 floating point	System.Double	double
bool	Boolean true or false	System.Boolean	boolean
decimal	Real accurate to 28 decimal places	System.Decimal	

The simple types are all examples of C# value types. They are called *value types* because when you pass an instance of a value type, you pass the value of the object instead of reference to it. Those familiar with Common Object Request

Broker Architecture (CORBA) can draw parallels to CORBA's structs, which behave similarly.

Value types are the same as classes except you introduce value types by the keyword `struct` instead of the keyword `class`. For example, by default this class:

```
public class fred
{
    int a;
}
```

is passed by reference, whereas this value type:

```
public struct barney
{
    int b;
}
```

is passed by value.

Just because `string` is a built-in alias for `System.String`, do not confuse it with the simple types. `System.String` is a class, not a struct. As in Java, you pass it by reference, not by value.

The Integer Types

The unsigned versions of the integer types can be a welcome sight to those who have programmed around their absence in Java. A 16-bit integer can represent 65,536 different values. In Java it always represents the values –32,768 to +32,767. This is the signed range of a 16-bit integer. In many languages it also represents 0 to +65,535, which is termed an *unsigned integer*. C# supports both the signed and the unsigned ranges of 8-bit, 32-bit, and 64-bit integers, too.

Like Java, you may not cast an integer to a `bool` (`boolean` in Java) in C#. If `i` is an integer variable, an expression such as the following will result in a compilation error:

```
boolean nonzero = i;
```

To perform this conversion, use an expression like this one:

```
bool nonzero = ( i != 0 );
```

The decimal *Type*

The decimal type has greater precision than the floating-point types but a smaller range. It is intended primarily for financial calculations.

Boxing

In Java, you must place primitive types in one of the wrapper classes (for example, Integer) before you can use them as Objects. This allows the primitive types to be passed to a method such as those found in the collection classes. For example:

```
int i = 42;
Object intObj = new Integer( i );
foo.methodThatTakesAnObject( intObj );
```

In C# this operation is called *boxing* and is performed implicitly without exposing the programmer to wrapper classes. In fact, the wrapper class is not visible or accessible to the programmer:

```
int i = 42;
object intObj = i;
foo.methodThatTakesAnObject( intObj );
```

A simple cast will not work:

```
int i = 42;
foo.methodThatTakesAnObject( (object)i ); // this won't compile
```

Wrapper classes are not explicitly referenced, so remember that a copy of the value is taken and any changes to the original variable will not affect the boxed value. For example:

```
int i = 42;
object o = i;
i = 43;
System.Console.WriteLine("o = {0}", o ); // writes "o = 42"
```

Boxing occurs for all value-type objects, not just simple types.

Introducing Variable Scope

Most languages that trace their roots to C allow you to reuse variable names in a nested block like so:

```
public void amethod()
{
    int i = 3;
    . . .
    if ( . . . )
    {
        int i = 5;
        . . .
    }
}
```

The value of this feature in modern programs is questionable as it makes bugs more likely, particularly during the maintenance phase of a program's life. C# does not allow this construct, and using the preceding code in C# will result in a compilation error.

Exploring Arrays

Using arrays in C# holds few surprises for the Java programmer. In C#, array parameters have a tighter syntax, and multidimensional arrays will simplify using rectangular arrays.

Specifying Array Parameters

You program C# arrays in a manner similar to Java. One difference is in declaring arrays and specifying array parameters.

In Java you have the option to declare a method that takes an array using either this:

```
public void func( String parms[] )
```

or this:

```
public void func( String[] parms )
```

In C# you must always use the form where you place the brackets next to the type, both when you declare parameters or variables:

```
public void func( string[] parms )
{
    int[] i = new int[5];
}
```

Creating Multidimensional Arrays

True multidimensional arrays are a welcome sight in C#. The patterns you are familiar with in Java will work, but using C# will save you time. To create a two-dimensional array in Java, you allocate one dimension and then each row of the second. The following example shows how to create a 10x15 array of integers in Java:

```
int a[][] = new int[15][];
for ( int i = 0; i < 15; i++ )
{
    a[i] = new int[10];
}
```

The same code in C# looks like this:

```
int[,] i = new int[10,15];
```

This code only works if the array is rectangular, however. Should the lengths of any dimension vary, allocate the dimensions individually as you would in Java. For example:

```
int a[][] = new int[100][];
for ( int i = 0; i < 100; i++ )
{
    a[i] = new int[ i+1 ];
}
```

Note that using this:

```
myarray[4][3]
```

is different from using this:

```
myarray[4,3]
```

In other words, you cannot interchange the syntax. Fortunately, such errors are detected at compile time.

Understanding Statements and Expressions

Most of the statements, operators, and expression rules you know from Java behave exactly the same way in C#. However, C# introduces a number of new statements and operators, and it modifies the behavior of some familiar ones. There are also differences in how some expressions behave. The following sections describe where C# differs from Java.

Using the switch Statement

At first glance, the switch statements for Java and C# appear to be identical. To a large extent this is true, but you cannot fall through from one case to the next by omitting the break statement. Should you forget to type in a break statement, as in the following example, your code will not compile:

```
switch( j )
{
    case 1:
        x = "one";
        break;
    case 2:
        x = "two";
    case 3:
        x = "three";
        break;
}
```

If you forget the break, you will welcome this compile-time feature. You could waste hours trying to catch a bug like this.

But what if you actually want to fall through? You can fall through by explicitly stating the case statement to continue at. Do this using a special form of the goto statement:

```
switch ( i )
{
    case -1:
        negative = true;
        break;
    case 0:
        negative = true;
        goto case 1;
    case 1:
        positive = true;
        break;
}
```

Because you are explicitly specifying the case to continue at, there is no need to arrange the case statements in an unnatural order to achieve the desired result. You may also fall through to a single case from several others instead of just one.

When targeting multiple cases at the same code, goto statements aren't needed. For example:

```
switch ( i )
{
    case 1:
    case 2:
    case 3:
        x = "chicken";
        break;
    case 4:
    case 5:
        x = "turkey";
        break;
}
```

The C# designers made this feature friendly to both usage patterns. They preserved the ability to fall through for those who want it (typically in performance-critical code) and saved many hours of debugging for the majority of programmers.

Finally, the default case does not need to come last in C#. For instance, it is legal to write the following:

```
switch ( i )
{
    case 2:
```

```
        x = "pancakes";
        break;
    default:
        x = "bacon and eggs";
        break;
    case 1:
        x = "omelet";
        break;
}
```

Using the goto Statement

The goto statement transfers control to the statement denoted by its label:

```
Int[] a = new int[10];
int i = 0;
again: a[i] = i;
i++;
if ( i < 10 )
{
    goto again;
}
```

The label applies to a statement and not a block as it does with Java's break and continue.

The break and continue statements in C# do not have forms that take labels. You use these forms of break and continue to jump out of nested loops in Java. Use a goto statement to achieve the same effect in C#.

NOTE   *The previous section covered the special form of* goto *used in a* switch *statement.*

Using the foreach Statement

To iterate over a collection in Java, a typical example would be the following:

```
Iterator iter = myCollection.iterator();
while ( iter.hasNext() )
{
    MyElement e = (MyElement)iter.next();
    // do something with e here
}
```

In C#, the foreach statement provides a neat shortcut for iterating over a collection and similar constructs. The equivalent of the preceding example is this:

```
foreach ( MyElement e in myCollection )
{
    // do something with e here
}
```

You can iterate any object of a class that implements the IEnumerable interface using foreach. Naturally, many of the collection classes in the System.Collections namespace satisfy this requirement. IEnumerable is not limited to classes in the System.Collections namespace. For instance, the System.Array class implements IEnumerable, allowing foreach to be used with any array you create. For example:

```
string[] sa = new string[3] { "one", "two", "three" };
foreach ( string s in sa )
{
    System.Console.WriteLine( s );
}
```

Many classes throughout the library implement IEnumerable, allowing them to be iterated in this fashion. The one caveat is that modifying the underlying collection while iterating is not permitted and results in an exception.

Using the lock Statement

The lock statement closely resembles Java's synchronized statement. It obtains an object's monitor lock, executes either the statement or the block it refers to, and then releases the lock. For example:

```
lock ( obj ) obj.count++;
```

In Java, you cannot obtain the monitor lock of a primitive type, and, similarly in C#, you cannot obtain the monitor lock of a value type.

Using the using Statement

The using statement has no counterpart in Java. It allows you to mimic the common C++ practice of using stack variables to manage object lifetimes.

You employ the using statement, as shown in Listing 2-1.

Listing 2-1. The using *Statement*

```
using System;
using System.IO;
using System.Net.Sockets;

namespace UsingExample
{
    /// <summary>
    /// Invokes the HTTP service on the local machine the hard way
    /// </summary>
    class UsingExample
    {
        static void Main(string[] args)
        {
            using ( TcpClient c = new TcpClient( "localhost", 80 ) )
            {
                using( StreamReader rdr = new StreamReader( c.GetStream() ) )
                {
                    using( StreamWriter wtr
                                        = new StreamWriter( c.GetStream() ) )
                    {
                        wtr.WriteLine( @"GET /" );
                        wtr.Flush();
                        System.Console.WriteLine( rdr.ReadToEnd() );
                    }
                }
            }
        }
    }
}
```

At the start of the block, the objects defined in parentheses are instantiated. The body of the block is then executed. At the end of the block, the Dispose method of each of the objects allocated at the beginning is called as if it were part of a finally block. This ensures that cleanup occurs even if an exception is thrown.

Classes must implement IDisposable to be managed by the using statement. IDisposable contains only one method, Dispose, which is used much as you use

Window.dispose in Java to release precious resources without waiting for garbage collection to run.

CAUTION   *Do not confuse the* using *statement with the* using *directive.*

Using the is Operator

The C# is operator behaves like Java's instanceof operator. It enables you to test whether an object is an instance or a descendant of a given Type.

Using the as Operator

When you cast an object to a type, and that object is not compatible with the desired type, you will generate an exception. This is not always convenient. When you expect a significant number of casts to fail, it is often more desirable to get a null reference to indicate the incompatibility than to handle an exception. This is the purpose of the as operator. When the cast fails, it returns a null reference.
    Given the following:

```
public class Class1
{
}
public class Class2 : Class1
{
}
public class Class3 : Class1
{
}

Class3 a;
Class1 b = new Class2();
Class1 c = new Class3();
```

if you then use this:

```
a = c as Class3;
```

then the variable a will contain a reference to the same object as c. If you try the following:

```
a = b as Class3;
```

then the variable a will contain null.

Using the checked and unchecked Statements and Operators

The checked and unchecked statements and operators control the behavior of the system when an overflow occurs during arithmetic operations.

In checked state, an overflow would cause a System.OverflowException to be thrown:

```
int x;
int max = System.Int32.MaxValue;
checked
{
    x = max + 1;    // throws System.OverflowException
}
```

In unchecked state, no exception is raised, and the result is simply truncated:

```
int y;
int max = System.Int32.MaxValue;
unchecked
{
    y = max + 1;    // no exception
}
```

There are also the operators for controlling checking within an expression. You could rewrite the two preceding examples as the following:

```
int max = System.Int32.MaxValue;
int x = checked( max + 1 );     // throws System.OverflowException
int y = unchecked( max + 1 );    // no exception
```

> **TIP**   *Using unchecked mode simplifies the code for creating checksums and sequence numbers.*

Using Equality

There are several places where equality testing may not behave as you expect in C#.

String Equality

You can compare strings in C# directly using the equality operator (==) instead of a special method. As in Java, strings are equal if they are the same length and have the same characters in the same positions. So, given the following code:

```
string s1 = "abcd    ";
string s2 = "abcd    ";
string s3 = "abcd";
```

s1 and s2 are considered equal in this code:

```
if ( s1 == s2 )
{
    // equal
}
```

but s2 and s3 are not equal, as you can see:

```
if ( s2 == s3 )
{
    // won't get here since they are different
}
```

> **NOTE**   *The ability to use the equality operator (==) instead of a special method is due to C#'s operator overloading feature. For more details on this, see the "Operator Overloading" section later in this chapter.*

Reference Equality

Comparing two reference variables is normally a comparison between the values of the references and not the objects themselves. Reference equality functions the same as it does in Java. However, in C# you can overload the equality (==) and inequality (!=) operators to change this behavior (see Listing 2-2).

Listing 2-2. Overloading the == and != Operators

```
public class Person
{
    private string m_name;

    public Person( string name )
    {
        m_name = name;
    }

    public string Name
    {
        get
        {
            return m_name;
        }
    }

    // two Person instances are considered equal if their names are equal
    public static bool operator == ( Person a, Person b )
    {
        return ( a.Name == b.Name );
    }
    public static bool operator != ( Person a, Person b )
    {
        return ( a.Name != b.Name );
    }

    static void Main( string[] argv )
    {
        Person jack = new Person( "Jack" );
        Person jill = new Person ( "Jack" );

        // this would normally compare the references - but not here
        if ( jack == jill )
        {
```

```
            System. Console.WriteLine ("Jack and Jill are the same!" );
        }
        else
        {
            System. Console.WriteLine ("Jack and Jill are not the same" );
        }
    }
}
```

NOTE   *You must overload the* == *and* != *operators as a pair or you will get inconsistent behavior.*

If you want to test whether two references have the same value, you must cast them to references to object first, thereby defeating the operator overload:

```
public static bool SameObject( Person a, Person b )
{
    object x = (object)a;
    object y = (object)b;
    return x == y;
}
```

Value Type Equality

You cannot compare value types unless the implementer provides equality and inequality operators. There are no default implementations, so provide implementations if users of your value types need to be able to compare them.

This is a better choice, rather than settling for a default implementation. A default implementation cannot cover all possibilities, and you could be lulled into believing you had equality covered. If you forget to address equality, you get a compile-time error to remind you.

Delegate Equality

There are special rules for testing delegates for equality, which will be explained in the "Delegates" section of this chapter.

Introducing Functions and Methods

Like Java, C# does not allow functions that are not methods of some type. However, in C#, methods may exist on a struct and not just a class.

Just as Java allows you to invoke methods written in a compiled language through Java Native Interface (JNI), C# allows you to invoke methods in a compiled language Dynamic Link Library (DLL) using platform invoke. Chapter 15, "Getting Outside the Box," will cover this topic more thoroughly.

Parameter Marshalling

As discussed previously, you pass all classes by reference and all structs by value. These are only the default rules. In reality, reference types are passed by value, too, but it is the value of the *reference* that is passed and not the value of the object to which it refers.

In Java, you cannot pass an int to a method that wants to modify its value. However, C# allows you to use the ref modifier on a parameter to pass a value type by reference:

```
class RefMarshallExample
{
    public static void Add( ref int a, int b )
    {
        a += b;
    }

    static void Main(string[] args)
    {
        int a = 5;
        int b = 6;

        RefMarshallExample.Add( ref a, b );

        System.Console.WriteLine( "a = {0}", a );
    }
}
```

Notice that you specify the ref modifier in both the declaration and the invocation.

A parameter specified with ref must have a value before the method is called, even if it is null. If you need a parameter that only has a value after the method invocation, you can use the out modifier to avoid initializing the variable before making the call (see Listing 2-3).

Listing 2-3. Using the out *Modifier*

```
public class OutMarshall
{
    public static int Combine( out string result, string a, string b )
    {
        result = a + b;
        return result.Length;
    }

    static void Main( string[] argv )
    {
        string a = "abcdef";
        string b = "ghijkl";

        string r; // notice I don't even set this to null

        Combine( out r, a , b );

        System.Console.WriteLine( "<{0}> and <{1}> combined makes <{2}>",
                                    a, b, r );
    }
}
```

You must set a value for a parameter with the out modifier before the method returns.

Method Modifiers

C# has more method modifiers than Java and is more unforgiving. In C#, you must use the method modifiers consistently.

Using the virtual and override Modifiers

The virtual modifier has the same effect as in Java; it makes the method virtual. However, in C# you need to specify that a method overrides the base class implementation by adding the override modifier. Failure to do this will result in a compiler warning, but more importantly, you will not get the virtual behavior.

If you need to invoke the base class implementation of a method, use the base prefix just as you would use the super prefix in Java (see Listing 2-4).

Listing 2-4. Using the base *Prefix*

```
namespace OverrideExample
{
    class Class1
    {
        public virtual void Hello()
        {
            System.Console.Write( "Hello from Class1" );
        }
    }

    class Class2 : Class1
    {
        public override void Hello()
        {
            base.Hello();
            System.Console.Write( " and hello from Class2 too" );
        }

        public static void Main( string[] args )
        {
            Class2 c2 = new Class2();
            c2.Hello();
        }
    }
}
```

This example results in the message *Hello from Class1 and hello from Class2 too.*

Using the new *Modifier*

Overriding a nonvirtual base class method requires the addition of the new modifier. Failure to do so will not result an error, just in a warning.

 **TIP**   *You should add the missing* new *modifier and elimi-nate the warning. If you do not, it will be unclear to other programmers whether you forgot the* new *modifier or the* virtual *and* override *modifiers.*

Variable Length Parameter Lists

To write a list of variables in Java, you use `System.out.println` and pass it a con-catenated string of the object values. You can do the same with `System.Console.WriteLine` in C#, but you will often see the form where the string contains tokens and the variables are passed as parameters:

```
System.Console.WriteLine( "Values are {0}, {1}, {2}", a, b, c );
```

It would be impossible to define a method like this in Java because the num-ber of parameters varies from call to call. To declare such a method in C#, use the `params` modifier and an array. You declare the version of `System.Console.WriteLine` shown like this:

```
public static void WriteLine( string format, params object[] arg );
```

The `params` modifier roughly translates as "gather up everything from this point to the end of the parameter list and put it in an array," allowing you to invoke the function with a variable number of parameters (after the minimum) as long as they are compatible with the array type. You are not restricted to using an array of `object`. The array may be of any type you choose.

Understanding Types and Objects

Classes and interfaces exist in C# as they do in Java—only C# often uses the col-lective term *types*. C# also introduces two more types: *structs* and *delegates*. A struct is similar to a class except that it is a value type and you pass it by value instead of reference. A delegate is similar to a method reference except the dele-gate also knows to which object instance you are referring.

Using Classes

Classes in C# are similar to classes in Java. There are enough details to make things interesting, but the basic concept remains the same.

Inheritance

In Java, a class may inherit from a base class and implement interfaces. It may not inherit from multiple base classes. C# classes behave the same way. The difference is the syntax.

You would write the following class declaration from Java:

```
public class ClassA extends ClassB implements Interface1
{
    . . .
}
```

as follows in C#:

```
public class ClassA : ClassB, Interface1
{
    . . .
}
```

Because only one of the types in the list following the colon may be a class, there is no ambiguity as to which the base class is.

The syntax for calling parent constructors also differs. Instead of using super in the method body, you use a more C++-like syntax. For example, in Java you might write the following:

```
public class ClassA extends ClassB implements Interface1
{
    public ClassA( int x, int y )
    {
        super( x, y );
        . . .
    }
}
```

whereas in C# you would write the same code like this:

```
public class ClassA : ClassB, Interface1
{
    public ClassA( int x, int y ) : base( x, y )
    {
        . . .
    }
}
```

You use a similar syntax to support default parameters in constructors. This avoids unnecessary code duplication. For example:

```
public class ClassB
{
    public ClassB( int x ) : this( x, 15 ) { }
    public ClassB( int x, int y )
    {
        . . .
    }
}
```

Using sealed, const, and readonly Instead of final

In Java, the keyword final can have several different meanings. C# uses three keywords in place of final: sealed, const, and readonly.

You can declare a Java class using the modifier final, which indicates it may not be inherited from. C# uses the modifier sealed for the same purpose:

```
public sealed class DontEvenThinkOfTryingToInheritFromThis
{
    . . .
}
```

You also use the final modifier on member variables in Java. These may be class variables (static) or instance variables. C# uses the readonly modifier for the same purpose (see Listing 2-5).

Listing 2-5. Using the readonly Modifier

```
using System;

namespace ReadOnlyExample
{
    public abstract class LogEntry
    {
        // the unique instance identifier that nobody can modify
        protected readonly Guid id = Guid.NewGuid();

        protected string message;

        public LogEntry( string m )
```

```
        {
            message = m;
        }
    }

    public class ConcreteLogEntry : LogEntry
    {
        public ConcreteLogEntry( string m ) : base( m )
        {
            // the following causes a compile error
            // id = Guid.NewGuid();
        }

        public string Record()
        {
            return id.ToString() + " " + message;
        }

        static void Main(string[] args)
        {
            ConcreteLogEntry le = new ConcreteLogEntry( "something happened" );

            System.Console.WriteLine( le.Record() );
        }
    }
}
```

The modifier const exists in most languages that trace their roots back to C, including C#. It designates a variable whose value may not be modified. Most Java programmers equate this with static final, which is the closest equivalent in Java, but there is a difference. You may only use the C# const modifier on variables that are initialized with a literal at compile-time. The equivalent of this Java statement:

```
static final int x = 1;
```

in C# is the following:

```
const int x = 1;
```

A const variable is by definition static.

In Java you can use the final modifier on a method when you want to prevent descendants from overriding it. However, there is no equivalent to this in C#.

Properties

The JavaBeans specifications introduced many of you to the notion of properties. You have probably followed the pattern and coded getX and setX methods many times. C# takes this concept a step further and formalizes the structure in the language itself.

In Java a property Bottles might be coded as this:

```java
private int bottles;
public int getBottles()
{
    return bottles;
}
public void setBottles( int bottles )
{
    this.bottles = bottles;
}

public void sayIt()
{
    System.out.println ( "There are " +
                            getBottles() +
                            " bottles of beer on the wall" );
}
```

The equivalent in C# would be this:

```csharp
private int m_bottles;
public int Bottles
{
    get
    {
        return m_bottles;
    }
    set
    {
        m_bottles = value;
    }
}

public void SayIt()
{
    System.Console.WriteLine( "There are {0} of beer on the wall", Bottles );
}
```

Note the property is accessed as if it were a field (not like a method.) Also, the get and set are always adjacent. The careless person on the team who never keeps the pairs together will have to find a new way to annoy you!

Access Control

It does not always make sense for a property to have both a set and get method. For instance, a state property may derive its value from other operations performed on the object. C# supports this by omitting the set method. For example:

```
public class SixPack
{
    private int m_bottles = 6;

    public bool UnOpened
    {
        get
        {
            return ( m_bottles == 6 );
        }
    }

    public void TakeBottle()
    {
        m_bottles--;
    }
}
```

The same principle applies when a property is readable but not writeable. Omit the get method instead.

Abstract Properties

You can declare a property abstract just like a method, which makes sense because it is really just a pair of methods. The creator of the base class has control over which of the accessors the children must implement (see Listing 2-6).

Listing 2-6. Using abstract
```
public abstract class SixPack
{
    public abstract bool UnOpened
```

```
        {
            get;
        }
    }

    public class BottleSixPack : SixPack
    {
        int bottles = 6;

        public override bool UnOpened
        {
            get
            {
                return ( bottles == 6 );
            }
        }

        public void TakeBottle()
        {
            bottles—;
        }
    }

    public class CanSixPack: SixPack
    {
        int cans = 6;

        public override bool UnOpened
        {
            get
            {
                return ( cans == 6 );
            }
        }

        public void TakeCan()
        {
            cans—;
        }
    }
```

If the UnOpened property had been declared as this:

```
public abstract bool UnOpened
{
    get;
    set;
}
```

then the child classes would have needed to implement both accessors.

Is It Just a Matter of Style?

If you are accustomed to coding a pair of getXXX() and setXXX() methods, you might wonder if this is simply a stylistic choice formalized into the language in the same way the setXXX() and getXXX() names were formalized by the JavaBeans standard. To some extent, the answer is yes.

To somebody using your class, a property looks just like a field. It separates the definition from the implementation transparently. They do not need to know if the method is called setXXX, SetXXX, or XXX. It is always XXX, just like it is always setXXX in a JavaBean.

 **NOTE** *The one downside to properties in C# is that you establish access at the property level, so there is no support for a* public get *and a* protected set *on the same property.*

Indexers

When accessing an element of a Java collection, as in:

```
x= coll.get( i );
```

you may have wished that you could write the following, as you can with an array:

```
x = coll[i]
```

C# has special methods called *indexers* supporting this syntax. Indexers bear a strong resemblance to properties. For example:

```
public object this[ int index]
{
    get
    {
        return myinternalarray[ index ];
    }
    set
    {
        myinternalarray[ index ] = value;
    }
}
```

You are not restricted to using integers as the index type; you can use any type. For example, the System.Collections.Specialized.StringDictionary uses strings. If it is appropriate you may provide multiple indexers as does System.Collections.Specialized.NameValueCollection. You may index this class by integer offset or by key string.

Indexers are not limited to a single index variable. If it makes sense to treat your class like a two-dimensional array, you could define the indexer like this:

```
public object this[ int i1, int i2 ]
{
    get
    {
        . . .
    }
    set
    {
        . . .
    }
}
```

As with properties, you may omit the get or set blocks to restrict access. If someone attempts to set an indexer that has no set block, they will get a compile-time error.

Operator Overloading

The ability to redefine an operator's behavior can take some getting used to. An operator overload is a method that takes the same number of parameters as the operator and returns the appropriate value. They are always public static methods.

A unary operator operates on a single parameter and returns a single value. Binary operators take two parameters and return single value. Listing 2-7 demonstrates overloading the binary addition (+) operator and the unary subtraction (-) operator.

Listing 2-7. Overloading + and –

```
namespace OperatorOverloadingExample
{
    class Point
    {
        protected int m_x;
        protected int m_y;

        public Point( int x, int y )
        {
            m_x = x;
            m_y = y;
        }

        public int X
        {
            get
            {
                return m_x;
            }
        }

        public int Y
        {
            get
            {
                return m_y;
            }
        }

        // overrides binary addition operator

        public static Point operator + ( Point a, Point b )
        {
            return new Point( a.X + b.X, a.Y + b.Y );
        }

        // overrides unary subtraction operator
```

```
    public static Point operator - ( Point a )
    {
        return new Point( - a.X , - a.Y );
    }

    static void Main(string[] args)
    {
        Point p = new Point( 3, 4 );
        Point q = new Point( 36, -5 );

        Point r = p + ( - q );

        System.Console.WriteLine( "Result: x = {0}, y = {1}", r.X, r.Y );
    }
}
}
```

Not all operators can be overloaded, so check the C# Language Specification carefully before attempting to overload a particular operator.

If you have a C++ background, you may be wondering why you do not see the array index and cast operators ([] and (), respectively) listed as overloadable operators in the C# Language Specification. Other C# features already take care of them. Indexers give you control of how [] behaves, and user-defined conversions replace ().

User-Defined Conversions

Although treated differently than operator overloading by the documentation, essentially user-defined conversions allow you to overload the cast operator. C# allows you to declare the conversion with either the implicit or explicit modifier.

Using the explicit modifier gives you the behavior you might expect. You must explicitly use a cast to invoke the conversion. Using the implicit modifier allows the compiler to use your conversion without the need for an explicit cast in the code (see Listing 2-8).

Listing 2-8. Using implicit *and* explicit *Conversions*

```
namespace UserDefinedConversionExample
{
    class AccountBalance
    {
        int m_balance;
```

```
    public AccountBalance( int b )
    {
        m_balance = b;
    }

    public static implicit operator int( AccountBalance a )
    {
        return a.m_balance;
    }

    public static explicit operator string( AccountBalance a )
    {
        return "$" + a.m_balance;
    }

    static void Main(string[] args)
    {
        AccountBalance bal = new AccountBalance( 777 );

        // since int conversion is implicit we can write

        int i = bal;

        // string conversion must be explicitly requested

        string str = (string)bal;

        // this causes a compilation error
        // str = bal;

        System.Console.WriteLine( "i = {0} \nstr = {1}", i, str );
    }
}
}
```

User-defined conversions are always static methods. You may use them with classes or structs.

Using true *and* false *Operators*

It seems odd that you can overload the true and false operators. It would appear that this is just a conversion to bool. The intent is to allow a decision on what a null reference means. If you need to tolerate a null reference, you need to overload these operators. Listing 2-9 treats a null reference as equivalent to false.

Listing 2-9. Overriding the true *and* false *Operators*

```
namespace TrueFalseOperatorExample
{
    public class FalseWhenNull
    {
        public static bool operator true ( FalseWhenNull e )
        {
            return  ( e == null ) ? false : e.b;
        }

        public static bool operator false ( FalseWhenNull e )
        {
            return  ( e == null ) ? true : !e.b;
        }

        public bool b;

        public FalseWhenNull( bool b )
        {
            this.b = b;
        }

        public static void Main( string[] args )
        {
            FalseWhenNull truefwn = new FalseWhenNull( true );
            FalseWhenNull falsefwn = new FalseWhenNull( false );
            FalseWhenNull nullfwn = null;

            if ( truefwn )
            {
                System.Console.WriteLine( "true" );
            }
            else
            {
                System.Console.WriteLine( "false" );
            }

            if ( falsefwn )
            {
                System.Console.WriteLine( "true" );
```

```
        }
        else
        {
            System.Console.WriteLine( "false" );
        }

        if ( nullfwn )
        {
            System.Console.WriteLine( "true" );
        }
        else
        {
            System.Console.WriteLine( "false" );
        }
      }
    }
}
```

The result of the false operator is a bool that indicates if the object is false—*not* the value of the object. If the object maps to false, the false operator returns true. This may be counterintuitive at first!

Structs

At first glance, a struct looks similar to a class. Both have methods, fields, and properties, but there are a few key differences:

- A struct may implement interfaces, but it cannot inherit from another struct or class.

- You pass structs by value unless you override the default behavior using the ref modifier.

- A struct variable is an instance of the struct, not a reference.

- Structs cannot have a default constructor (in other words, one that takes no parameters); instead all variables in a struct are initialized to zero.

So, why use a struct? Aren't you going to just end up copying a lot of data? Because a struct variable is not a reference, it does not create another object that has to be garbage collected separately. In fact, a local struct variable will be allocated on the stack and therefore never need garbage collection.

Pass by value semantics are sometimes desirable. If you want to pass callers a copy of your object, it is easier to use a struct than to clone an instance of a class. When passing data across a network connection, giving someone a reference can result in many network hops. By using a struct, a copy of the state is sent in the original message. This behavior is analogous to that of IDL structs in CORBA. Listing 2-10 demonstrates the use of structs.

Listing 2-10. Using a Struct

```
namespace StructExample
{
    public struct Point
    {
        public int x;
        public int y;

        public Point( int x, int y )
        {
            this.x = x;
            this.y = y;
        }

        public void Print()
        {
            System.Console.WriteLine( "x = {0}, y = {1}", x, y );
        }
    }

    class StructExample
    {
        static void Main(string[] args)
        {
            Point p = new Point( 3, 4 );

            Point q = p;        // takes a copy

            q.x = 5;            // only changes q not p

            p.Print();          // so we still see x = 3, y = 4
        }
    }
}
```

Interfaces

You already know about interfaces. There are just a few caveats related to value types.

A struct may implement an interface just like a class. When you cast a struct to one of its interfaces, boxing occurs. So, modifying a struct through an interface reference will not modify the original struct.

Delegates

In Java, if you want to call back to other objects, you have to define an interface. Any class that wants to interact with you must implement your interface and then register with you. You need to manage the list of registered parties and implement the logic for iterating the list and invoking the appropriate method.

You can do the same in C#. When dealing with a single method, there is a more elegant solution: *delegates*. A delegate is like a method template. The .NET Framework uses them heavily. I will show you a simple example to demonstrate how to use them.

This is the classic observer pattern from *Design Patterns* by Erich Gamma, Richard Helm, Ralph Johnson, and John Vlissides (Addison-Wesley, 1995). It resembles the listener interface used heavily in JavaBeans and Swing. Instead of defining an interface that the observer classes need to implement, you need to define a delegate. The definition of the delegate specifies the method signature you want to call back to:

```
public delegate void NotifyCallback( decimal newPrice );
```

The observer class then implements a method that matches the signature defined in the delegate:

```
public class MyObserver
{
    . . .
    public void ProcessPriceChange( decimal price )
    {
        . . .
    }
    . . .
}
```

Now you need to allow observers to register with the notifier class. The method to do this should take an instance of the delegate type. You combine this delegate with an instance that the notifier maintains. You can use the `Combine` method, but the += operator is more convenient.

```
public class MyNotifier
{
    . . .
    NotifyCallback observers;

    public void AddObserver( NotifyCallback ncb )
    {
        observers += ncb;
    }
    . . .
}
```

The observer has to create a delegate instance that it uses to register with the notifier:

```
public class MyObserver
{
    . . .
    public void RegisterInterest( MyNotifier notifier )
    {
        NotifyCallback cb = new NotifyCallback( this.ProcessPriceChange );
        notifier.AddObserver( cb );
    }
    . . .
}
```

When an event occurs that must be communicated to the observers, the notifier invokes the delegate, and the registered method is invoked on each observer instance:

```
public class MyNotifier
{
    . . .
    public decimal Price
    {
        . . .
        set
        {
            m_price = value;
            observers( value );
```

```
            }
        }
        . . .
}
```

When an observer no longer needs to be notified, it can call the -= operator
(or some other method you provide) to unregister itself:

```
public class MyNotifier
{
    public void RemoveObserver( NotifyCallback ncb )
    {
        observers -= ncb;
    }
}
```

Several issues arise when multiple object instances are registered in a delegate. If the method has a return value, only the result from the last instance in the
list will be returned. Also, if one of the instances throws an exception, it is immediately propagated and none of the remaining instances are processed.

You can overcome these limitations by processing the invocation list manually. System.Delegate has a GetInvocationList method that returns the list as an
array. You can then invoke the individual instances and handle the return value
or exceptions however you want (see Listing 2-11).

Listing 2-11. Explicitly Processing a Delegate's Invocation List

```
public delegate bool NotifyCallback( decimal newPrice );

public class MyNotifier
{
    . . .
    public decimal Price
    {
        . . .
        set
        {
            bool vetoed = false;
            m_price = value;

            foreach ( NotifyCallback ncb in observers.GetInvocationList() )
            {
                try
                {
```

```
                    vetoed = ncb( value );
            }
            catch( Exception e )
            {
                // should do something here of course
            }
             if ( vetoed )
            {
                break;
            }
        }

        if ( vetoed )
        {
            throw new PriceChangeVetoedException();
        }
        else
        {
            m_price = value;
        }
    }
  }
  . . .
}
```

These examples show delegates that use methods on class instances. A delegate may also match a static method. Both may be mixed in the same invocation list as long as the signatures match that of the delegate.

Equality

Two delegates are equal if their invocation lists contain the same elements in the same order. Being practical about this, equality testing of delegates probably only makes sense when you expect them to contain a single reference.

Events

You can further simplify the preceding example by using *events*. Events formalize the observer pattern into the language and can therefore eliminate much of the code.

You could rewrite the notifier from the previous example as follows:

```
public class MyEventNotifier
{
    public event NotifyCallback Notify;

    private decimal m_price;

    public decimal Price
    {
        get
        {
            return m_price;
        }
        set
        {
            m_price = value;
            if ( Notify != null )
            {
                Notify( value );
            }
        }
    }
}
```

Declaring the event `Notify` creates an implicit private delegate, yet exposes the operators `+=` and `-=` for it so that observers can easily register for it as follows:

```
public void RegisterInterest( MyEventNotifier notifier )
{
    NotifyCallback cb = new NotifyCallback( this.ProcessPriceChange );
    notifier.Notify += cb;
}
```

The previous example does not follow the normal conventions established by the framework. Many classes use events according to these conventions. An event XXX is typically invoked through a method OnXXX, so you need an OnPriceChange method. The delegate usually takes two parameters: the object raising the event and an `EventArgs` descendant. This changes the code for the notifier to that shown in Listing 2-12.

Listing 2-12. Using Events according to the Framework Conventions

```
public delegate void NotifyCallback( object sender, PriceEventArgs e );

public class MyEventNotifier
{
    public event NotifyCallback Notify;

    protected void OnPriceChange( PriceEventArgs eva )
    {
        if ( Notify != null )
        {
            Notify( this, eva );
        }
    }
    private decimal m_price;
    public decimal Price
    {
        get
        {
            return m_price;
        }
        set
        {
            m_price = value;
            PriceEventArgs peva = new PriceEventArgs( m_price );
            OnPriceChange( peva );
        }
    }
}

public class PriceEventArgs : EventArgs
{
    private decimal m_price;
    public PriceEventArgs( decimal price )
    {
        m_price = price;
    }
    public decimal Price
    {
        get
        {
            return m_price;
        }
```

```
        }
}
```

Events are integral to many parts of the .NET Framework, including both WinForms and WebForms.

Introducing Enumerations

In Java, if a variable represents a finite set of possibilities—for instance, gender— you would typically define a number of constant values as in the following:

```
public class Gender
{
    static final int MALE = 1;
    static final int FEMALE = 2;
    . . .
}
```

C# uses *enumerations* to achieve the same thing. This is a concept taken from C++ and further enhanced for C#. An enumeration is an integral type that has a set of named values. The keyword enum is used instead of the longer enumeration. In C#, the preceding example looks like this:

```
enum Gender
{
    Male,
    Female
}
```

By default the underlying type of an enumeration is int. In this case it would consume less space if you used a byte. In C# you can specify the underlying integer type as in the following:

```
enum Gender : byte
{
    Male,
    Female
}
```

Typically the integer values used to represent the names are not important. The default behavior is to assign the first name to zero, the second name to one, and so forth. If you want to change this, you can specify the mapping as in the following:

```
enum Gender : byte
{
    Male =1,
    Female =2
}
```

or even like this:

```
enum Gender : byte
{
    Male =1,
    Female = Male + 1
}
```

Understanding Exceptions

C# has exceptions that on the surface behave much as they do in Java. They all descend from System.Exception as opposed to java.lang.Throwable. There is no distinction between exceptions and errors as there is in Java. That said, user exceptions should normally inherit from System.ApplicationException.

The big change is that you do not declare the exceptions you throw. In fact, there is no mechanism to do this.

C# uses the familiar try . . . catch . . . finally construct. An additional general form of the catch statement exists for situations where you do not care about the type of exception being thrown:

```
try
{
    x = location.X;
    y = location.Y;
}
catch
{
    // if anything goes wrong ensure both variables are set to null;
    x = null;
    y = null;
}
```

You can use this form of the catch statement in conjunction with specific catch clauses to handle anything that they do not filter out. It must be the last catch clause in the list. The other difference is in how exceptions are rethrown. To rethrow the current exception in a catch block, use the throw statement without a target:

```
try
{
    . . .
}
catch ( MyException e )
{
    throw;
}
```

Using Namespaces and the using Directive

If you come from a C++ background you know that a *namespace* is essentially the same as a Java package. The syntax for namespaces is different, as C# does not have the restriction of one public class per compilation unit. In Java, the package com.apress.book would be specified as this:

```
package com.apress.book;

public class NamespaceExample
{
    . . .
}
```

In C#, the equivalent would be this:

```
namespace com
{
    namespace apress
    {
        namespace book
        {
            public class NamespaceExample
            {
                . . .
            }
        }
    }
}
```

or more succinctly, it would be this:

```
namespace com.apress.book
{
    public class NamespaceExample
    {
        . . .
    }
}
```

There is no convention in C# regarding namespaces. You can continue following Java's use of your domain in reverse to avoid collisions. The `using` directive is analogous to Java's `import` directive. It enables you to avoid fully qualifying a name everywhere you use it. The most common way of employing this `using` directive:

```
using com.apress.book;
```

brings in all the names in a namespace. You could think of it as equivalent to this:

```
import com.apress.book.*;
```

in Java but the `using` directive also brings in any enclosed namespaces allowing you to refer to class `com.apress.book.Chapter2.Example` using `Chapter2.Example`.

The other form of the `using` directive allows you to solve the problem of name collisions by aliasing. Imagine you have two namespaces that each contain a `Date` (not that anyone would ever do this of course!). In Java you must fully qualify the class name to ensure you get the correct type, or you must remember the precedence rules. In C# you could qualify the class names, or you could specify the aliases `CoreDate` and `DBDate` to disambiguate the `Date` classes, as in the following:

```
using mycore;
using mydatabase;
using CoreDate = mycore.Date;
using DBDate = mydatabase.Date;
```

The alias form is not restricted to classes but may be used at any level in the hierarchy.

NOTE *Do not confuse the* using *directive with the* using *statement, which performs a very different function.*

Using Documentation Comments

The familiar /*   */ and // comments are available in C# without differences from their Java counterparts. Documentation comments differ substantially, however.

Documentation comments in C# serve a similar purpose to those in Java. Instead of extending the block comment for this purpose, C# extends the line comment.

You place C# documentation comments on lines where the first nonwhite-space characters are ///. You must repeat them on each line of the comment. For example:

```
/// This is
/// a doc comment
/// in C#
```

The special @xxx tags in Java are actually XML tags in C#. I will only cover a subset of the most useful tags in this section, but you can refer to the documentation for a full list.

When using the compiler directly, process the comments by adding the /doc:outputfilename option to your compile command. There is no separate tool such as javadoc to generate documentation. The result of processing the comments is not a set of Web pages but an XML file. How you process the XML into HTML pages or some other form is left to you.

Those using Visual Studio .NET are more fortunate. You can generate HTML pages for a single project or an entire solution using the menu option Tools ➤ Build Comment Web Pages. If you prefer the option of processing the comments into some other form, you can use the compiler option to emit XML.

The most useful tag is <summary>. You use it to give a short description of a type or member. You should enter longer descriptions inside a <remarks> tag. You can document individual parameters using <param> tags and return values using a <returns> tag. Users of Visual Studio .NET will be pleasantly surprised if they type /// above a method to find the appropriate tags generated for them to fill out.

Using these tags, you could document a class as shown in Listing 2-13.

Listing 2-13. Documenting a Class

```
namespace DocumentationComments
{
    /// <summary>
    /// A documentation sample - the short description goes here
    /// </summary>
    /// <remarks>Where a longer description would go</remarks>
    class ClassExample
    {
        /// <summary>
        /// A member variable
        /// </summary>
        private string m_str;

        /// <summary>
        /// A property example
        /// </summary>
        /// <remarks>
        /// You would put a more in depth description inside remarks tags
        /// </remarks>
        public string PropertyExample
        {
            get
            {
                return m_str;
            }
        }

        /// <summary>
        /// A method example
        /// </summary>
        /// <param name="val">a new value to be saved</param>
        /// <returns>the length of the string</returns>
        public int MethodExample( string val )
        {
            m_str = val;
            return val.Length;
        }

        /// <summary>
        /// The main method for the program
```

```
        /// </summary>
        /// <param name="args">command line arguments</param>
        static void Main(string[] args)
        {
        }
    }
}
```

The comments are still readable in spite of the XML tags and are easily added, especially if you have Visual Studio .NET to generate a skeleton for you.

Using the Preprocessor

If, like me, you used C or C++, you may have bemoaned the absence of the preprocessor when you first started programming in Java. C# has a preprocessor, though it is not as powerful as the preprocessor in C or C++.

If you have never used the C/C++ preprocessor, you may be wondering what is so wonderful about it. Have you ever inserted debugging code and then commented it out rather than deleting it in case you needed it again? Have you ever added a flag to a class to make turning on a feature easier and wished you did not pay the price of all those if statements in production? If you can say you have even thought of such things, you will love the preprocessor.

You may have heard the argument that the C/C++ preprocessor is bad because it leads to cryptic code. This argument refers mostly to the macro capability and is not relevant to C# because the C# preprocessor does not support macros.

The C# preprocessor supports the following statements:

```
#define
#undef
#if
#elif
#else
#endif
#warning
#error
#line
#region
#endregion
```

Of these, #define, #if, #elif, #else, and #endif are of greatest value on a day-to-day basis. They enable you to select between alternate sections of code at compile-time.

The following example carries out a little extra validation when the DEBUG symbol is defined. When the symbol is not defined, no runtime overhead occurs to omit the test, and the compiler does not generate the instructions:

```
public string Postcode
{
    get
    {
        return m_postcode;
    }
    set
    {
#if DEBUG
        if ( value == null )
        {
            System.Console.WriteLine( "Error: null value passed to postcode!"
);
        }
        else
        {
            m_postcode = value;
        }
#else
        m_postcode = value;
#endif
    }
}
```

In the C/C++ preprocessor, you could associate a symbol with a value such as this:

```
#define MAXGUESSES=5
```

The C# preprocess does not support this. Think of how you would handle it in Java. If it is a constant that belongs in the source code, declare it as a const field in the appropriate class. If it is a parameter, you may want to change at runtime, use a configuration file (analogous to a properties file in Java), and retrieve the value at runtime.

In addition to defining symbols in source code files, you can define symbols at compile-time by specifying /define:XXX as an option to the compiler command. The #warning and #error directives support defensive programming. If you provide several explicit choices and none are selected, you can generate a compiler warning or an error:

```
#if IPV4
    int ipaddress;
#elif IPV6
    long ipaddress;
#else
    #error One of IPV4 or IPV6 must be defined
#endif
```

No comment may appear on the same line as a #error or #warning. It would be treated as part of the message.

The #line is for tools that generate C# source code.

Writing Unsafe Code

Why Microsoft chose to use such a negative name for this feature of C# eludes me. *Unsafe code* is code that is unverifiable.

So what does *safe* mean in this context? In Java, you are aware of verifiable code. This is code that the byte code verifier can determine does not manipulate memory it does not own. Safe code in C# is the same as verifiable code in Java.

To create code in Java that is not verifiable, you need to resort to JVM assembly language. You could use the .NET intermediate language to achieve this in .NET, but C# has the ability to manipulate memory directly without resorting to such measures.

Chapter 15, "Getting Outside the Box," will cover exactly how you do this.

Standardizing C#

Microsoft has submitted the C# language to the European Computer Manufacturers Association (ECMA) for standardization. This means that other people can freely implement the language on other platforms. At the time of writing, there are already efforts underway outside Microsoft to implement C# on Linux. Microsoft has also submitted the .NET runtime to ECMA, so these ports should be compatible with the language as it is used on Windows.

C# improves on both C++ and Java. I expect to see implementations appear on many other platforms once the standard has been finalized.

Summary

C# is a rich and powerful language that offers features beyond those you have become familiar with in Java. Many of these differences, used correctly, result in more maintainable programs. Java programmers will find that C#'s similarity to Java makes it comparatively painless to learn. Microsoft is everywhere, and knowing C# can only increase your marketability in today's world.

You should be in a good position to start developing C# programs now. For a more thorough treatment of the C# language, I strongly recommend *A Programmer's Introduction to C#* by Eric Gunnerson (Apress, 2000).

CHAPTER 3

Introducing the .NET Platform

If C# IS THE EQUIVALENT OF the Java language, then the .NET platform is the equivalent of the Java Virtual Machine (JVM) and the class libraries—not just the standard edition libraries, but the Java 2 Enterprise Edition (J2EE) libraries.

Unfortunately, the Microsoft marketing machine has taken the .NET tag and plastered it on products having nothing to do with the .NET platform. For instance, there is MSN Messenger .NET and .NET Passport, which were renamed before the .NET platform was even released. In fact, I would not be surprised to see a .NET label on a mouse or a keyboard in the near future. Therefore, it can be difficult to recognize what is part of the .NET platform and what is merely marketing. However, Microsoft's widespread adoption of the .NET tag reflects the importance of the .NET platform to Microsoft's future.

This chapter introduces you to the .NET platform, its constituent parts, and how they relate to Java.

The Pieces of the .NET Platform

The .NET platform, as most developers know, has two major components: the Common Language Runtime (CLR) and the associated libraries installed together as the .NET Framework Redistributable. The CLR is the virtual machine and a core set of libraries. There are additional libraries that provide the full functionality of the .NET platform.

You install the .NET Framework Redistributable when you install the .NET Software Development Kit (SDK) or Visual Studio .NET. Your customers would install it as part of your product installation if some previous product had not already done so. In many respects you can equate the .NET Framework Redistributable to a runtime version of the J2EE platform without the reference server implementations.

Just as you compile Java programs to JVM byte codes, you compile .NET programs to an intermediate language creatively called Microsoft Intermediate Language (MSIL). Even though your C# programs compiled down to .exe and .dll files, the actual code is in MSIL byte codes.

Understanding the Class Libraries

The .NET class libraries are organized into namespaces in a similar manner to the J2EE libraries, and they correspond to named features:

WinForms: This is the name of the .NET windowing library. It corresponds to Java Foundation Classes (JFC)/Swing or Abstract Windowing Toolkit (AWT) in Java.

ASP.NET: This is the Web server feature of .NET. ASP.NET WebForms are analogous to Java Server Pages (JSP). Web Services are also part of ASP.NET.

ADO.NET: This is the database access element of .NET. Like Java Database Connectivity (JDBC), ADO.NET supports a number of database implementations.

Remoting: This is the equivalent of Remote Method Invocation (RMI) for .NET programs and is a close relative of Web Services.

.NET components: These are analogous to JavaBeans or ActiveX controls.

COM+:   Both COM+ and Enterprise JavaBeans (EJB) provide support for enterprise business objects. They do, however, have significant differences. COM+ is not unique to .NET but is fully supported by it.

Microsoft Message Queue (MSMQ):   This is supported by a message-queuing library in .NET. Unlike Java Message Service (JMS), it is not a general Message-Oriented Middleware (MOM) library.

Directory services: These are supported in .NET, obviously with good support for Active Directory. This is comparable to Java Naming and Directory Interface (JNDI).

Windows services: Java provides no special support for Windows services or Unix daemons. Doing either correctly typically requires a native code launcher be written. The .NET Framework libraries contain support that makes writing Windows services easier than ever before.

Native code: Sun may have been unhappy with the proprietary extensions Microsoft added to its JVM and compiler, but the extensions greatly simplified interoperability with native Windows code. Naturally there is excellent support for this in .NET.

Understanding the Common Language Runtime

The CLR is often thought to be the .NET virtual machine. It is in fact the virtual machine *and* the core class libraries. The CLR provides many of the same services that the JVM does. It interprets the MSIL byte codes, provides garbage collection, and enforces the appropriate security for programs running under its control.

Code running under the control of the CLR is termed *managed code.* All other code is *unmanaged code.* It is not possible to write unmanaged code in C#. The C# compiler will not emit native machine code. When an .exe file (a binary executable) containing managed code is invoked, an instance of the CLR is launched to process the byte codes in the file.

A CLR process contains logical subdivisions called *application domains.* Code running in separate domains behave much as if they were in separate processes but avoid some of the overhead of launching and running multiple processes. This has benefits in environments such as ASP.NET where many short-lived programs run under the control of a master program.

There are actually two versions of the CLR. One is optimized for single-processor workstation environments and the other for multiprocessor (MP) server environments. The workstation version is used by default when managed code is run from the command line or the explorer. The server version must be requested when the CLR is invoked and requires a special loader program to be written. ASP.NET uses the server version of the CLR when running on an MP machine.

The SDK provides two tools that enable you to dig deeper into managed code. The ildasm tool is an MSIL disassembler, and the ilasm tool is an MSIL assembler. If you invoke ildasm on the HelloWorld.exe file you built in Chapter 1, "Introducing C#," with this command:

```
ildasm HelloWorld.exe
```

and then double-click the Main method, you can see the MSIL the compiler generated for it:

```
.method public hidebysig static void  Main(string[] args) cil managed
{
  .entrypoint
  // Code size       11 (0xb)
  .maxstack  8
  IL_0000:  ldstr      "Hello world from C#"
  IL_0005:  call       void [mscorlib]System.Console::WriteLine(string)
  IL_000a:  ret
} // end of method HelloWorld::Main
```

If you have any experience with an assembly language, you will soon deduce that it puts a reference to the string on the stack and calls the familiar System.Console.WriteLine method that is located in the mscorlib assembly (assemblies are similar to libraries).

Now create a file called HelloWorld.il containing the following code:

```
.assembly HelloWorld {}
.assembly extern mscorlib {}
.method static public void Main() cil managed
{
  .entrypoint
  .maxstack  8
  ldstr      "Hello world from IL"
  call       void [mscorlib]System.Console::WriteLine(string)
  ret
}
```

and compile it using this command:

```
ilasm HelloWorld.il
```

You will find you have a HelloWorld.exe file that you can run in the normal way. You just wrote an MSIL program!

The Benefits of .NET

Although far from an exhaustive list, standardization, language independence, and platform independence all promise significant benefits to users of the .NET platform.

Standardization

Not only has Microsoft submitted the C# language to the European Computer Manufacturer's Association (ECMA) for standardization, it has also submitted the Common Language Infrastructure (CLI). CLI is composed of the CLR virtual machine and a limited set of core class libraries. Although the class libraries are a small subset of those available in the .NET SDK, they go beyond the minimum necessary to support the C# language.

The CLI submission talks about several *profiles*. These profiles discuss which class libraries need to be present to conform to the standard. Rather than reflecting degrees of compliance, these profiles are more directed at permitting compliance on restricted platforms (for example, phones, refrigerators, heart monitors, and so on). In these cases, the full libraries are generally too bulky and may contain features that embedded hardware does not support.

Microsoft has created a version of the .NET runtime called the Compact Framework. This has fewer libraries than the full .NET runtime and targets Windows CE devices such as the Pocket PC.

The standards submission benefits efforts to create ports of .NET on other platforms without a license from Microsoft. It remains to be seen how Microsoft will react to third-party class libraries that mimic such features as ASP.NET because the libraries are a subset of those supplied in Visual Studio .NET and the .NET SDK.

The team responsible for standardizing the CLI is ECMA TC39/TG3. You can find the standards submissions at msdn.microsoft.com/net/ecma/. Surprisingly enough, the ECMA site (www.ecma.ch) does not link to these documents.

Language Independence

Java was not the first platform-independent language/runtime environment, but it brought the concept into the mainstream. Microsoft's .NET firmly pushes language independence out of the lab and onto desktops everywhere.

There have been several languages ported to the JVM since its release, but none are widely used as an alternative to Java. The .NET virtual machine has been designed to support multiple languages, and Microsoft is launching it with C#, C++, Visual Basic (VB), and JScript (JavaScript/ECMAscript). Microsoft even has a variant of Java called J# currently in beta.

Other vendors quickly exploited this aspect of .NET using the information contained in the standards submission. Eiffel was one of the first non-Microsoft languages for .NET. Fujitsu has COBOL for .NET, and ActiveState has Perl and Python compilers. Visit the MSDN site (msdn.microsoft.com) for a growing list of other languages.

Language independence in .NET goes beyond the compilers that generate the virtual machine byte codes. In the past, you have been able to call functions written in other languages but with many restrictions, such as the following:

- Language X may be able to call language Y but not vice versa.

- The library of language P conflicts with the library of language K.

All .NET languages share the same libraries, so the conflict issue is irrelevant. They all use the same calling conventions, so functions in different languages are interchangeable. But the feature that takes language independence to its next level is that all languages implement objects in the same way. This means that a VB .NET class may inherit from a C# base class and be tagged with an attribute written in MC++.

In the following example, the C# class `Base` defines an abstract method called `GetFrom`:

```
namespace MixedLanguageInheritanceExample
{
    public abstract class Base
    {
        protected abstract string GetFrom();

        public void SayIt()
        {
            System.Console.WriteLine( "Hello from " + GetFrom() );
        }
    }
}
```

The VB .NET class `Child` overrides `GetFrom` as if everything were in the same language:

```
Module Module1

    Class Child : Inherits MixedLanguageInheritanceExample.Base

        Protected Overrides Function GetFrom() As String
            GetFrom = "multiple languages"
        End Function

    End Class

    Sub Main()
        Dim c As Child = New Child()
        c.SayIt()
    End Sub

End Module
```

Platform Independence

Because .NET languages compile to byte codes, which are executed by a virtual machine, they have the same potential for platform independence as Java. You face different obstacles when porting .NET and Java.

A Java port requires the following steps:

1. Obtain a license from Sun.

2. Port the Java Development Kit (JDK) reference implementation source code provided by Sun.

3. Optimize for your target platform.

A .NET port requires the following:

1. Obtain the ECMA specifications.

2. Implement those specifications.

3. Add the pieces that are not part of the standard.

Because Microsoft has submitted the CLI as a standard, everyone has access to the specifications and there is no need to obtain a license. However, currently there is no source code to leverage when creating your port. Microsoft and Corel have announced they are working on a shared source implementation of the CLI and C# for Windows and FreeBSD. Once available, this reference implementation is likely to increase the number of ports to other platforms.

The ECMA standard only covers the core libraries, presenting a problem for porting efforts that want to achieve full compatibility with Microsoft. For instance, if these ports provide a compatible implementation of ASP.NET, how will Microsoft react? There has been no mentioning of licensing the features not covered by the standard, so this is unknown territory. How Microsoft resolves this issue could accelerate or undermine porting efforts.

Even without a reference implementation, there are several efforts underway to port the CLI/CLR to Linux. Ximian's Mono project is probably the best known of these. It remains to be seen how well these will be received outside the Windows community.

Summary

Now you understand the core of the .NET platform, including the CLR. You also know not to confuse the .NET tag with the .NET platform.

Armed with this knowledge, and the understanding of C# you gained in the previous chapter, you are ready start digging a little deeper into various aspects of the .NET platform. You will start with the equivalent of JFC and AWT: the graphical user interface, WinForms.

Using WinForms

THE WINFORMS CLASSES IN .NET are the equivalent of Java Foundation Classes (JFC)/Swing in Java. WinForms are not quite the equivalent of Abstract Windowing Toolkit (AWT), as WinForms bears a closer resemblance to Swing. At the end of the day, they all serve the same purpose of creating a graphical user interface (GUI) for your application.

This chapter covers building WinForms applications using Visual Studio .NET and how WinForms compare to Swing.

Creating HelloWorld in WinForms

In this section, you will build a simple WinForms HelloWorld program to use as a basis for starting your comparison. The only cost-effective way to build most WinForms applications is to use Visual Studio .NET. You could build the application by hand (without the aid of any design tools), but it would almost certainly result in wasted time and money. The hours saved by using Visual Studio .NET more than offset its cost.

Building the Project and Adding the Controls

Follow these steps to build the HelloWorld program:

1. Create a new project in Visual Studio .NET and select the Visual C# Projects project type and the Windows Application template. Name it **HelloWorld** for variety.

2. When Visual Studio .NET has created the project, you will see the forms designer. Click the Toolbox tab, which makes the Toolbox appear. Then click on the button with the pushpin icon so that it stays open. You will want easy access to the Toolbox when creating WinForms applications.

3. You will add three controls to the form, starting with a Label. Select
    a Label from the Toolbox and drag it onto the form, then drop it onto the
    form, as shown in Figure 4-1.

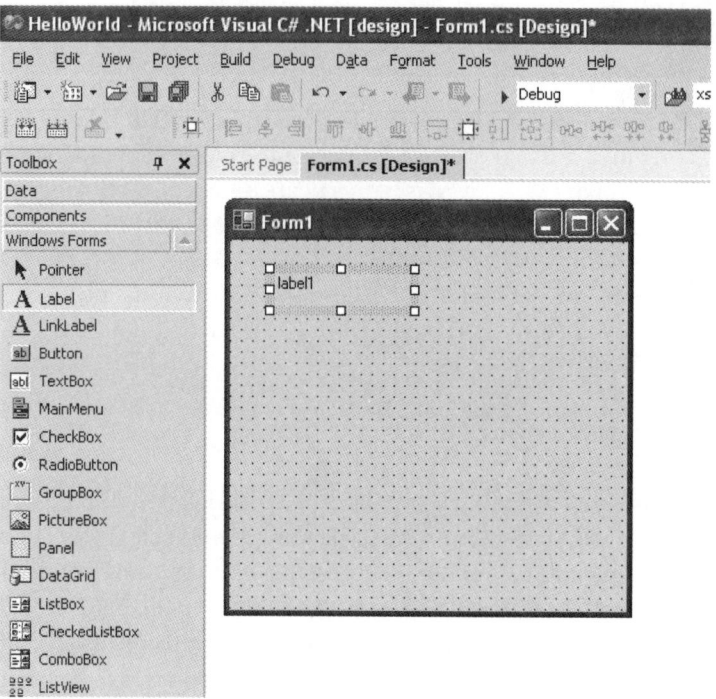

Figure 4-1. Dragging a label from the Toolbox to the form

4. Now scroll down in the Properties panel until you get to the row labeled
    Text. It should have the value label1. If not, do not worry—you are going
    to change it anyway. Change the value to **Hello World**, and you should
    see that reflected in the forms designer, as shown in Figure 4-2.

Figure 4-2. Changing the Label *control's* Text *property*

5. Now select a TextBox from the Toolbox and drop it on the form. Find its Text property and make it blank by deleting the value.

6. Last you need a Button, so drag one from the Toolbox to the form. Change the button's Text property to **Say hello**.

7. To make it more interesting, double-click the button you just created. You will flip from the design view to the code view, with the cursor on a method that looks like the following:

```
private void button1_Click(object sender, System.EventArgs e)
{

}
```

8. Take the contents of the textbox and construct a new Text property for the label, so make this method read like the following example:

```
private void button1_Click(object sender, System.EventArgs e)
{
    label1.Text = "Hello " + textBox1.Text;
}
```

9. Now compile and run the application. When the form opens, enter your name in the textbox and click the button. The result should look similar to Figure 4-3.

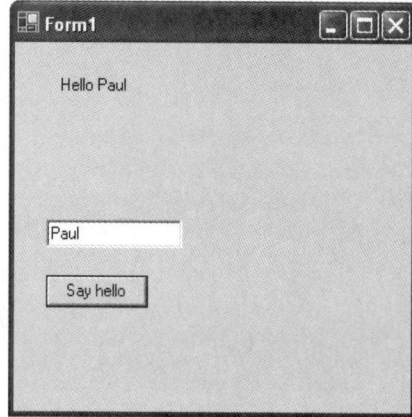

Figure 4-3. The completed WinForms application

Congratulations, this is your first WinForms application.

Looking Inside the WinForms HelloWorld

If you look at the code again you will see that the main class `Form1` inherits from the `System.Windows.Forms` class. `Form`. `System.Windows.Forms` is the primary namespace for WinForms classes and could be thought of as the equivalent of `javax.swing`. However, `System.Windows.Forms` is not subdivided the way the `javax.swing` package is.

The `Form` class is roughly equivalent to a `JFrame`. But as the `Form` class is used for all windows, it also replaces `JDialog` and `JInternalFrame`. In this example, `Form1` is the main window class, so a `Form1` instance is passed as the parameter to `Application.Run` in the `Main` method. Creating a `Form` instance is not equivalent to creating a `JFrame`, as the former does not start the message loop. Invoking `Application.Run` passing the `Form` as a parameter starts the message loop:

```
static void Main()
{
    Application.Run(new Form1());
}
```

This variant of the Run method adds an event handler for the Closed event of the specified Form so that closing this form exits the application. You do not have to worry about processing the closed event as you would in Swing, unless you need special shutdown logic (for example, a Mother may I? dialog box).

Look at the controls you added in the designer. You can easily locate the instance variables for the controls, which all come from the WinForms namespace:

```
private System.Windows.Forms.Label label1;
private System.Windows.Forms.TextBox textBox1;
private System.Windows.Forms.Button button1;
```

The first time you look at the code, you might wonder where all the initialization logic is hidden. By default, Visual Studio .NET uses the special #region and #endregion preprocessor directives to hide code it has generated. Look carefully and you will find a line that reads like this:

```
Windows Form Designer generated code
```

If you look in the left margin, you will see a small box with a plus in it. Click the plus, and the code that has been generated by the designer will be revealed. Hiding code generated by design tools is common in Visual Studio .NET.

In this case, a method called InitializeComponent was hidden in the designer-generated code region. The hidden code contains the logic to create the controls and to set the properties configured in the designer. Let's look at button1—it is the most interesting. button1 is instantiated in a normal way along with the other controls:

```
private void InitializeComponent()
{
    this.label1 = new System.Windows.Forms.Label();
    this.textBox1 = new System.Windows.Forms.TextBox();
    this.button1 = new System.Windows.Forms.Button();
```

and later configured by this:

```
//
// button1
//
this.button1.Location = new System.Drawing.Point(24, 168);
this.button1.Name = "button1";
this.button1.TabIndex = 2;
this.button1.Text = "Say hello";
this.button1.Click += new System.EventHandler(this.button1_Click);
```

The control is positioned on the form using absolute coordinates, and the size of the control is specified explicitly. The various layout mechanisms from Swing have no parallel in WinForms.

Also in this block of code is the statement that registers a handler for the button's Click event. This statement was added when you double clicked the button in the designer.

The other important piece of code inside InitializeComponent is the following, which actually adds the controls to the Form:

```
this.Controls.AddRange(new System.Windows.Forms.Control[] {
    this.button1,
    this.textBox1,
    this.label1});
```

There is other initialization logic in InitializeComponent, which I leave you to investigate yourself.

NOTE   *The use of the* InitializeComponent *method is a Visual Studio .NET convention. It is not part of the class hierarchy.*

Using WinForms Controls

The System.Windows.Forms namespace contains most of the controls you might expect in a Windows user interface (UI) library. The easiest way to see them is to switch to design view in Visual Studio .NET and look at the Toolbox.

The classic set of controls you expect to find in any UI toolkit is there. Button, RadioButton, CheckBox, TextBox, ListBox, and ComboBox all have analogies in both Swing and AWT. Whereas Swing has JTextField and JTextArea, WinForms has the MultiLine attribute on its TextBox control. Data binding is a nice feature of the ListBox and ComboBox classes, and it allows you to populate the choices using an array, without having to loop through and add the array elements one at a time. Table 4-1 lists the standard WinForms controls with their Swing and AWT equivalents.

Table 4-1. WinForms to Swing and AWT Control Mapping

WINFORMS CONTROL	SWING CONTROL	AWT CONTROL
Label	JLabel	Label
LinkLabel		
Button	JButton	Button
RadioButton	JRadioButton	CheckBoxGroup
CheckBox	JCheckBox	CheckBox
TextBox (MultiLine=false)	JTextField	TextField
TextBox (MultiLine=true)	JTextArea	TextArea
ListBox	JList	List
ComboBox	JComboBox	Choice
Panel	JPanel	Canvas
TreeView	JTree	
ToolBar	JToolBar	
StatusBar	JStatusBar	
TrackBar	JSlider	
TabControl	JTabbedPane	
ToolTip	JToolTip	
ProgressBar	JProgressBar	
DomainUpDown		
NumericUpDown		
Splitter	JSplitter	
OpenFileDialog	JFileChooser	
SaveFileDialog	JFileChooser	
ColorDialog	JColorChooser	
FontDialog		
RichTextBox	JEditorPane	
	JTable	
ListView		

(*continued*)

Table 4-1. WinForms to Swing and AWT Control Mapping (continued)

WINFORMS CONTROL	SWING CONTROL	AWT CONTROL
DateTimePicker		
MonthCalendar		
MainMenu	JMenuBar	MenuBar
ContextMenu	JPopupMenu	
NotifyIcon		

The `Panel` control serves the same role as a `JPanel`. `Panel` allows you to group controls and manipulate them as a unit.

The `DomainUpDown` and `NumericUpDown` have no Swing counterpart, and they behave like a `TextBox` control combined with a `VScrollBar` control. The `NumericUpDown` allows a user to select a number within a range either by typing it in or by using the scroll buttons. Similarly, `DomainUpDown` allows the user to select from a list of string values.

In Swing you use a `JSplitPane` to provide two adjacent resizable areas you can put controls into. In WinForms you add a `Splitter` control to the `Form` and anchor controls to either side, to achieve the same effect. Remember to anchor the controls, or the `Splitter` will not function correctly.

Swing contains some sophisticated controls and dialog boxes, which you previously would have had to purchase as aftermarket controls. The most useful of these was the `JFileChooser` dialog box, which has counterparts in `OpenFileDialog` and `SaveFileDialog`. Other utility dialog boxes are `ColorDialog`, which corresponds to `JColorChooser`, and `FontDialog`, which has no Swing counterpart.

The WinForms `RichTextBox` is the closest analogy to `JEditorPane`. It supports only Rich Text Format (RTF).

There is no direct analogy to `JTable`. The WinForms `ListView` control has similar behavior to the right panel of the Windows Explorer and so may be appropriate in some cases. The other candidate is a `DataGrid`, which is heavily geared to database access.

Two sophisticated controls provided in WinForms are `DateTimePicker` and `MonthCalendar`, which have no Java equivalent outside third-party control libraries. The `MonthCalendar` displays a monthly calendar, as shown in Figure 4-4. It allows single or range selection of dates.

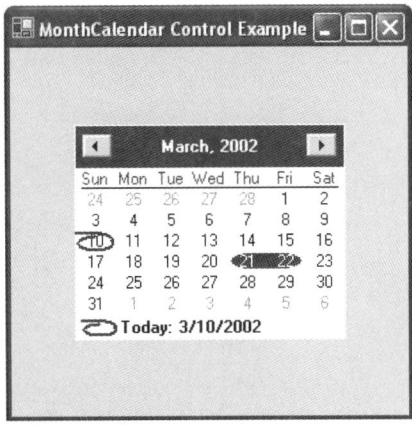

Figure 4-4. The MonthCalendar *control*

The DateTimePicker combines the MonthCalendar with a TextBox providing an alternative format for single date entry.

Looking Deeper at Layout

The rich selection of layout managers available in Swing has no parallel in WinForms, but the layout mechanism bears a closer look if you want your forms to behave in a user-friendly manner.

When you design a Form or Panel, lay out the controls as they will appear when the Form or Panel is at its default size. Run the HelloWorld example again and see what happens when you resize the form. You were probably expecting the controls to move relative to one another or stretch as you dragged the edges of the form around. The controls stayed exactly in the same spot, even when you dragged the edges of the form so that they were hidden! This was probably not the behavior you wanted.

Take a look at the properties of anyone of the controls. Down at the bottom is a section called Layout, which contains a property Anchor. By default this is set to Top, Left. What happened when you tried to manipulate HelloWorld's form was that the controls were maintaining their position relative to the form's top and left edges. If you click the drop-down arrow for the Anchor property value, you can chose which edges the control is anchored to, as shown in Figure 4-5.

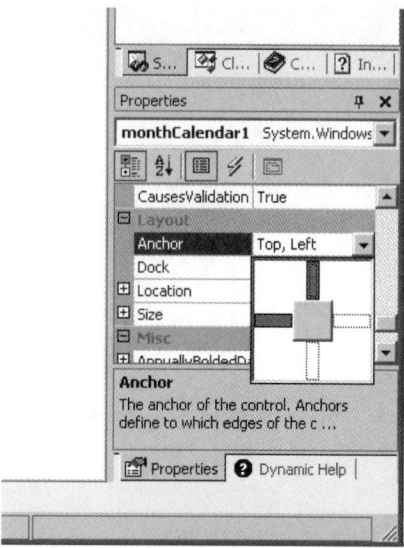

Figure 4-5. Configuring the `Anchor` *property of a control*

Experiment with the different controls to see how the various attachment modes make them behave. For example, if you experiment with the `TextBox` from HelloWorld, you will see that setting `Anchor` to `Left, Right` makes it resize horizontally, but `Top, Bottom` does nothing size-wise unless you set `MultiLine` to `true`.

The other layout related property is `Dock`. `Dock` behaves like the `BorderLayout` in Swing. Its most obvious use is with `ToolBar` and `StatusBar`, which dock with the top and bottom of the `Form` (respectively). It is also useful with `Panel`, `TreeView`, and `ListView`. Instead of using compass points to describe the locations, `Dock` uses `Top`, `Bottom`, `Left`, `Right`, and `Fill`.

Creating Menus

Menus in WinForms are similar to menus in Swing. Instead of starting with a `JMenubar`, start with a `MainMenu`. The individual items are `MenuItem` instances, instead of `JMenuItem` instances. Follow these steps:

1. Create a new Windows Application project called **MenuExample**. Drag a `MainMenu` from the Toolbox onto the form, as shown in Figure 4-6.

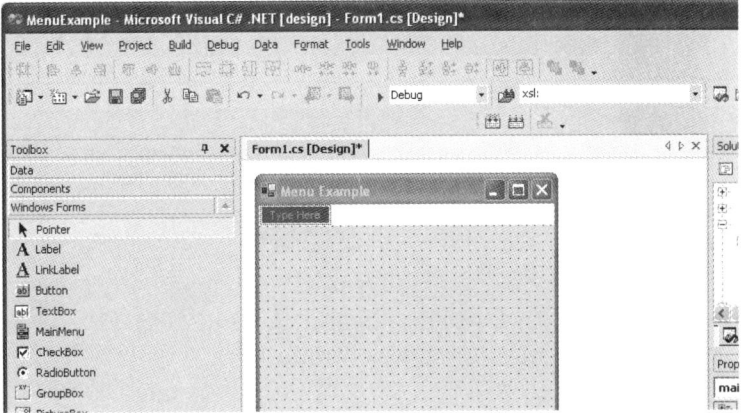

Figure 4-6. The form after adding the `MainMenu`

2. Build up your menu structure by typing the various items directly into the `MainMenu` in the designer. In this case, set a single top-level menu item to **Say**, and add two child items named **Hello** and **Goodbye**. Your form should now look like Figure 4-7.

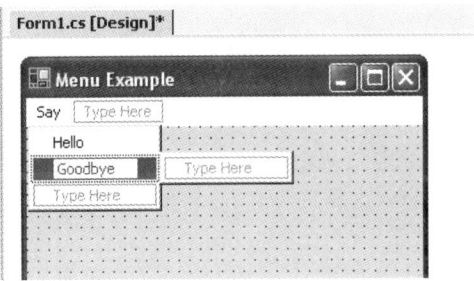

Figure 4-7. The menu after adding the items

3. Add a `Label` to the form so that the menu has something to manipulate. Set its `Text` property to **What shall I say?** Now double-click the Hello menu item to add a click handler that should be completed as follows:

```
private void menuItem2_Click(object sender, System.EventArgs e)
{
    label1.Text = "Hello!";
}
```

4. Repeat the process for the Goodbye menu item. Change its handler to the following:

```
private void menuItem3_Click(object sender, System.EventArgs e)
{
    label1.Text = "Goodbye!";
}
```

5. Now build and run the application. As you expect, selecting the menu items changes the label accordingly.

6. Menus should be keyboard friendly as well as mouse friendly. You add accelerator keys, which are used in conjunction with the Alt key, by placing an ampersand (&) before the letter in the menu item, which is used as the accelerator key. In Figure 4-8, Alt+S is the accelerator for the Say menu item, Allt+H for Hello, and Alt+Y for Goodbye" Notice how the ampersands are changed to an underline as they will appear at runtime.

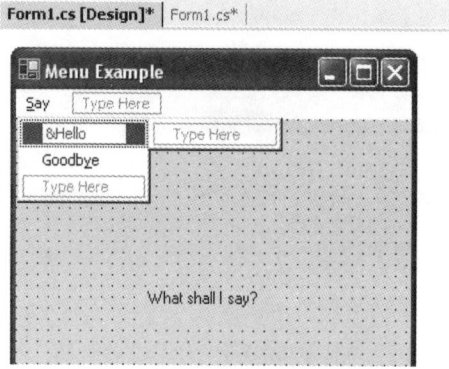

Figure 4-8. The menu after adding accelerator keys

7. A shortcut key provides a way to invoke a menu item without navigating the menu hierarchy. They are often invoked using the Ctrl key. Add a shortcut key by setting the Shortcut property of the menu item, as shown in Figure 4-9.

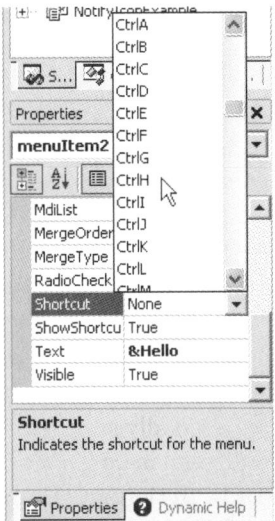

Figure 4-9. Setting the Shortcut *property for a menu item*

8. The ShowShortcut property enables you to control whether the shortcut is shown on the menu. Make Ctrl+H the shortcut for Hello and Ctrl+Y the shortcut for Goodbye. The application now looks like Figure 4-10.

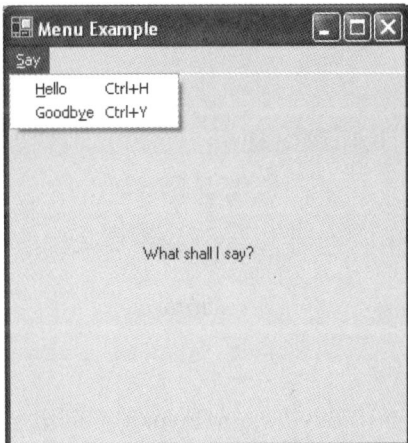

Figure 4-10. The menu shortcuts as they appear at runtime

9. A ContextMenu, the equivalent of a JPopupMenu in Swing, is built in a similar fashion to a MainMenu. After you drag the control to the form, select it and build up the menu in the same area used to build the MainMenu. Drag a ContextMenu from the Toolbox onto the example and add two items and name them **Say hello** and **Say goodbye**, as shown in Figure 4-11.

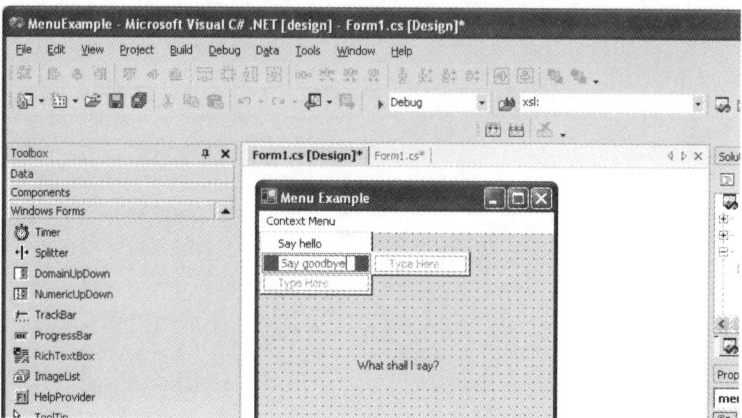

Figure 4-11. Creating a context menu

10. Associate a ContextMenu with a control by setting the control's ContextMenu property in the designer. In this case, set the property for the label as shown in Figure 4-12.

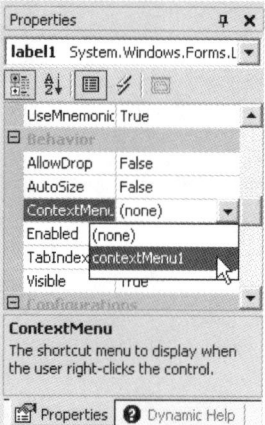

Figure 4-12. Adding the context menu to the Label *control*

11. Build and run the application. The context menu appears when you right-click the label, as shown in Figure 4-13.

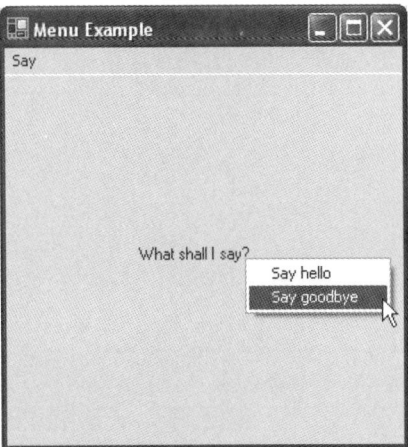

Figure 4-13. The context menu at runtime

Creating Toolbars

Toolbars in WinForms behave in a similar way to JToolBars in Swing. They act as a place to hold other controls, usually buttons. You add a toolbar by dropping a ToolBar control on a form in the designer. The ToolBar always docks with the top of the form. Follow these steps:

1. Create a new Windows Application project called **ToolBarExample**. Drag a ToolBar control from the Toolbox onto the form, as shown in Figure 4-14.

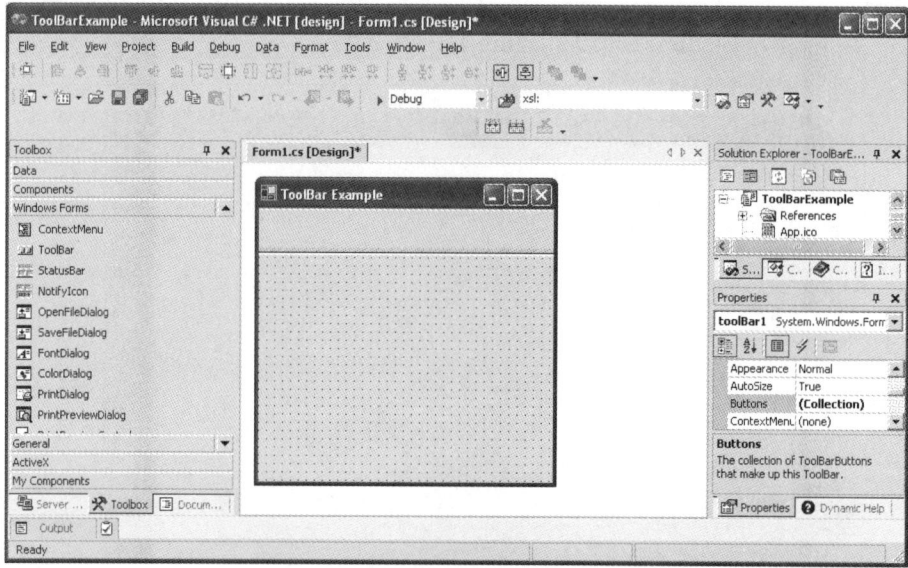

Figure 4-14. The ToolBar *control when first added to the form*

2. Notice the Buttons property is highlighted in the Properties panel of Figure 4-14. You use this to add buttons to the ToolBar. Press the ellipsis button to display the dialog box shown in Figure 4-15. This enables you to manipulate the buttons on the ToolBar.

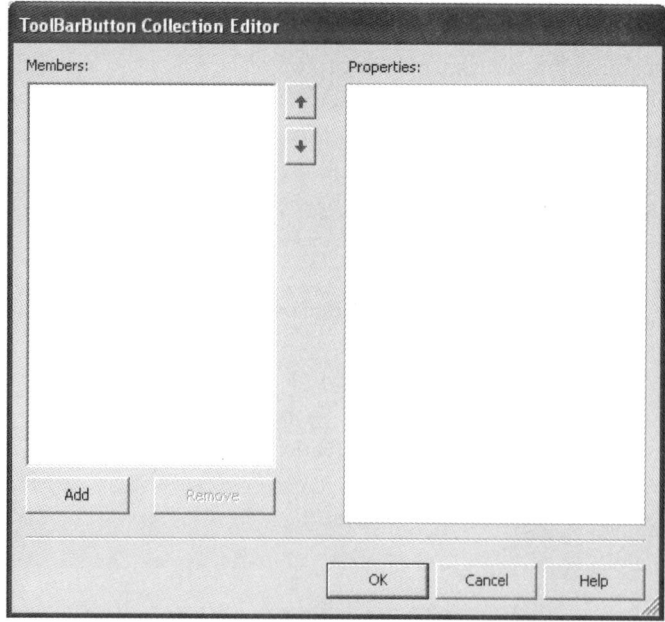

Figure 4-15. The dialog box for manipulating toolbar buttons

3. Add two buttons with their Text properties set to **Hello** and **Goodbye** respectively, as shown in Figure 4-16.

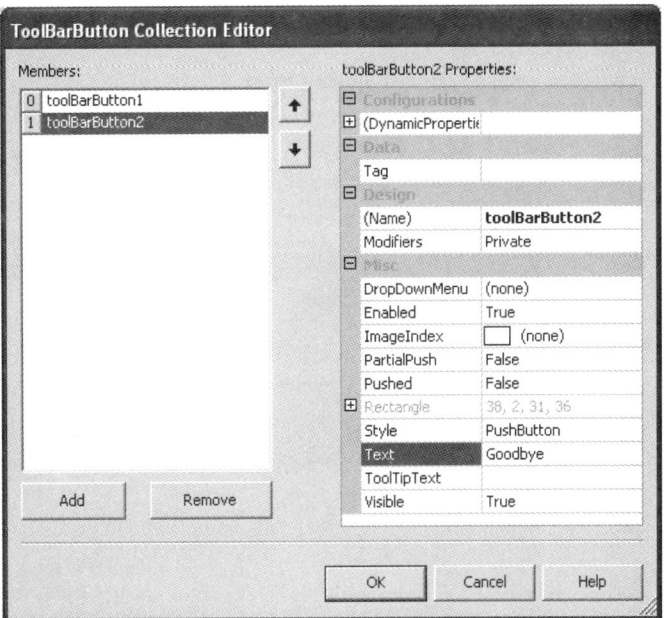

Figure 4-16. Buttons added to the toolbar button dialog box

4. Now add a label to the form with its Text property set to **What shall I say?** Double-click the ToolBar to add a button click handler that reads as follows:

```
private void toolBar1_ButtonClick( object sender,
                System.Windows.Forms.ToolBarButtonClickEventArgs e )
{
    if ( e.Button == toolBarButton1 )
    {
        label1.Text = "Hello to you too!";
    }
    else if ( e.Button == toolBarButton2 )
    {
        label1.Text = "Goodbye!";
    }
}
```

You cannot create a separate handler for each button, so you are forced to determine which one was pressed using the Button property of the ToolBarButtonClickEventArgs parameter.

5. Normally you display an icon in a toolbar button, not text. Add two icons to the project by selecting Project ➤ Add New Item . . . ➤ Icon File and name them **Hello.ico** and **Goodbye.ico**. Select Image ➤ Current Icon Image Types ➤ 16 x 16, 16 Colors to change each of the icons to the correct format, as shown in Figure 4-17.

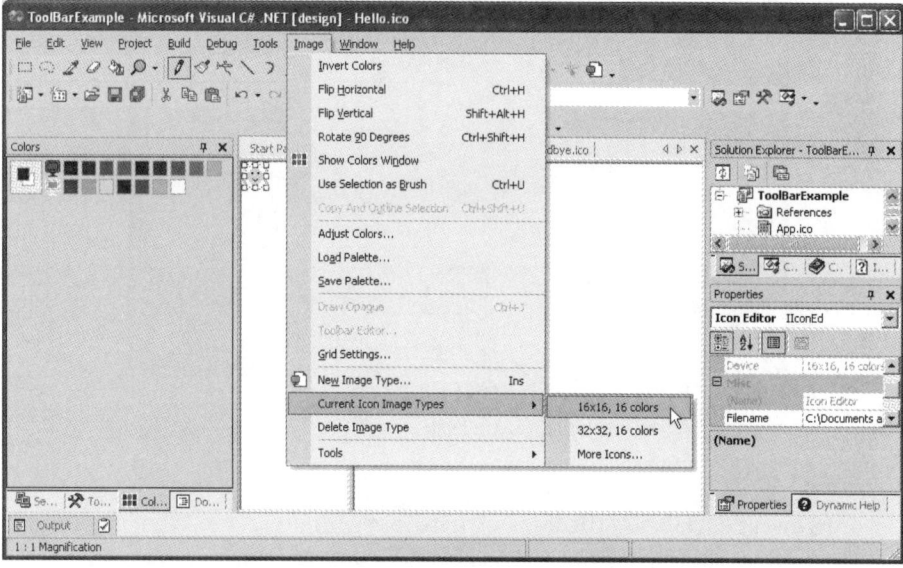

Figure 4-17. Modifying the icon format for use on the toolbar

6. Modify the icons to images that convey hello and goodbye and save them. Now, add an ImageList control to the form. Open its Images property so that you can add the icons to the collection. The dialog box that appears is almost identical to that shown in Figure 4-15. Clicking the Add button allows you to add Hello.ico and Goodbye.ico to the list. Click OK to save the collection.

7. Select the ToolBar and modify its ImageList property to reference the ImageList you just created. Reopen the Buttons collection and modify the ImageIndex property of each button to refer to the appropriate image in the ImageList, as shown in Figure 4-18.

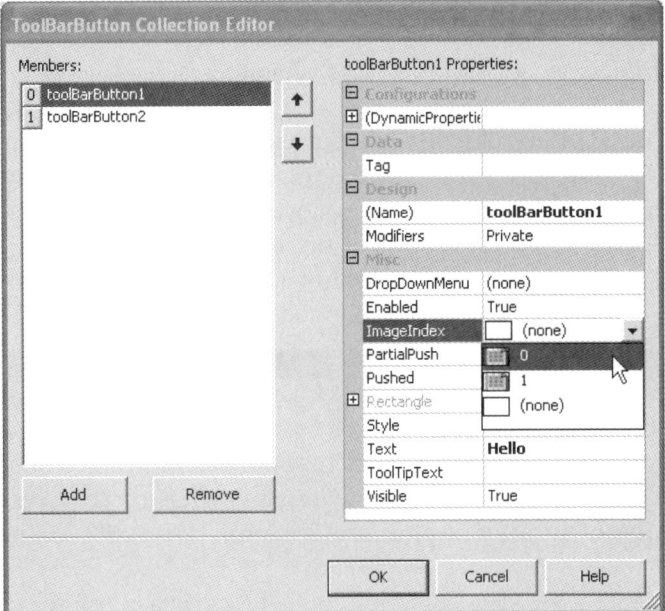

Figure 4-18. Selecting the image for a toolbar button

8. Clear the Text property of each button so that only the icon will be displayed. Now when you run the application it will look similar to Figure 4-19.

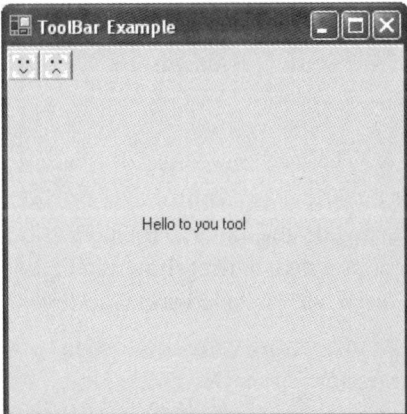

Figure 4-19. The completed toolbar example

Adding Help

Help in WinForms is based around standard Windows HTML Help (.chm) files. This means you have a wide range of authoring options from which to choose.

From the application developer standpoint, it is relatively easy to add help support. Once a `HelpProvider` control has been added to the application and configured with the desired help file, it is a matter of configuring the help settings for each control to display the appropriate topic.

Printing

Support for printing in Java is provided by the `java.awt.print` classes. These give you control over how the data is rendered onto the printer, and they also give you limited user configuration. The print controls in WinForms support or allow full configuration of the printing process and of print preview. Follow these steps:

1. Create a new Windows Application project called **PrintExample**. Add a `MainMenu` with the items shown in Figure 4-20.

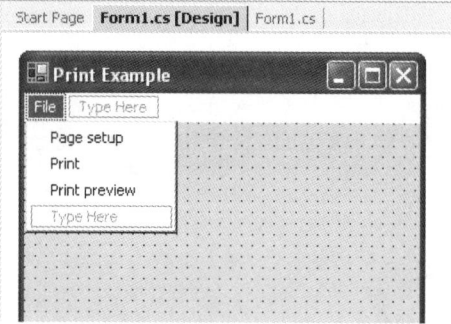

Figure 4-20. The menu for `PrintExample`

2. Drag a `PrintDocument` control from the Toolbox onto the form. This is the core of the printing support in .NET. The other print controls all use a reference to the `PrintDocument`. Double-click the `PrintDocument` control to add a print page handler, which should be modified as follows:

```
    private int currentPage;

    private void printDocument1_PrintPage( object sender,
                            System.Drawing.Printing.PrintPageEventArgs e )
    {
        e.Graphics.DrawString( "Page " + currentPage,
            new Font( "Times New Roman", 15 ),
            Brushes.Black,
            e.MarginBounds.Left,
            e.MarginBounds.Top );
        currentPage++;
        if ( currentPage > 3 )
        {
            e.HasMorePages = false;
        }
        else
        {
            e.HasMorePages = true;
        }
    }
```

3. The Graphics property of the PrintEventArgs parameter contains the Graphics object needed to render the page. It is your responsibility to track which page is being printed and to indicate when all the pages have been printed by setting the HasMorePages property of the PrintPageEventArgs parameter.

4. You could invoke the PrintDocument's Print method in the handler for the Print menu item, but users expect to be given a choice of printer when they select that menu item. Drag a PrintDialog control from the Toolbox and set its Document property to the PrintDocument instance. Now double-click the Print menu item and modify its click handler as follows:

```
    private void menuItem2_Click(object sender, System.EventArgs e)
    {
        if ( printDialog1.ShowDialog( this ) == DialogResult.OK )
        {
            currentPage = 1;
            printDocument1.Print();
        }
    }
```

This only prints the document if the user clicks OK in the Print dialog box displayed by the `PrintDialog` control.

5. Users also expect to preview their documents before printing them. Drag a `PrintPreviewDialog` from the Toolbox onto the form and set its `Document` property. Now double-click the Print Preview menu item and change the handler to read:

```
private void menuItem3_Click(object sender, System.EventArgs e)
{
    currentPage = 1;
    printPreviewDialog1.ShowDialog( this );
}
```

6. Now you can run the application and preview the pages before printing.

7. Your users also expect to be able to configure the page layout before printing. Drag a `PageSetupDialog` to the form and set its `Document` property. Double-click the Page Setup menu item and modify the handler to invoke the dialog box:

```
private void menuItem4_Click(object sender, System.EventArgs e)
{
    pageSetupDialog1.ShowDialog( this );
}
```

Your print page handler is responsible for honoring many of the settings, but the dialog box provides a convenient way for the user to configure the page layout. The print controls enable you to add significant functionality to your application with little effort.

Exploring Multithreading Issues

You already know not to call a method on a Swing component from a thread that is not the event loop thread. You use the `invokeLater` or `invokeAndWait` methods of the `SwingUtilities` class to have the method executed on the event loop thread.

The same issue exists in WinForms. You must make UI changes on the thread that created the form. The `Control.Invoke` method serves exactly the same function as the `SwingUtilities.invokeXXX` methods.

Using the NotifyIcon Control

While looking through the Toolbox or the System.Windows.Forms documentation you will eventually stumble across the oddly named NotifyIcon class. NotifyIcon will allow you to write an application that lives in the Windows system tray (as an icon naturally).

The *system tray* is the collection of icons usually found at the right of your taskbar. It contains such things as your Messenger status, your new mail notification, and your volume control.

Let's create a minimal application that demonstrates how to create an application that uses the system tray:

1. Create a new Windows Application project called **NotifyIconExample**. Once the Form is displayed, drag over a Button and a NotifyIcon. Change the Text property of the button to **Hide in tray** and then double-click the button.

2. You want clicking on the button to hide the application in the system tray, so make the event handler look like the following:

```
private void button1_Click(object sender, System.EventArgs e)
{
    notifyIcon1.Visible = true;
    this.Visible = false;
}
```

3. Next, you need to make the reverse happen when you double-click the tray icon. To do this you need to handle the DoubleClick event for the NotifyIcon instance. This is not readily achieved in the designer, so do it the old-fashioned way and add the event handler by hand. First, create the handler. Find the button1_Click handler and add the following code after it:

```
private void notifyIcon1_DoubleClick(object sender,
                                    System.EventArgs e)
{
    notifyIcon1.Visible = false;
    this.Visible = true;
}
```

4. Now register the handler in the form's constructor:

```
public Form1()
{
    //
    // Required for Windows Form Designer support
    //
    InitializeComponent();

    //
    // TODO: Add any constructor code after InitializeComponent call
    //
    this.notifyIcon1.DoubleClick +=
            new System.EventHandler(this.notifyIcon1_DoubleClick);
}
```

5. Prior to running, you need to specify an icon for the NotifyIcon control so the application can be seen in the system tray. There is no default provided by the designer. In this case you will use the icon already present in the project as App.ico. Select the NotifyIcon control and change its Icon property to specify this file.

6. You also want to specify the text that displays when you hover over the icon, so make the Text property say **Hello from NotifyIconExample**. Finally, make the NotifyIcon control initially invisible by changing its Visible property to **False**.

 **TIP**   *If you want to modify the icon, double-click the file App.ico in the Solution Explorer and you will be placed in the icon editor.*

7. Okay, now you are ready to try the example. When the form opens, click the button and the icon will appear in the system tray. When you double-click the system tray icon, the form will reappear.

If you desire more sophisticated functionality, you could display a context menu in response to a right-click on the icon and follow other conventions for system tray applications.

Incorporating ActiveX Controls

Windows controls have historically been *ActiveX* (also known as OCX or OLE) controls. These are specialized Component Object Model (COM) components. COM is the component architecture used extensively in Windows prior to .NET. At some point you will probably need to incorporate an ActiveX control into one of your applications.

For this example let's use the Web Browser ActiveX control:

1. Create a new Windows application called **ActiveXExample**.

2. Next you would normally drag the control from the Toolbox to the form, but because the Toolbox does not contain ActiveX controls as installed, you need to add them yourself the first time you want to use them. You could add the control to an existing tab of the Toolbox, but I prefer to keep ActiveX controls on a tab with the name ActiveX. To create the new tab, right-click anywhere inside the Toolbox (even on a component) and select Add Tab from the context menu. Rather than opening a dialog box as you might expect, a textbox appears at the bottom of the Toolbox for you to enter the name of the new tab. Type in **ActiveX** and press Enter.

3. You should now have a new tab in your Toolbox named "ActiveX", so go ahead and select it. As created, the tab contains only the pointer tool, but you need to add the Web Browser ActiveX control. Right-click the Toolbox and select Customize Toolbox. . . . A dialog box, like the one shown in Figure 4-21, will open so you to select the component to add.

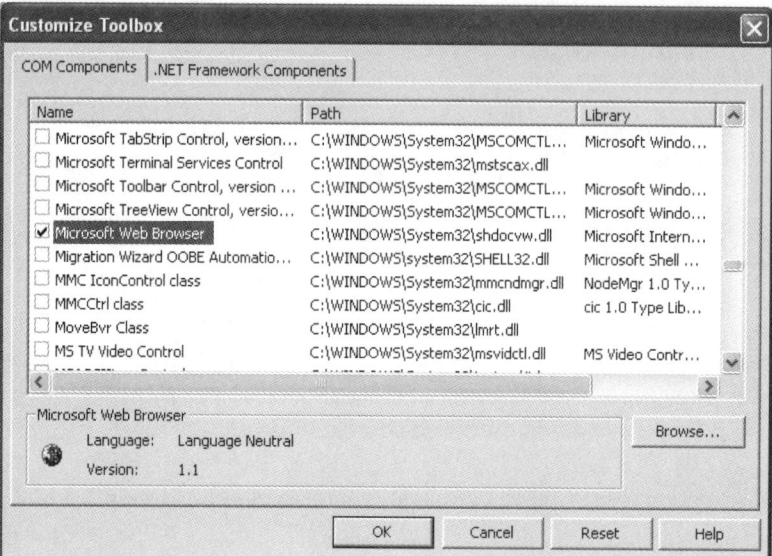

Figure 4-21. Selecting an ActiveX control to add to the Toolbox

4. ActiveX controls are COM components, so select the COM Components
tab and scroll down until you find Microsoft Web Browser. Check the box
as shown in Figure 4-21 and press OK.

5. Your ActiveX Toolbox tab will now contain an Explorer item, as shown in
Figure 4-22, which you can drag onto your form as if it were a normal
WinForms control. You can also position and size it as if it were
a WinForms control.

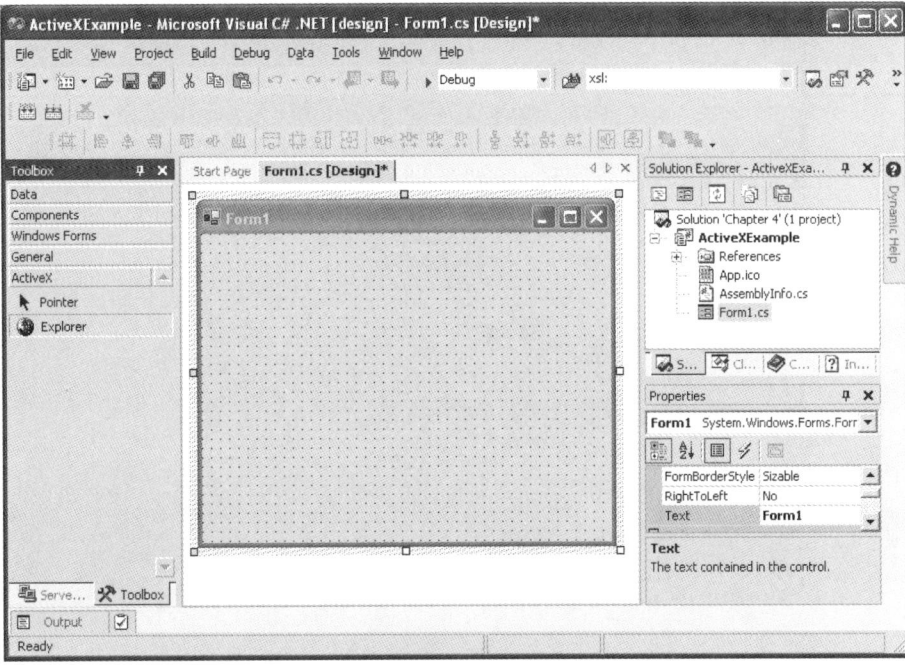

Figure 4-22. The Web Browser ActiveX control in the Visual Studio .NET Toolbox

You may have noticed some activity in your Solution Explorer when you dropped the control on your form. Let's look at that a little more closely. If you examine the References folder, you will see two new entries: SHDocVw and AxSHDocVw. These were generated by Visual Studio .NET and are proxies that make the control appear to be the same as any other WinForms control. SHDocVw is the Runtime Callable Wrapper (RCW) that provides a proxy between managed code and COM. AxSHDocVw is the proxy that sits on top of the RCW and makes the ActiveX control appear to be a WinForms control.

TIP *If you need to generate proxies for an ActiveX control outside Visual Studio .NET, you can use the* axlmp *command-line tool.*

6. Add a `TextBox` and a `Button` to the form so you can enter a URL and request that it be displayed in the Web Browser control. You do not always have to be content with the names the designer picks for components. Rename these to **textBoxUrl** and **buttonUrl** by editing the names in the Properties panel. The entry is labeled (`Name`) and is in the Design section, as shown in Figure 4-23.

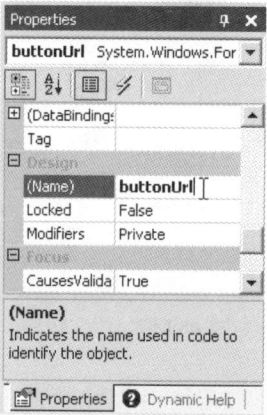

Figure 4-23. Renaming the `Button` *control*

7. Now you need to add code to satisfy that request. Double-click the button so that you are placed in the button click handler. Add the following code to request the Web Browser control to display the URL entered in the textbox:

```
private void buttonUrl_Click(object sender, System.EventArgs e)
{
    object flags = null;
    object frame = null;
    object post = null;
    object headers = null;
    axWebBrowser1.Navigate( textBoxUrl.Text,
            ref flags, ref frame, ref post, ref headers );
}
```

8. Now, when you build and run the project, you can enter a URL in the textbox and click the button to navigate to the specified page, as shown in Figure 4-24.

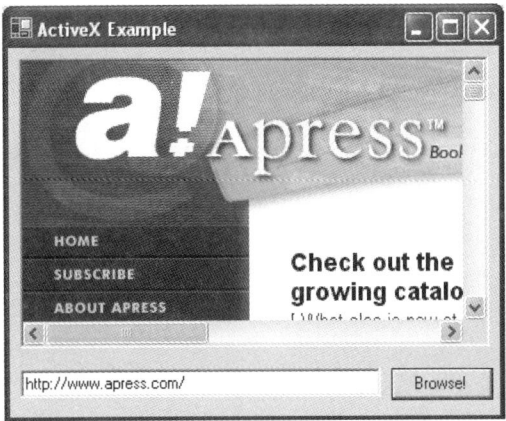

Figure 4-24. The completed application using the Web Browser ActiveX control

The ability to easily interoperate with existing ActiveX controls is essential to making migration to .NET as painless as possible for existing Windows developers.

Summary

The WinForms classes have many parallels to the Swing classes, which should give you an advantage over programmers moving from other GUI frameworks such as Microsoft Foundation Classes (MFC) or Motif. Visual Studio .NET is a productive environment for building WinForms applications. You can achieve a high level of functionality in a comparatively short period of time.

Building Web Sites with ASP.NET

Active Server Pages for .NET (ASP.NET) is the name for the Web server support in .NET. It encompasses Web pages and Web Services. Chapter 8, "Understanding Networking," will cover Web Services, along with other networking mechanisms. ASP.NET WebForms are the equivalent to Java Server Pages (JSP). There is another lesser-known feature of ASP.NET called an *HttpHandler*, which bears a strong resemblance to a servlet.

You can readily discern the type of an ASP.NET page by its suffix, as shown in Table 5-1.

Table 5-1. ASP.NET Page Types by Suffix

SUFFIX	TYPE
.aspx	WebForms page
.ascx	WebForms user control
.ashx	HttpHandler page
.asmx	Web Service

This chapter describes how to use the first three of these to build Web sites and how they compare to using JSP and servlets. You will also learn how to create ASP.NET server controls in addition to user controls.

Creating a Simple WebForms Page

Let's revisit our old friend HelloWorld, but this time in WebForms.

Building HelloWorld in WebForms

To create a simple HelloWorld program in WebForms, follow these steps:

1. Create a new ASP.NET Web Application project called **WebFormsHelloWorld**. Once Visual Studio .NET has created the project, you will be left in design mode on a new blank form. Now, you are going to repeat the steps you took for HelloWorld in WinForms (in Chapter 4, "Using WinForms"), even though it is a Web page.

2. First drag a Label to the form and change its Text property to **Hello World**. Next, drop a TextBox on the form and make sure its Text property is blank. The third control should be a Button with the Text property set to **Say Hello**. Your screen should look similar to Figure 5-1.

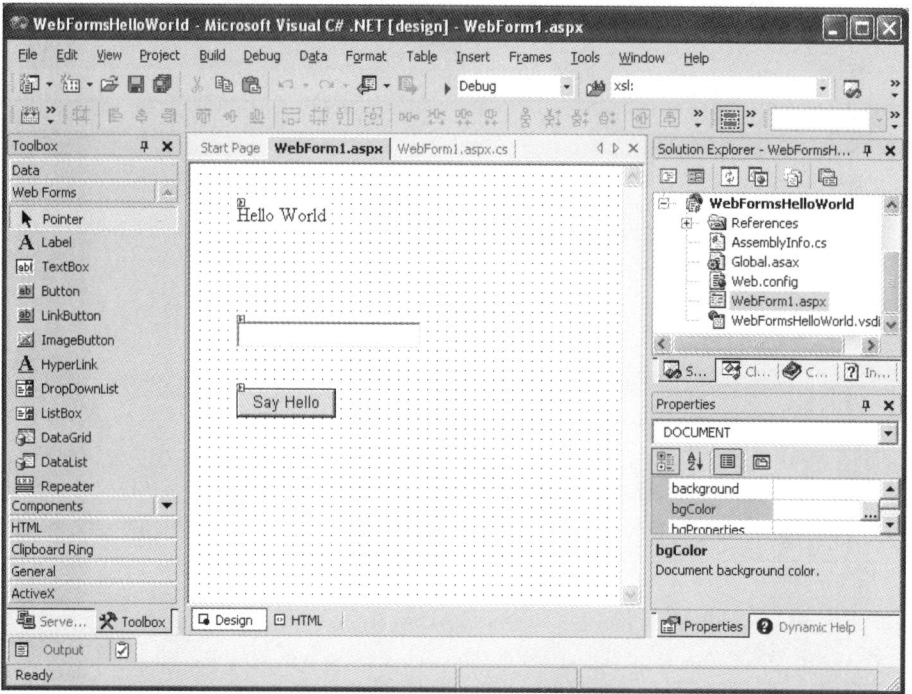

Figure 5-1. Design view of the completed HelloWorld page

3. So far there is nothing unusual—you could do the same in any What-You-See-Is-What-You-Get (WYSIWYG) HTML editor. But now it gets interesting! Double-click the button and you see the following:

```
private void Button1_Click(object sender, System.EventArgs e)
{

}
```

4. Now change the event handler to read as follows:

```
private void Button1_Click(object sender, System.EventArgs e)
{
    Label1.Text = "Hello " + TextBox1.Text;
}
```

5. Go ahead and run it. It behaves just as expected. But this is a Web page, how can you have a button click handler? Let's look a little closer.

Looking Deeper Inside the WebForms HelloWorld

Switch the WebForm from design to HTML view by clicking the button at the bottom left of the design panel. Many examples (tutorials, conference presentations, and so on) show a WebForms page with the code inline enclosed in <%...%> blocks as you would in JSP (see Listing 5-1).

Listing 5-1. A Simple WebForms Page

```
<%@ Page language="c#" %>
<HTML>
    <HEAD>
        <title>Inline ASP.NET WebForm Example</title>
    </HEAD>
    <body>
        <form method="post">
            <%
            if ( Request.Params[ "who" ] != null )
            {
                %>Hello <%= Request.Params[ "who" ] %><%
            }
            else
            {
                %>Hello World<%
            }
            %>
            <P><INPUT type="text" name="who"></P>
            <P><INPUT type="submit" value="Submit"></P>
        </form>
    </body>
</HTML>
```

Although Listing 5-1 is perfectly legal, it does not reflect how Visual Studio .NET generates ASP.NET pages. Look at the first line of WebForm1.aspx, and you will see this directive:

```
<%@ Page language="c#" Codebehind="WebForm1.aspx.cs"
    AutoEventWireup="false" Inherits="WebFormsHelloWorld.WebForm1" %>
```

This directive specifies that the code is in a separate file called WebForm1.aspx.cs. Such a file is known as a *code-behind file*. Visual Studio .NET always uses the code-behind model for ASP.NET pages. The code-behind file WebForm1.aspx.cs was the file you actually edited to fill in the body of the button click event handler.

To look at the controls themselves, open WebForm1.aspx in design view as before. At the bottom-left of the design panel there are two buttons: Design and HTML. If you press the HTML button, you will see the file generated by the designer, including the controls themselves (see Listing 5-2).

Listing 5-2. The WebForms Controls in WebForm1.aspx

```
<body MS_POSITIONING="GridLayout">
    <form id="Form1" method="post" runat="server">
        <asp:Label id="Label1"
            style="Z-INDEX: 101; LEFT: 40px;
                    POSITION: absolute; TOP: 32px"
            runat="server">Hello World</asp:Label>
        <asp:TextBox id="TextBox1"
            style="Z-INDEX: 102; LEFT: 40px;
                    POSITION: absolute; TOP: 128px"
            runat="server"></asp:TextBox>
        <asp:Button id="Button1"
            style="Z-INDEX: 103; LEFT: 40px;
                    POSITION: absolute; TOP: 184px"
            runat="server" Text="Say Hello"></asp:Button>
    </form>
</body>
```

The controls have an `asp:` prefix, as if they are part of a JSP taglib. If you look at the HTML source for the page rendered to your browser, you will see regular HTML controls (see Listing 5-3).

Listing 5-3. HTML Controls

```
<body MS_POSITIONING="GridLayout">
    <form name="Form1" method="post" action="WebForm1.aspx"
            id="Form1">
```

```
    <input type="hidden" name="__VIEWSTATE" value="..." />
    <span id="Label1" style="...">Hello World</span>
    <input name="TextBox1" type="text" id="TextBox1"
        style="..." />
    <input type="submit" name="Button1" value="Say Hello"
        id="Button1" style="..." />
    </form>
</body>
```

NOTE   *Some of the values in the HTML have been replaced with ellipses (...) for clarity.*

The WebForms controls generate HTML just like a taglib. So where does the button click handler fit in? The ASP.NET framework processes the parameters returned by the page and routes them to the appropriate controls. The controls then fire events to trigger processing of the parameters. This model allows you to program WebForms in a similar fashion to WinForms.

The WebForms event model is quite different from the JSP model you are familiar with and may seem awkward at first. It will, however, save considerable time because it eliminates the need for much of the mundane housekeeping code that JSP demands.

The controls are instantiated in the class generated from the .aspx file. The class created by this process inherits from the one in the code-behind file. That is the meaning of `Inherits="WebFormsHelloWorld.WebForm1"` in the `Page` directive. If you are wondering why it is necessary to even specify that, consider the scenario where the code-behind file contains more than one descendant of `System.Web.UI.Page`. Without the `Inherits` attribute, how would ASP.NET know which class to use?

Using the WebControls

At the time of writing, there are no standard taglibs in JSP, so you will look at the WebControls in the context of the HTML form elements.

The basic building blocks are the `Label`, `TextBox`, `Button`, `CheckBox`, `RadioButton`, and `HyperLink` controls. Configure these in the designer. The event handlers are fairly intuitive, as demonstrated in the preceding example.

The next group of controls is based on lists. In JSP, you would typically generate a number of individual objects and add them to the control one by one. You can do this in WebForms, but it is easier to create an array of values and then use those values in the `DataSource` property for the control. An example is a `ListBox`, which may be populated as follows:

```
public string[] strs = new string[] { "a", "b", "c", "d" };

private void Page_Load(object sender, System.EventArgs e)
{
    ListBox1.DataSource = strs;
    ListBox1.DataBind();
}
```

A `ListBox` control ultimately generates an HTML `<select>` tag, as does a `DropDownList`. The `CheckBoxList` and `RadioButtonList` provide convenient ways to generate multiple `CheckBox` and `RadioButton` controls, respectively.

The `Table`, `TableRow`, and `TableCell` controls enable you to create an HTML table, which can be manipulated programmatically at runtime. For displaying database information, use a `DataGrid` control.

Another useful control is the `Calendar` control. This displays a monthly calendar and allows date selection in a user-friendly fashion. It has no counterpart in HTML but is rather a complex control built up of many HTML controls.

The `DataGrid` and `DataList` controls are for use with `DataSet`s, which typically contain database information.

Using Validation Controls

Validation controls validate the input to other controls. You can add validation controls to a page, and they will display an error message should the validation fail. If ASP.NET determines that the browser supports client-side scripts, it generates the appropriate code to perform the validation locally, eliminating the overhead of a roundtrip to the server.

The most useful validation controls are the `RequiredFieldValidator`, `RangeValidator`, and `RegularExpressionValidator`. The `RequiredFieldValidator`, when attached to a control, makes it easy to indicate that some form of entry is required. The `RangeValidator` is for specifying upper and lower boundaries on a numeric entry in a control. The `RegularExpressionValidator` control is for specifying a regular expression to be used in validating the control. The latter even provides a choice of canned expressions. The `RequiredFieldValidator` may be combined with other validations so you can require an entry and validate the value. The next example shows how to use validation controls to check a U.S. Social Security number entry. Follow these steps:

1. Create a new Web Application project called
    WebFormsValidationExample.

2. Drag a TextBox and a Button over to the form. Change the button text to
    Try it. Now drag over a RequiredFieldValidator to the right of the
    TextBox. Change its ErrorMessage property to **You must make an entry**.

3. Next, change the ControlToValidate property to the name of the TextBox
    control, **TextBox1**. The result should be similar to Figure 5-2.

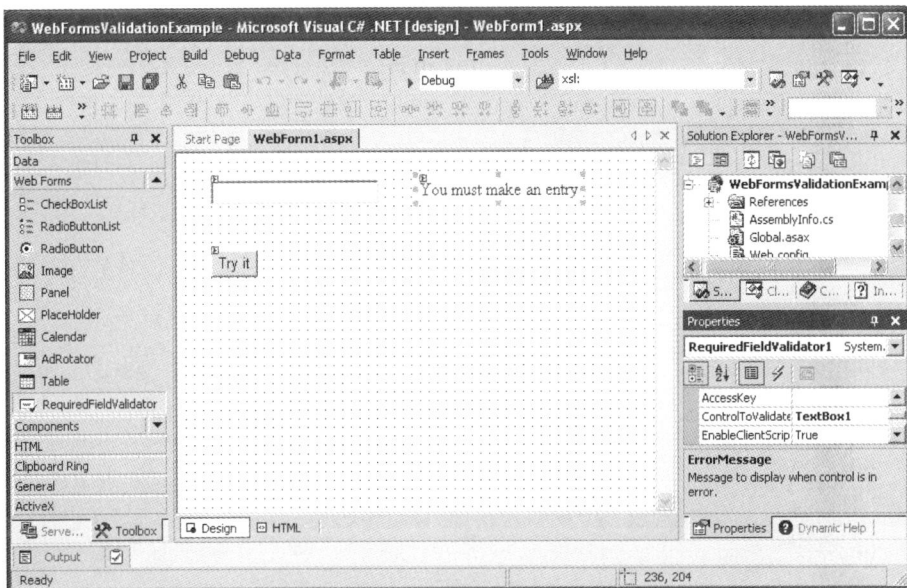

Figure 5-2. Design view of the page after adding RequiredFieldValidator

4. Build and run the project to see the effect of the validation control. Click
    the button without entering anything in the box and an error message
    appears. Enter something and the message goes away.

5. Now use a RegularExpressionValidator control to make the textbox
    entry conform to a U.S. Social Security number. Drag
    a RegularExpressionValidator to the form and place it on top of the
    RequiredFieldValidator so the error messages appear in the same place.
    You will not be permitted to drop the RegularExpressionValidator in
    exactly the same place using the mouse. Drop it as close to the
    RequiredFieldValidator as possible and then use the arrow keys to com-
    plete the positioning.

6. Change the `ControlToValidate` property of the `RegularExpressionValidator` to **TextBox1** and the `ErrorMessage` property to **Not a valid Social Security number**.

7. The key to the `RegularExpressionValidator` is the `ValidationExpression` property. In this case, make it [0-9]{3}-[0-9]{2}-[0-9]{4}. To do this, select the `ValidationExpression` property and press the ... button. When the dialog box shown in Figure 5-3 appears, leave the Standard Expressions on (Custom). Enter **[0-9]{3}-[0-9]{2}-[0-9]{4}** in the Validation Expression field and click OK.

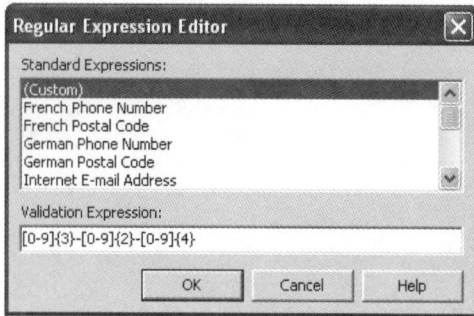

Figure 5-3. The Regular Expression Editor dialog box

This time when you run the project, you will get an error message if you enter nothing or if you fail to enter a correctly formatted U.S. Social Security number.

Informing the user of the validation errors is important, but your program will almost certainly need to behave differently depending on the success or failure of validation. The validation controls all have an `IsValid` property that you can use to determine the outcome of each validation programmatically. Follow these steps:

1. Add a `Label` control to the form and clear its `Text` property. Double-click the button to create a button click handler and change it as follows:

```
private void Button1_Click(object sender, System.EventArgs e)
{
    if ( RequiredFieldValidator1.IsValid &&
        RegularExpressionValidator1.IsValid )
    {
        Label1.Text = TextBox1.Text + " is valid";
    }
```

```
        else
        {
            Label1.Text = "";
        }
    }
```

2. Now when you run the project and enter a valid social security number, the label is populated.

This addition points out another interesting feature of the validation controls. You are probably using Internet Explorer (IE) 6 as it is required by Visual Studio .NET. For "smart" browsers, such as IE 6, the validation is performed by a client-side script to avoid unnecessary trips to the server. Therefore, you cannot rely on the server getting control when validation fails.

To demonstrate this, enter a valid U.S. Social Security number and then an invalid U.S. Social Security number in your form. The label should have been cleared, but because the validation error was displayed by the client-side script, the code to clear the label was never executed. Now change the `EnableClientScript` property of each of the validation controls to **false** and run the project again. This time the label is cleared when the invalid U.S. Social Security number is entered, but at the expense of a trip to the server.

Avoid Using a Control When HTML Will Do

It is not always appropriate to use a WebControl—sometimes HTML will do. An example of this is a label that is not changed at runtime. Why incur the overhead of a control, when you are never going to use it?

In the Toolbox you will find an HTML palette. This contains simple HTML design-time controls, which can also be used when building WebForms pages. Although you can manipulate these at design-time in the same way as the WebControls, they result in simple HTML in the body of the page. These can also be useful when assembling your own controls.

Building Your Own Controls

Building controls using JSP taglibs can be fairly complex. ASP.NET supports building controls at two different levels: user controls and server controls. User controls allow you to create page fragments that you can parameterize and reuse. If you need more power than user controls offer, you can create server controls, which have all the capabilities of the stock WebControls.

Creating WebForms User Controls

A user control is a page fragment stored in its own file with an .ascx suffix. The user control can have its own code-behind file and is fully supported by Visual Studio .NET. Employing user controls allows you to break down pages into reusable chunks (similar to modular programming). Follow these steps:

1. Create a new Web Application project called **WebFormsUserControlExample**. To add a user control, right-click the project and select Add ➤ Add Web User Control. . . . This will then prompt you for the name of the file to create; take the default of WebUserControl1.

2. Assemble the control as you would a page. For this example, add a Label and a HyperLink for a typical footer. Make the Text property of the Label **For questions about this page send mail to ** and the Text property of the HyperLink to **paul@csharpwebservices.com**. Now set the NavigateUrl property of the HyperLink to **mailto:paul@csharpwebservices.com**.

3. To use the control on a page in the project, drag the control from the Solution Explorer onto the page. Try it with the WebForm already provided in the project. Open the page in design view and drag the control onto it. This will create two new lines in WebForm1.aspx. The first establishes a reference to the control for the page:

    ```
    <%@ Register TagPrefix="uc1" TagName="WebUserControl1"
        rc="WebUserControl1.ascx" %>
    ```

    The second creates an instance of the control on the page:

    ```
    <uc1:WebUserControl1 id=WebUserControl11
        runat="server"></uc1:WebUserControl1>
    ```

4. Now run the project and you will see the contents of the control appear on the page. If you reuse the control on several pages in an application, you can make changes in the .ascx file that are reflected in all the pages that embed the control.

Creating WebForms Server Controls

Server controls have more in common with JSP taglibs but are more complex to develop than user controls, as they support the roundtrip. Server controls are contained in code only. Typically they inherit from System.Web.UI.Control or, more commonly, System.Web.UI.WebControls.WebControl. Follow these steps to create a control that wraps a text input field:

1. Start by creating an ASP.NET Web Application project, and call it **WebFormsServerControlExample**. Now add a code file for the control. Right-click the project and select Add ➢ Add Class...➢ Web Custom Control and accept the default name WebCustomControl1.cs.

2. To use the control on a form, it must be added to the Toolbox. First, build the project so that WebCustomControl1.dll exists. Now select Tools ➢ Customize Toolbox...➢ .NET Framework Components ➢ Browse...and navigate to WebCustomControl1.dll in C:\inetpub\wwwroot\WebFormsServerControlExample\bin. Check WebCustomControl1 when it appears in the list. Now the control will be listed in the Toolbox on the general palette.

3. Drag the control onto the form and change its Text property to **test**. Run the project and the word *test* should appear in the browser.

4. Now change the HTML produced by the control. This is carried out in the Render method and will create a text input box:

    ```
    protected override void Render(HtmlTextWriter output)
    {
        output.WriteBeginTag( "input" );
        output.WriteAttribute( "type", "input" );
        output.WriteAttribute( "name", UniqueID );
        output.WriteAttribute( "id", UniqueID );
        output.WriteAttribute( "value", Text );
        output.WriteEndTag( "input" );
    }
    ```

5. To make the control handle the post back data, you must implement the IPostBackDataHandler interface. You do this by implementing the LoadPostData and the RaisePostDataChangedEvent methods. The former handles the actual changing of the data and the latter notifying interested parties. The separation allows the framework to effect all changes to the data, before any other objects start reacting to the change. Add

a using statement for System.Collections.Specialized and then implement LoadPostData as follows:

```
public virtual bool LoadPostData( string postDataKey,
                                  NameValueCollection postCollection )
{
    String currText = Text;
    String newText = postCollection[postDataKey];
    if (currText != newText)
    {
        Text = newText;
        return true;
    }
    else
    {
        return false;
    }
}
```

6. Implement RaisePostDataChangedEvent as follows:

```
public virtual void RaisePostDataChangedEvent()
{
    // typically change events would be fired here
}
```

7. Remember to declare that you have implemented the IPostBackDataHandler interface:

```
public class WebCustomControl1 :
    System.Web.UI.WebControls.WebControl,
    IPostBackDataHandler
```

Now when you run the form, enter a text value, and press Enter, the value is posted back and with the appropriate event logic you have a usable control.

Creating ASP.NET Applications

An ASP.NET application is comprised of files held in an Internet Information Services (IIS) virtual root, or *vroot*. Each Visual Studio .NET project is its own application. The IIS vroot is created when the project is created. You are already familiar with the page generation files and content files. In addition to these, each application contains two additional files, web.config and global.asax.

The web.config file is an XML file that configures many options for the application as a whole. To view the type of information a web.config file contains, open one from any of the example projects you have already created.

The global.asax generated by Visual Studio .NET is little more than a directive that refers to its code-behind file global.asax.cs. If you attempt to open it, you will be placed in a design view, which is of little use. Switch to code view and you will see the code in Listing 5-4.

Listing 5-4. The global.asax File

```
public class Global : System.Web.HttpApplication
{
    protected void Application_Start(Object sender, EventArgs e)
    {
    }
    protected void Session_Start(Object sender, EventArgs e)
    {
    }
    protected void Application_BeginRequest(Object sender,
        EventArgs e)
    {
    }
    protected void Application_EndRequest(Object sender,
        EventArgs e)
    {
    }
    protected void Session_End(Object sender, EventArgs e)
    {
    }
    protected void Application_End(Object sender, EventArgs e)
    {
    }
}
```

These event handlers allow you to perform specialized processing at various stages in the application lifecycle for all requests. An example is a custom logging mechanism that needs to record all accesses to the application.

Maintaining State

Web pages are not as stateless as purists would have everyone believe. The strategies you may have used to maintain state in JSP will pave your way in ASP.NET. The techniques are the same; only the implementation details differ.

View State

One useful strategy is to pass data in a hidden form field. This works well for small amounts of noncritical data, as a clever user could easily access and modify the value. It also has the advantage that it stays in the context of the page, so when the user hits Back a few times, the correct value is returned.

ASP.NET WebControls use a special hidden form field called __VIEWSTATE to maintain state across page views. Each page has a property called ViewState, which is a collection of name-value pairs. When the page is rendered, the contents of ViewState are serialized into the __VIEWSTATE form field. This is more convenient than creating your own hidden fields. The contents are also obscured, which reduces the risk of tampering, although you should not rely on ViewState for sensitive data.

You could rewrite the Text property of the server control from the preceding section as follows:

```
public string Text
{
    get
    {
        return (string)ViewState[ "Text" ];
    }

    set
    {
        ViewState[ "Text" ] = value;
    }
}
```

The contents of ViewState become part of the page and are transferred to and from the browser. This makes it unsuitable for large volumes of information.

Session State

ASP.NET has the same concept of user sessions as JSP. Like JSP, it can use cookies or URL rewriting to track sessions.

There is a Session object accessible to all pages a given user visits within an application. You manipulate data stored in the Session object by key, as in:

```
Session[ "Who" ] = "Paul";
```

In a *Web farm* (multiple Web servers serving an individual site) configuration, session data is available to all the servers in the farm.

Application State

ASP.NET application state is analogous to JSP application state. ASP.NET application state is stored in an HttpApplicationState object accessible through each page's Application property. Information stored in the application state is available to all pages in the application, regardless of the user. A typical use might be to store small amounts of frequently accessed information.

Information is stored in the HttpApplicationState object using name-value pairs. The name is used as an index:

```
Application[ "TestKey" ] = NewValueTextBox.Text;
```

Be aware that the application state object is not inherently thread safe. Use the Lock and Unlock methods to serialize access:

```
try
{
    Application.Lock();
    Application[ "TestKey" ] = NewValueTextBox.Text;
}
finally
{
    Application.UnLock();
}
```

In a Web farm configuration, application state is not available across the servers. Even within the same server, each ASP.NET process has an independent copy of application state. This makes application state inappropriate for storing global data that changes on each page hit.

Cookies

The equivalent of javax.servlet.http.Cookie in ASP.NET is System.Web.HttpCookie. These classes provide basically the same functionality, although many of the methods in the Java version are replaced by properties in the ASP.NET version. The ASP.NET HttpCookie class also provides a convenient mechanism for storing several values in the same cookie.

The HttpCookie class can hold either a single value or a set of values accessed by a string indexer. It also provides a HasKeys property to determine whether it contains a single value or multiple subkeys.

The cookies for a given request or response are accessible through the Cookies property of the appropriate HttpRequest or HttpResponse instance:

```
HttpCookie cookie = new HttpCookie( "Sample" );
cookie[ "A" ] = TextBox1.Text;
cookie[ "B" ] = TextBox2.Text;
cookie[ "C" ] = TextBox3.Text;
Response.Cookies.Add( cookie );
```

Using HttpHandler Pages

ASP.NET pages that have an .ashx suffix fulfill a similar role to Java servlets. Instead of inheriting from System.Web.UI.Page, they implement System.Web.IHttpHandler.

Visual Studio .NET does not directly support creating such pages, so you need to start with a Web application project. You can then add a xyz.ashx file and a xyz.ashx.cs file. You may keep the code in the .ashx file, but it is advantageous to put it in a separate code-behind file. This enables you to take advantage of the Visual Studio .NET support that is present for .cs files.

Let's create a handler that returns a simple plain text file. Follow these steps:

1. Create a new Empty Web project called **HandlerExample**. Then create a reference to the System.Web library. Right-click References, and select Add Reference. . . . When the dialog box comes up, scroll the list down and double-click System.Web.dll. Then click OK.

2. Now use Add ➢ Add New Item... ➢ Text File, but call the file **Handler.ashx**. Enter the following in the file:

    ```
    <%@ WebHandler Language="c#" Codebehind="Handler.ashx.cs"
        class="HandlerExample.Handler" %>
    ```

    Notice that the directive specifies WebHandler instead of Page.

3. You can now create the code-behind file. Right-click the project and
    select Add ➤ Add New Item...➤ Code File and call it **Handler.ashx.cs**.
    The following is a good template to begin with, so enter the following
    into the blank file:

```
using System.Web;

namespace HandlerExample
{
    public class Handler : IHttpHandler
    {
        public void ProcessRequest(HttpContext context)
        {
            HttpRequest request = context.Request;
            HttpResponse response = context.Response;
        }

        public bool IsReusable
        {
            get
            {
                return true;
            }
        }
    }
}
```

There are no equivalents of doGet, doPost and so on in IHttpHandler.
There is only ProcessRequest, which is more like the service method in
HttpServlet.

4. Now add the code to ProcessRequest so it actually returns something.
    Change ProcessRequest so it reads as follows, and then build the project:

```
public void ProcessRequest(HttpContext context)
{
    HttpRequest request = context.Request;
    HttpResponse response = context.Response;

    response.ContentType = "text/plain";
    response.Write( "Hello World!" );
    response.End();
}
```

5. Before you can run the handler you need to do a few more things. First open the Properties panel for Handler.ashx and change the Build Action property to **Content**. This enables the Set as Start Page option on the context menu for Handler.ashx, which you should select.

6. The other thing you need is a web.config file for the project. From the project's context menu select Add ➢ Add New Item... ➢ Web Configuration File. There is no need to change the default web.config settings for this example.

7. You should now be able to run the project just as you would a WebForms project. When your browser opens the page, you will see the familiar message: Hello World!

You can return textual data other than HTML from a regular .aspx page. If you want full control of the output stream, an HttpHandler is a better choice. Listing 5-5 shows the `ProcessRequest` method that returns the contents of a GIF file.

Listing 5-5. The `ProcessRequest` Method

```
public void ProcessRequest(HttpContext context)
{
    HttpRequest request = context.Request;
    HttpResponse response = context.Response;

    response.ContentType = "image/gif";

    FileStream fs = new FileStream( @"c:\inetpub\wwwroot\winxp.gif",
        FileMode.Open,
        FileAccess.Read,
        FileShare.Read );
    long rem = fs.Length;

    byte[] buffer = new byte[ 4096 ];
    while ( rem >= 4096 )
    {
        fs.Read( buffer, 0, 4096 );
        response.BinaryWrite( buffer );
        rem -= 4096;
    }
    if ( rem > 0 )
    {
        buffer = new byte[ rem ];
```

```
        fs.Read( buffer, 0, (int)rem );
        response.BinaryWrite( buffer );
    }
    fs.Close();

    response.End();
}
```

Comparing ASP.NET to ASP

Active Server Pages (ASP) is the equivalent of JSP and ASP.NET for unmanaged code. Although there are similarities between all three technologies, ASP has some significant differences from both JSP and ASP.NET.

The biggest difference is that ASP uses scripting languages rather than compiled languages. To overcome this limitation, performance-critical code for an ASP page is typically written as a COM object using a compiled language.

The concept of code behind does not exist in ASP. Code is executed as it is encountered, starting at the top of the page as with JSP. ASP uses the familiar <%...%> construct to encapsulate code. If you embed code within an ASP.NET page, function definitions and global variables must be enclosed like this:

```
<script language="c#" runat="server">
...
</script>
```

in blocks reminiscent of JSP's <jsp:declaration> or <%!...%> blocks. The <%...%> construct is used in ASP.NET more like <jsp:scriptlet> is in JSP.

ASP has no equivalent of reusable code similar to ASP.NET user controls and server controls or JSP taglibs.

ASP.NET and ASP are quite different. The main thing to understand is that ASP.NET is a significant improvement over ASP, and any comparisons between JSP and ASP you may have read about will not apply.

Summary

WebForms raise the productivity level of your Web page development. Your knowledge gained developing JSP pages will only enhance your understanding of what the framework is doing for you. The ability to build your own controls and reuse them across pages and projects is a big advance from JSP include files.

This is one of the areas where .NET with Visual Studio .NET takes a big step beyond what you have in Java today.

Exploring ADO.NET

A<small>CTIVE</small>X D<small>ATA</small> O<small>BJECTS</small> for the .NET Framework (ADO.NET) is your database interface in .NET, the equivalent of Java's Java Database Connectivity (JDBC). This chapter covers database access using ADO.NET and how it differs from JDBC. It closely looks at the DataSet object, which is the core of the ADO.NET disconnected model and how to use data binding to WinForms controls and ASP.NET controls, in particular the DataGrid controls. First, you will discover the tools provided by Visual Studio .NET to assist with database development.

Using Visual Studio .NET Database Features

Although not strictly ADO.NET, this is an ideal time to touch on the Visual Studio .NET tools that facilitate database development. After all, you need to set up a database to develop and run the examples in this chapter. These tools are geared to Microsoft SQL Server development. However, Visual Studio .NET includes a copy of Microsoft SQL Server 2000 Desktop Engine (MSDE), which is what I used to develop these examples.

You might be used to using SQL Enterprise Manager and SQL Query Analyzer to administer SQL Server, but some functions are readily performed from within Visual Studio .NET, making it unnecessary to launch a different tool. It is also important to realize you cannot do everything from the Integrated Development Environment (IDE).

By default, the Server Explorer is a separate tab in the same slide-out panel that holds the Toolbox. You can use the Server Explorer to connect to SQL Server instances on the local or remote systems. Once connected, you can manipulate databases, tables, and stored procedures, providing you have permission to do so.

You cannot modify permissions using the Visual Studio .NET Server Explorer. You will need to launch SQL Enterprise Manager to manipulate these.

Creating Databases

To create a new database, select the SQL Server instance. In this case, choose the local MSDE instance, which will be called VSDOTNET. Right-click the node to open the context menu and select New Database, as shown in Figure 6-1.

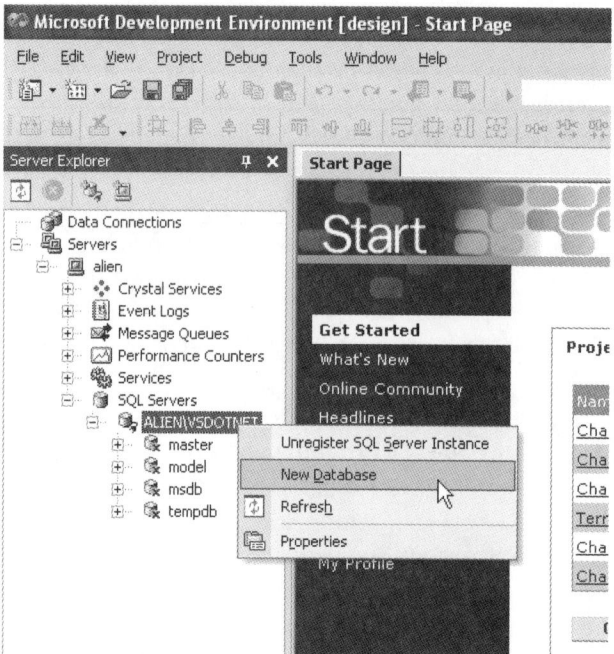

Figure 6-1. Creating a new database

When the Create Database dialog box appears, as in Figure 6-2, supply a name for the database. In this case, enter **chapter6** in the New Database Name box, and click OK. Note that although this is convenient for development purposes, you are not able to control any aspect other than the name. Everything else such as the location, log location, and so on used their default values.

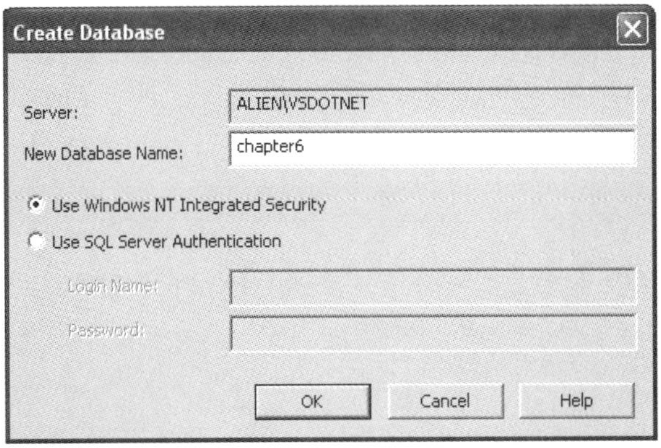

Figure 6-2. *Naming a new database*

Creating Tables

The first step to create a table is to expand the new database node. You will see a Tables node. Open the context menu for the Tables node and select New Table, as in Figure 6-3.

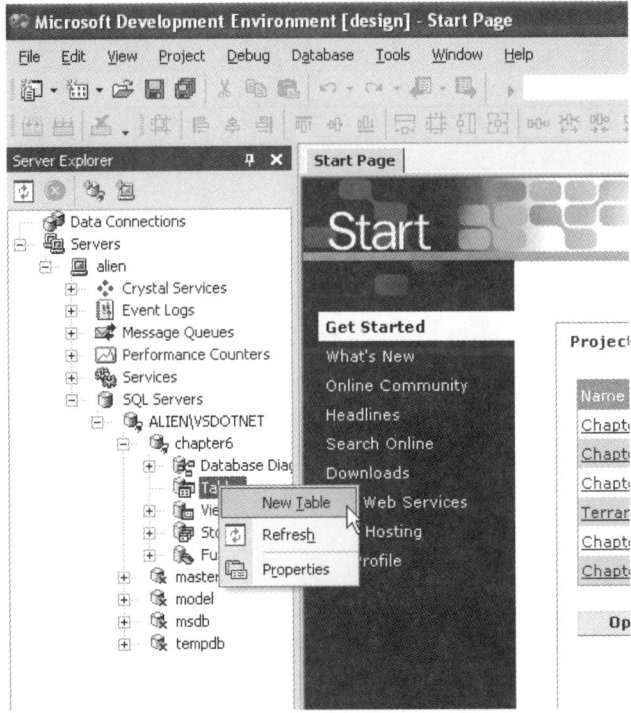

Figure 6-3. *Creating a new table*

You will then be placed in the design view for a table. This enables you to specify the characteristics for the rows and specify any indexes or constraints. Figure 6-4 shows the rows for a table to hold details of .NET languages.

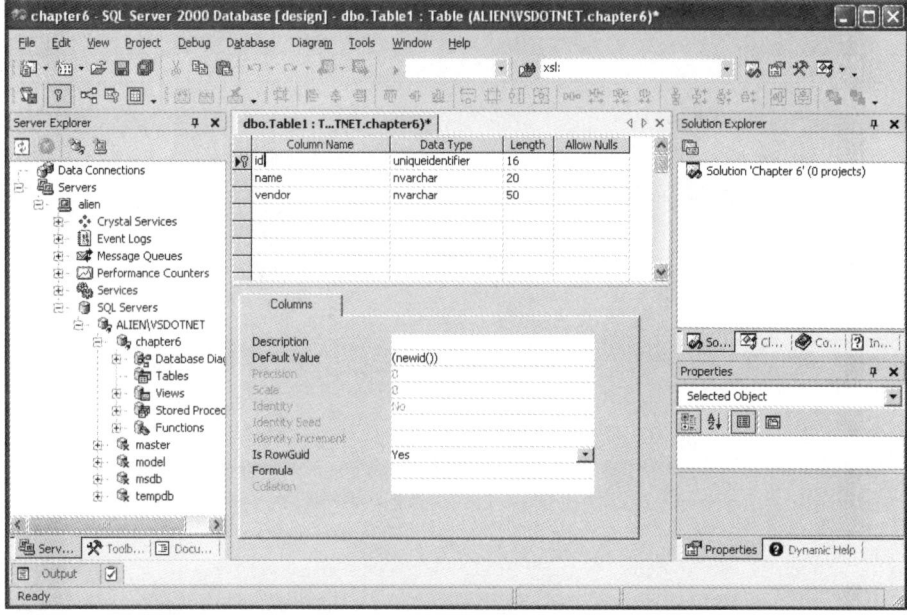

Figure 6-4. Designing a table

Up to this point, the table has been assigned a dummy name, in this case Table1. When you save the table, you will be prompted to enter a name, as shown in Figure 6-5. For this example, enter the name **dotnetlanguages**.

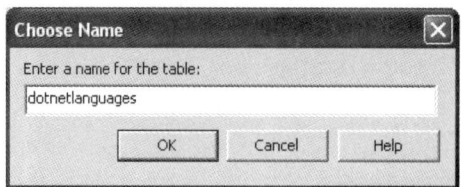

Figure 6-5. Naming a new table

Now you have created the table, you need to enter some data. Select the table and open its context menu. Select Retrieve Data from Table, as shown in Figure 6-6.

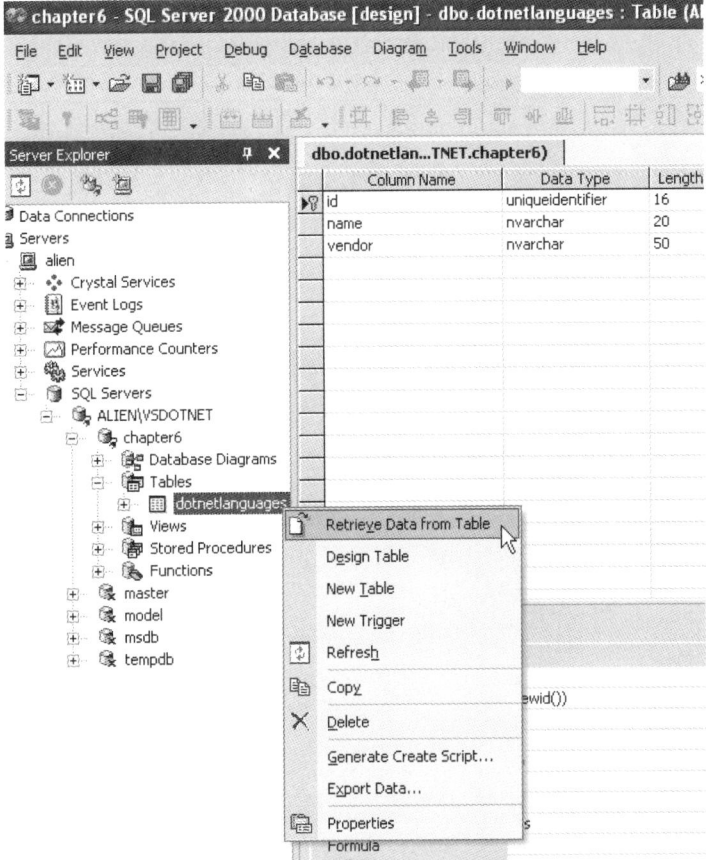

Figure 6-6. Retrieving data from a table

This opens a DataGrid control, which allows you to insert, edit, and delete rows from the table. At this point you need to enter some rows. Providing you correctly set the default for the id column to newid() as shown in Figure 6-4, you can just enter data into the name and vendor columns. As you enter each row, it appears to vanish, but if you rerun the query, by selecting Query ➤ Run or by pressing the toolbar button with the red exclamation mark (!), you will see that the rows are part of the table. If you make a mistake, press the Esc key to abandon entry into a cell or type over your error. If you create a row you do not want, right-click in the left column and select Delete. You should end up with something similar to Figure 6-7.

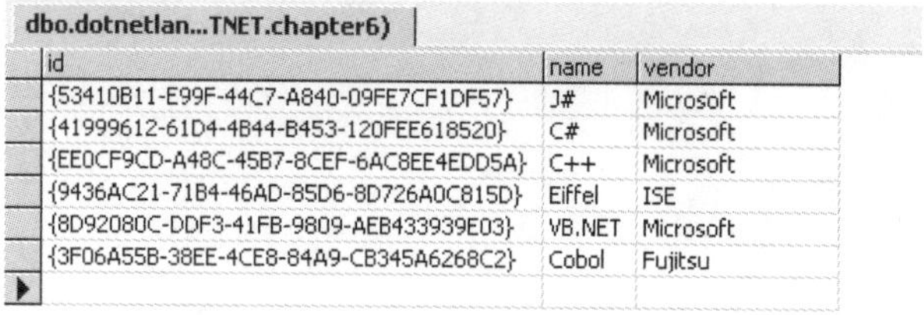

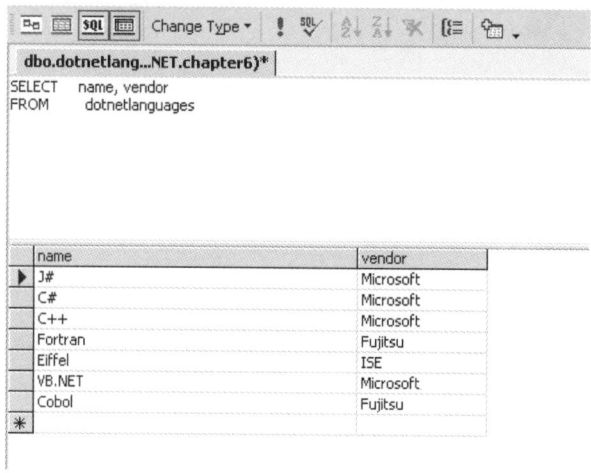

Figure 6-7. Editing rows in a table

If you need to restrict the rows, select View ≻ Panes ≻ SQL to open a panel, which allows you to enter SQL much as you would in the SQL Query Analyzer. When you run the query, the results are shown in the DataGrid control. Figure 6-8 shows the dotnetlanguages table without the id field, which is an easier way to enter data in this case.

Figure 6-8. Using the SQL pane

Developing Stored Procedures

Creating and editing stored procedures is also made easy using the Server Explorer. Select the Stored Procedures node and open its context menu. Then select New Stored Procedure, as shown in Figure 6-9.

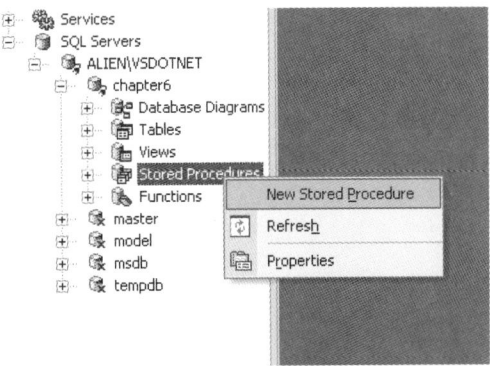

Figure 6-9. Creating a new stored procedure

You will be given the following skeleton stored procedure to start from in an edit panel:

```
CREATE PROCEDURE dbo.StoredProcedure1
/*
    (
        @parameter1 datatype = default value,
        @parameter2 datatype OUTPUT
    )
*/
AS
    /* SET NOCOUNT ON */
    RETURN
```

You can then edit this template to create your procedure. Create the following from the template:

```
CREATE PROCEDURE dbo.ListLanguagesForVendor
(
    @vendor nvarchar(50)
)
AS
    SELECT name
    FROM dotnetlanguages
    WHERE vendor = @vendor

    RETURN
```

Now save it by selecting File ➤ Save. If you have not changed the procedure name from the one suggested in the template, you will be prompted to enter one at this time.

To test the new procedure, open its context menu and select Run Stored Procedure. A dialog box will prompt you for any parameters, in this case @vendor. The Output panel will display the results.

Comparing a Simple Query in JDBC and ADO.NET

You will now create a simple query in JDBC and then again in ADO.NET to examine the differences between these two technologies.

Using JDBC

To use JDBC to create a simple query, follow these steps:

1. First create a typical JDBC query for the table dotnetlanguages on the local MSDE database chapter6 that you created in the preceding section.

2. Start by obtaining a Connection object:

```
String cstr = "jdbc:microsoft:sqlserver://localhost:1494; "
    + "DataBaseName=Chapter6;User=sa";
Connection conn = null;
Statement stmt = null;
ResultSet rs = null;

try
{
    Class.forName("com.microsoft.jdbc.sqlserver.SQLServerDriver");
    conn = DriverManager.getConnection( cstr );
```

NOTE *Determining which port MSDE is listening on can be difficult. Check the ERRORLOG.1 file located at* C:\Program Files\Microsoft SQL Server\MSSQL$VSdotNET\LOG.

3. Next create the `Statement` object and execute a SQL statement using it.
    As you are performing a query, use the `executeQuery` method. This will
    return a `ResultSet` object:

```
stmt = conn.createStatement();
rs = stmt.executeQuery( "select * from dotnetlanguages" );
```

4. The next step is to iterate over the rows in the `ResultSet` and extract the
    fields you are interested in:

```
while( rs.next() )
{
    System.out.println( rs.getString( "name" ) );
}
```

5. Finally, ensure everything gets closed to avoid waiting for garbage col-
    lection. In most cases there are not finalizers to close the `ResultSet`,
    `Statement`, or `Connection` objects:

```
}
finally
{
    if ( rs != null )
    {
        rs.close();
    }
    if ( stmt != null )
    {
        stmt.close();
    }
    if ( conn != null )
    {
        conn.close();
    }
}
```

Using ADO.NET

Listing 6-1 shows the equivalent .NET code.

Listing 6-1. The .NET Code

```
using System;
using System.Data;
using System.Data.SqlClient;
using System.Data.SqlTypes;

namespace SimpleQuery
{
    class SimpleQuery
    {
        [STAThread]
        static void Main(string[] args)
        {
            string cstr = @"Server=.\VSdotNET;"
                + @"Database=Chapter6;"
                + @"Integrated Security=SSPI";
            using ( SqlConnection conn = new SqlConnection( cstr ) )
            {
                conn.Open();

                SqlCommand cmd
                    = new SqlCommand( "select * from dotnetlanguages", conn );
                SqlDataReader rdr = cmd.ExecuteReader();

                while ( rdr.Read() )
                {
                    System.Console.WriteLine( "{0}", rdr.GetString( 1 ) );
                }
                rdr.Close();
            }
        }
    }
}
```

Start in a similar way to JDBC by creating a connection object. However, you must explicitly open the connection before using it:

```
string cstr = @"Server=.\VSdotNET;"
    + @"Database=Chapter6;"
    + @"Integrated Security=SSPI";
```

```
using ( SqlConnection conn = new SqlConnection( cstr ) )
{
    conn.Open();
  ....
}
```

In this case you create a `SqlConnection` instance because you are using the SQL Server managed data provider. Whereas JDBC and Microsoft's own OLE DB and ODBC use a factory pattern to return abstract interfaces to the database drivers/providers, ADO.NET uses separate providers whose classes you use directly. This is not a return to chaos, as the providers are built on top of a base class hierarchy and therefore follow a consistent pattern.

There are three managed database providers available at the time of writing: the SQL Server provider used in this example, an OLE DB provider, and an ODBC provider. The ODBC provider is not part of the base install and must be downloaded separately.

The connection string will vary with the provider and driver, just as it does in JDBC. In the SQL Server managed data provider case, the `Server` parameter specifies the server machine and SQL Server instance. Using the MSDE from Visual Studio .NET, my system results in `Server=.\VSdotNet`. If you are not using the local machine, you must substitute your own system name. If you use a full version of SQL Server rather than the MSDE that comes with Visual Studio .NET, remove `\VSdotNET`, unless your DBA instructs you to use a specific SQL Server instance name which would replace `VSdotNET`. The `Database` property specifies which database on the server to use. If you accepted the default authentication option when you installed MSDE, you choose Windows Authentication. In this case, use the `Integrated Security` parameter and specify the value `SSPI`. In this mode, the underlying Windows logon is used to authenticate to SQL Server or MSDE. This avoids the need to hard-code user credentials in the connection string. If you choose mixed authentication, you will have specified a password for the internal SQL Server user account sa during installation. sa is the SQL Server administrator account. Replace the `Integrated Security` parameter with `User ID` and `Password` parameters. The result should be similar to this:

```
string cstr = @"Server=.\VSdotNET;"
    + @"Database=Chapter6;"
    + @"User ID=sa;Password=xxxx";
```

If you did not install SQL Server, you will have to consult you system or database administrator to find out which mode and accounts to use.

 **NOTE** *If you need to adjust your connection string for this example you will need to make similar changes in the connection strings for all other database examples in this book.*

The ADO.NET equivalent of the JDBC Statement is the command object, SqlCommand in this case. There is no separation equivalent to Statement and PreparedStatement in ADO.NET. In place of the ResultSet, obtain a data reader (a SqlDataReader in this example) by invoking the ExecuteReader method of the command as follows:

```
SqlCommand cmd =
    new SqlCommand( "select * from dotnetlanguages", conn );
SqlDataReader rdr = cmd.ExecuteReader();
```

Iterating over the rows in the data reader is similar to performing the same operation on a ResultSet. A data reader is forward only, and you cannot reposition the current record pointer the way you can with a ResultSet:

```
while ( rdr.Read() )
{
    System.Console.WriteLine( "{0}", rdr.GetString( 1 ) );
}
```

When extracting the fields from a data reader's row, use the field index. You cannot use field names with a data reader.

In JDBC closing the ResultSet can be an optional step (however, not closing the ResultSet can tie up resources when using some databases, such as Oracle). In ADO.NET you cannot use the connection for anything else until you have closed the data reader:

```
rdr.Close();
```

In C#, employ the using statement to simplify the code and implicitly call Dispose to close the connection:

```
using ( SqlConnection conn = new SqlConnection( cstr ) )
{
    conn.Open();

    ...
}
```

 **NOTE** *The data reader classes do not implement* IDisposable, *so you cannot employ a* using *statement in those cases.*

Most of the time, ADO.NET providers close the connection in their finalizer if you have not already done so. However, as garbage collection is inherently unpredictable, it would be unwise to rely on it for such a precious resource.

Using CommandBehavior.CloseConnection

You will find many examples that use the following form of ExecuteReader:

```
SqlDataReader rdr =
    cmd.ExecuteReader( CommandBehavior.CloseConnection );
```

This form of ExecuteReader specifies that the connection is to be closed when the data reader is closed. You might use CommandBehavior.CloseConnection in situations where you open a connection, execute a single SQL statement, read the results, and then close the connection. Listing 6-2 is an example of this.

Listing 6-2. Typical Usage of CommandBehavior.CloseConnection *(Do Not Do This)*

```
string cstr = @"Server=.\VSdotNET;"
    + @"Database=Chapter6;"
    + @"Integrated Security=SSPI";
SqlConnection conn = new SqlConnection( cstr );

conn.Open();
SqlCommand cmd
    = new SqlCommand( "select * from dotnetlanguages", conn );
SqlDataReader rdr
    = cmd.ExecuteReader( CommandBehavior.CloseConnection );

while ( rdr.Read() )
{
    System.Console.WriteLine( "{0}", rdr.GetString( 1 ) );
}

rdr.Close();
```

Examining this code reveals that there is no guarantee that the connection will be closed when an error occurs. This is not acceptable in a production application. Your next thought might be to ensure the reader gets closed by adding a try...catch block. Even if you do this there is still a window between the connection being opened and the reader being created, which could suffer a failure and result in the connection being left open. You could add another try...catch block around the whole thing to ensure the connection gets closed. At this point you have added a try...catch block to close the connection, just to avoid having to explicitly close the connection!

Forget CommandBehavior.CloseConnection and employ a using statement to ensure the connection gets closed. This results in much cleaner and more maintainable code (see Listing 6-3).

Listing 6-3. Employing a using Statement to Ensure the Connection Gets Closed

```
string cstr = @"Server=.\VSdotNET;"
    + @"Database=Chapter6;"
    + @"Integrated Security=SSPI";
using ( SqlConnection conn = new SqlConnection( cstr ) )
{
    conn.Open();

    SqlCommand cmd =
        new SqlCommand( "select * from dotnetlanguages", conn );
    SqlDataReader rdr = cmd.ExecuteReader();

    while ( rdr.Read() )
    {
        System.Console.WriteLine( "{0}", rdr.GetString( 1 ) );
    }
    rdr.Close();
}
```

Using Command Parameters

ADO.NET does not have separate objects that parallel JDBC's Statement and PreparedStatement. The command object you have already seen can be used with parameters.

When using providers other than the SQL Server managed provider, parameters look much as they do in JDBC. The SQL statement itself is passed to the command with question marks (?)where the parameters are to be substituted:

```
string selstr =
    "select vendor from dotnetlanguages where name = ?";
OleDbCommand cmd = new OleDbCommand( selstr, conn );
```

In the SQL Server managed provider, the parameters are named and preceded by an at (@) symbol:

```
string selstr =
    "select vendor from dotnetlanguages where name = @name";
SqlCommand cmd = new SqlCommand( selstr, conn );
```

For each parameter, you must specify the type by creating an instance of the appropriate parameter class, such as `SqlParameter` or `OleDbParameter`. With the SQL Server managed provider, the name identifies the parameter within the SQL statement:

```
SqlParameter name =
    cmd.Parameters.Add( "@name", SqlDbType.NVarChar, 15 );
```

In all other cases, the order they are added to the command's `Parameters` property determines the question mark placeholder to which they correspond. The parameter name is irrelevant, although it must be specified:

```
OleDbParameter name =
    cmd.Parameters.Add( "@name", OleDbType.VarChar, 15 );
```

The `Value` property of the parameter object is set to the desired value prior to each call.

```
name.Value = textBox1.Text;
```

Using Stored Procedures

In JDBC you use the `Connection.prepareCall` method to specify the stored procedure and its parameters and may use question marks (?) as you would in `prepareStatement`. You can then specify which are output or input/output parameters by invoking methods on the `CallableStatement` returned by `prepareCall`.

In ADO.NET you create the command object specifying only the stored procedure name in place of the SQL statement. You then set the `CommandType` property of the command to `StoredProcedure`. You instantiate the parameter objects as you would with a regular command, but by specifying its `Direction` property you can indicate that a parameter is output or input/output. You can also designate one parameter as the return value of the stored procedure by specifying a `Direction` of `ParameterDirection.ReturnValue`.

Using the following SQL Server stored procedure in the button handler of a WinForms Form demonstrates this:

```
CREATE PROCEDURE dbo.QueryVendor
(
    @name nvarchar(15),
    @vendor nvarchar(15) = NULL OUTPUT
)
AS
    SELECT @vendor = vendor
    FROM dotnetlanguages
    WHERE name = @name


    RETURN @@ROWCOUNT
```

Listing 6-4 is equivalent to the SQL used previously, but it uses parameters exclusively and demonstrates input, output, and return value parameter types.

Listing 6-4. Invoking a Stored Procedure with Parameters

```
private void button1_Click(object sender, System.EventArgs e)
{
    string cstr = @"Server=.\VSdotNET;"
        + @"Database=Chapter6;"
        + @"Integrated Security=SSPI";
    using ( SqlConnection conn = new SqlConnection( cstr ) )
    {
        conn.Open();

        // stored procedure name is used in place of SQL statement
        // and type is set to stored procedure
        SqlCommand cmd = new SqlCommand( "QueryVendor", conn );
        cmd.CommandType = CommandType.StoredProcedure;

        // input parm
        SqlParameter name =
            cmd.Parameters.Add( "@name", SqlDbType.NVarChar, 15 );
        name.Value = textBox1.Text;

        // output parm
        SqlParameter vendor =
            cmd.Parameters.Add( "@vendor",
                                SqlDbType.NVarChar,
                                15 );
        vendor.Direction = ParameterDirection.Output;
```

```
    // return value
    SqlParameter rowCount =
        cmd.Parameters.Add( "@rowCount", SqlDbType.Int );
    rowCount.Direction = ParameterDirection.ReturnValue;

    // use this since we return no rows - just parms
    cmd.ExecuteNonQuery();

    if ( (int)rowCount.Value > 0 )
    {
        MessageBox.Show( this,
                         textBox1.Text +
                         " is available from " +
                         vendor.Value );
    }
    else
    {
        MessageBox.Show( this,
                         textBox1.Text +
                         " is not available yet" );
    }
  }
}
```

If your stored procedure returns rows as well as output or return parameters, be aware that the values of the parameters will not be available until the data reader has been closed.

Using DataSets

Although the data reader is the closest analogy to a JDBC ResultSet, Microsoft is promoting the DataSet as the normal way to use ADO.NET. A DataSet has some of the characteristics of a JDBC CachedRowSet in that it provides a way to assemble a set of data and then disconnect from the database before processing it, possibly remotely.

The Simple Query Revisited

Re-create the example from the start of this chapter using a DataSet instead of a data reader to show how they differ:

1. First, create the `DataSet` to hold the data:

```
DataSet dset = new DataSet();
```

2. The connection is then obtained as in the previous example, but instead of creating a `SqlCommand`, a `SqlDataAdapter` is instantiated using the desired SQL statement:

```
SqlDataAdapter da =
    new SqlDataAdapter( "select * from dotnetlanguages", conn );
```

3. Next use the `DataAdapter` to populate a `DataTable` in the `DataSet`. A name is given to the table in the `DataSet`, but it does not need to match the name of the original table in the database:

```
da.Fill( dset, "languages" );
```

4. Now, by placing the data in a `DataSet` you can safely close the connection before processing the data:

```
using ( SqlConnection conn = new SqlConnection( cstr ) )
{
    conn.Open();

    SqlDataAdapter da =
        new SqlDataAdapter( "select * from dotnetlanguages",
                            conn );
    da.Fill( dset, "languages" );
}
```

5. Now iterate the rows in the table and access the required fields by name. Specify the name for the `DataTable` that you used in the `Fill` method:

```
foreach( DataRow dr in dset.Tables[ "languages" ].Rows )
{
    System.Console.WriteLine( "{0}", dr[ "name" ] );
}
```

Beyond the Single Table DataSet

In the preceding example you were able to read the results of a query into a collection and close the connection before processing it. However, a DataSet can do more than store the results of a single query.

Tables

A DataSet is made up of a collection of DataTable objects. In the example, you added one DataTable. If the application required several queries to be run against a database they could all have been placed in the same DataSet. A DataSet can be serialized and transmitted to a remote client for processing. Sending a single DataSet containing all the necessary tables is more efficient than sending several individual ones.

One great feature of using a DataSet is that the tables can come from several databases. It is possible to assemble all the data a client needs into one DataSet and then send all of the data in a single transfer, isolating the client program from the details of how the tables are mapped to databases.

Relationships

Having multiple tables in a DataSet is useful, but what if you do not know exactly which rows you need at the time you make the query? You could extract all the data you might need (providing it is constrained enough) and process it later, but then you lose the power of SQL to select the data you need. With a little additional logic, you can model the relationships between the tables in the DataSet and use them when you process the data.

Imagine the following scenario. You have a WinForms application that displays the language skills of a development team. By using the application, you can discover the languages a given developer knows or see which developers are proficient in a given language. This is a *many-to-many* relationship typically modeled using a simple link table. Figure 6-10 shows the design view of the developers' table, and Figure 6-11 shows the design view of the link table, called devlanglink.

dbo.developers...TNET.chapter6)				◁ ▷
Column Name	Data Type	Length	Allow Nulls	
empno	int	4		
name	nvarchar	50		

Figure 6-10. The design view of the developers' table

dbo.devlangli...TNET.chapter6)				◁ ▷
Column Name	Data Type	Length	Allow Nulls	
langid	uniqueidentifier	16		
empno	int	4		

Figure 6-11. The design view of the link table, `devlanglink`

Notice that `devlanglink` has a composite primary key. To set this while designing the table in Visual Studio .NET, select both rows, right-click to open the context menu, and then select Set Primary Key, as shown in Figure 6-12.

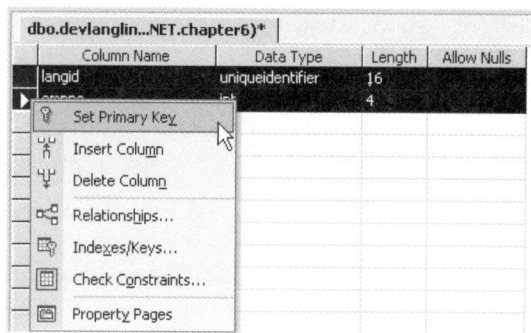

Figure 6-12. Creating the composite primary key for `devlanglink`

You can extract the list of languages for a developer using the following:

```
SELECT l.name from dotnetlanguages as l
JOIN devlanglink as k ON l.id = k.langid
JOIN developers as d ON d.empno = k.empno
WHERE d.name = @devname
```

You can obtain the developers who know a language using this:

```
SELECT d.name from developers as d
JOIN devlanglink as k ON d.empno = k.empno
JOIN dotnetlanguages as l ON l.id = k.langid
WHERE l.name = @langname
```

Unfortunately, this requires a trip to the database each time. Over a slow connection the user interface would respond slowly, and it would be impossible to work offline. If you extract the data into a DataSet, you can use relationships between the DataTables to obtain the subsets without contacting the database each time.

The following example demonstrates how you can use DataSet relationships:

1. Create a new Windows Application project called **RelationExample**. Modify the form so that its Text property reads **Relation Example** and its Size is **500, 300**.

2. Drag a Panel control from the Toolbox onto the form. Set its Dock property to **Bottom** and its Size to **492, 50**. Drag a Button control onto the Panel. Set its name to **loadDataButton**, its Text property to **Load Data**, and its Dock property to **Fill**.

3. Drag a TabControl control onto the form and set its Dock property to **Left**.

4. Drag a Splitter control onto the form. It should dock to the right of the TabControl control.

5. Drag a TextBox control onto the form and set its Name to **listTextBox**. Set its MultiLine property to **true**, its Dock property to **Fill**, and clear its Text property.

6. Select the TabControl and open its TabPages collection by clicking on the button with the ellipsis (. . .). You will see the usual collection dialog box. Click Add to add a TabPage to the collection. Set the page's name to **languageTabPage** and its Text property to **language**. Click Add again and this time set the name to **developerTabPage** and the Text property to **developer**. Click OK to close the dialog box.

7. Select the Language tab.

8. Drag a Label control onto the tab. Position it near the top of the page. Change its Text property to **Choose a language**.

9. Drag a ComboBox control onto the tab and position it below the Label. Change the name of the ComboBox to **languageComboBox** and clear its Text property.

10. Drag a Button control onto the tab. Set its name to **languageButton** and its Text property to **Which developers know this language?** Change the

Dock property to **Bottom** and then increase the Size property to **192, 50** so that all the text is visible.

11. The form should now look like that shown in Figure 6-13.

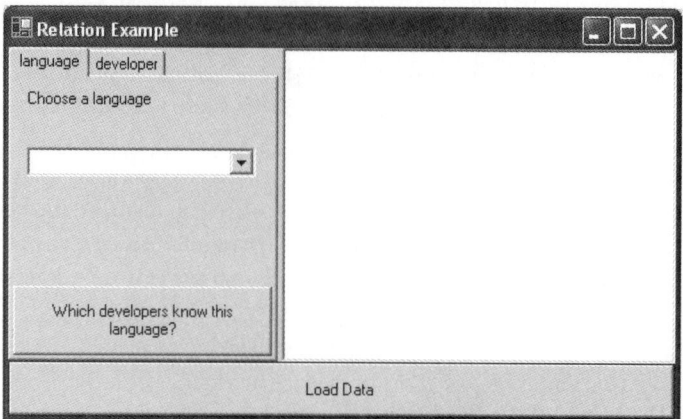

Figure 6-13. The form with the Language tab completed

12. Select the Developer tab.

13. Drag a Label control onto the tab. Position it near the top of the page. Change its Text property to **Choose a developer**.

14. Drag a ComboBox control onto the tab and position it below the Label. Change the name of the ComboBox to **developerComboBox** and clear its Text property.

15. Drag a Button control onto the tab. Set its name to **developerButton** and its Text property to **What languages do they know?** Change the Dock property to **Bottom** and then increase the Size property to **192, 50** so that all the text is visible.

16. The form should now look like that shown in Figure 6-14.

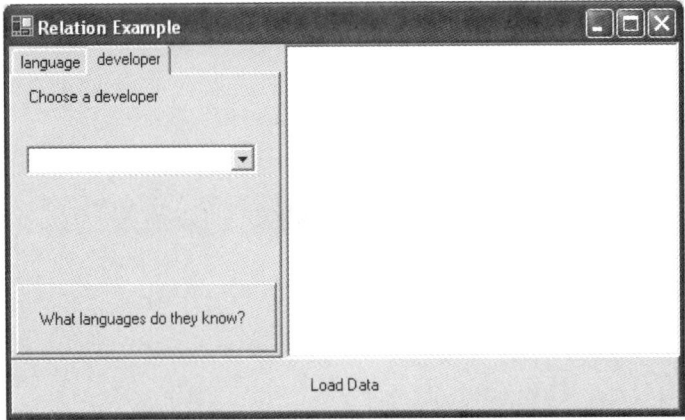

Figure 6-14. The form with the Developer tab completed

17. Double-click loadDataButton to create a button click handler. Change the code to that shown in Listing 6-5. Start by populating the DataSet with rows from the dotnetlanguages, developers, and devlanglink tables. To set up the relationships, create DataRelation objects and add them to the Relations property of the DataSet. A DataRelation specifies how columns in one table relate to columns in another table. You specify the columns as DataColumn objects.

Listing 6-5. Loading the Data into the DataSet *and Setting Up the* DataRelation *Objects*

```
const string connstr = @"Server=.\VSdotNET;"
    + @"Database=Chapter6;"
    + @"Integrated Security=SSPI";

private DataSet ds = null;

private void loadDataButton_Click(object sender,
                                  System.EventArgs e)
{
    ds = new DataSet();

    using ( SqlConnection conn = new SqlConnection( connstr ) )
    {
        conn.Open();

        // get the raw data
```

```
        SqlDataAdapter da1
            = new SqlDataAdapter( "select * from dotnetlanguages",
                                  conn );
        da1.Fill( ds, "dotnetlanguages" );

        SqlDataAdapter da2
            = new SqlDataAdapter( "select * from developers",
                                  conn );
        da2.Fill( ds, "developers" );

        SqlDataAdapter da3
            = new SqlDataAdapter( "select * from devlanglink",
                                  conn );
        da3.Fill( ds, "devlanglink" );

        // create the relationships

        ds.Relations.Add( "langlink",
            ds.Tables[ "dotnetlanguages" ].Columns[ "id" ],
            ds.Tables[ "devlanglink" ].Columns[ "langid" ] );

        ds.Relations.Add( "devlink",
            ds.Tables[ "developers" ].Columns[ "empno" ],
            ds.Tables[ "devlanglink" ].Columns[ "empno" ] );

        // establish data binding

        languageComboBox.DataSource = ds.Tables[ "dotnetlanguages" ];
        languageComboBox.DisplayMember = "name";

        developerComboBox.DataSource = ds.Tables[ "developers" ];
        developerComboBox.DisplayMember = "name";
    }
}
```

18. Now you can use these relationships to filter the rows in the DataSet and extract the desired rows. Double-click the languageButton on the Languages tab to create a button click handler. Enter the code as shown in Listing 6-6. Given a row from the dotnetlanguages table, you can use the GetChildRows method to locate the rows it maps to in the devlanglink table. Then iterate those rows and use the GetParent method to locate the related developers. Figure 6-15 shows how this appears in the application.

Listing 6-6. Using the Relationships in the `DataSet` *to List Developers Given a Language*

```
private void languageButton_Click(object sender,
                                System.EventArgs e)
{
    if ( ds == null )
    {
        MessageBox.Show( this, "You must load the data first" );
    }
    else
    {
        listTextBox.Text = "";
        // languageComboBox combobox is databound to the
        // languages DataTable
        DataRow lang
            = ( (DataRowView)languageComboBox.SelectedValue ).Row;
        foreach( DataRow row in lang.GetChildRows( "langlink" ) )
        {
            DataRow dev = row.GetParentRow( "devlink" );
            listTextBox.Text += dev[ "name" ].ToString() + "\r\n";
        }
    }
}
```

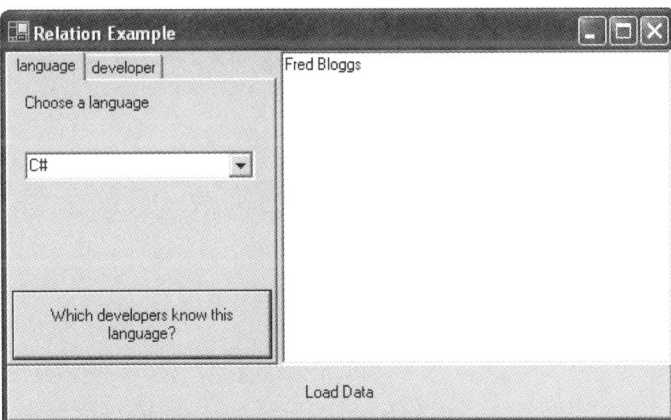

Figure 6-15. Using relationships to list developers who know a given language

19. Similarly, you can use these relationships to locate the languages a given developer knows. Double-click the `developerButton` on the Developer tab and enter the code shown in Listing 6-7. Figure 6-16 shows the result of implementing this button click handler.

Listing 6-7. Using the Relationships in the `DataSet` *to List Languages Given a Developer*

```
private void developerButton_Click(object sender,
                       System.EventArgs e)
{
    if ( ds == null )
    {
        MessageBox.Show( this, "You must load the data first" );
    }
    else
    {
        listTextBox.Text = "";
        // developerComboBox combobox is databound to the
        // developers DataTable
        DataRow dev
            = ( (DataRowView)developerComboBox.SelectedValue ).Row;
        foreach( DataRow row in dev.GetChildRows( "devlink" ) )
        {
            DataRow lang = row.GetParentRow( "langlink" );
            listTextBox.Text += lang[ "name" ].ToString() + "\r\n";
        }
    }
}
```

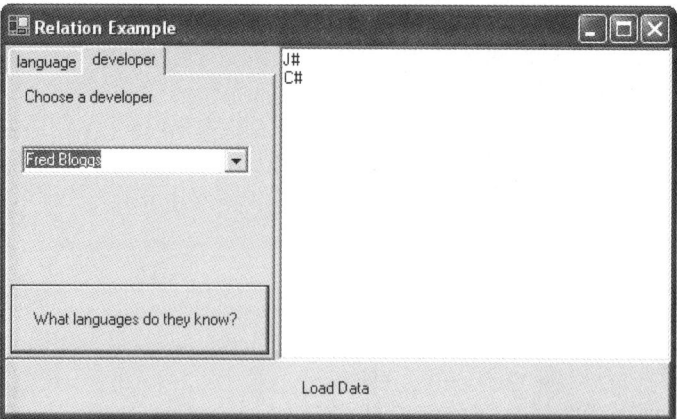

Figure 6-16. Using relationships to list the languages a given developer knows

20. Build and run the application.

Most examples of relationships use the equivalent of a two-way join. I deliberately chose the equivalent of a three-way join to show that it is almost as easy to accomplish.

By setting up the relationships between tables in a DataSet, you can avoid potentially costly roundtrips to the database, and you can even operate in situations where the database is unavailable.

Completing the Roundtrip

So far you have used DataSets to hold the results of queries, but they are not restricted to read-only operations. Like a CachedRowSet, a DataSet can be used to update a database, too.

Updates

When changes are made to a DataSet, they are tracked so that at some point in the future they may be reconciled with the original database. This occurs when you invoke the DataAdapter object's Update method. Just like the Fill method, the table's name is specified to indicate which one to update. The DataAdapter need not be the same instance used to populate the DataSet, and in most cases it will not be.

Take your developers' table from the previous example and add a new developer. Loading the data into the DataSet is the same as before:

```
SqlDataAdapter da =
    new SqlDataAdapter( "select * from developers", conn );
da.Fill( ds, "developers" );
```

At this point close the connection to the database.

When you are ready to add a new row, create a DataRow with the same columns as those in the DataTable. Fortunately, the DataTable has a NewRow method that does this for you. Then set the values for the fields and add the row to the Rows collection:

```
DataRow row = ds.Tables[ "developers" ].NewRow();
row[ "empno" ] = ++empno;
row[ "name" ] = developerTextBox.Text;
ds.Tables[ "developers" ].Rows.Add( row );
```

You edit the values of existing rows in the DataSet in a similar way.

Once you are ready to commit the changes to the database, you need to reconnect:

```
using ( SqlConnection conn = new SqlConnection( connstr ) )
{
    conn.Open();

    SqlDataAdapter da =
        new SqlDataAdapter( "select * from developers", conn );
```

So far, you have only supplied a select statement, and you need some combination of insert, update, and delete statements to make the required changes to the database. The SqlDataAdapter has properties that take a SqlCommand for each of these. In this example where you are adding the row, you could do the following:

```
da.InsertCommand = new SqlCommand(
    "INSERT INTO developers( empno, name ) values ( @empno, @name )",
    conn );
da.InsertCommand.Parameters.Add( "@empno",
                                 SqlDbType.Int,
                                 4,
                                 "empno" );
da.InsertCommand.Parameters.Add( "@name",
                                 SqlDbType.NVarChar,
                                 15,
                                 "name" );
```

which creates the insert command and maps the appropriate columns to the parameters.

To process updates and deletes, add the appropriate SqlCommand objects to the UpdateCommand and DeleteCommand properties of the SqlDataAdapter. The other alternative in this situation is to create a SqlCommandBuilder on the SqlDataAdapter that constructs the commands automatically:

```
SqlCommandBuilder cb = new SqlCommandBuilder( da );
```

This only works for tables populated by simple single table selects but eliminates all the parameter mapping code when it is an option.

Whichever method you use to populate the commands, your ultimate goal is to have the changes made to the DataSet reflected in the database. Accomplish this by invoking the DataAdapter object's Update method:

```
da.Update( ds, "developers" );
```

Invoke `Update` for each table changed. If the tables came from separate databases, you need to use a `DataAdapter` connected to the appropriate database for each table.

Conflicts

Running a single copy of the preceding example will not cause any conflicts between the `DataSet` and the database, but if you launch multiple copies you will soon create duplicate employee numbers. This is a classic optimistic locking problem, and the strategies for dealing with it and their shortcomings are well known. It is up to you to detect and handle conflicting updates according to the strategy you feel is most appropriate to your application.

At first glance this optimistic locking stuff looks ugly, but let me put it in perspective. Whenever you display an ASP.NET page to a user that allows them to update information, you do not usually lock the database rows waiting for a response. You must expect that when you get the response the underlying database rows may have changed in a manner that renders the updates made by the user obsolete. Your reaction may simply be to resend the original update page with the new data, but you deal with the situation somehow.

You can control the types of changes that are applied in a given `Update` invocation by extracting the rows with the desired change and only passing them to `Update`. Specify the rows by selecting out the `DataRow` instances with a given `DataViewRowState` such as `Added`, `Deleted`, or `ModifiedCurrent`. This could be important to satisfy constraints on the rows in the database, such as when you delete a row and then add a new one with the same unique key.

Constraints

Just as you can specify foreign key constraints and unique constraints in a database, you can specify them in a `DataSet`. This can help you validate data in a client, but remember that it only applies to the subset of rows in the `DataSet`, so you may still get errors when you invoke `Update` against the complete table.

You apply foreign key constraints by creating an instance of `ForeignKeyConstraint` and adding it to the `Constraints` property of the `DataTable`. Similarly, you apply unique constraints by creating an instance of `UniqueConstraint` and adding it to the same property. In both cases, you may specify multiple columns.

Understanding Pooling

Connection pooling in JDBC is typically provided by specialized class libraries that exploit the façade pattern to provide pooled connection objects. When these connection objects are closed, they do not close the underlying database connection but rather return it to the pool.

The SQL Server managed provider contains its own pooling mechanism, making the specialized class library unnecessary. Should pooling be undesirable in a given application it can be disabled in the connection string by specifying `Pooling='false'`.

The OLE DB and ODBC providers do not provide pooling themselves but rely on existing pooling mechanisms in the OLE DB or ODBC layers.

Implementing Data-Bound Controls

The WinForms and WebForms discussion touched briefly on the subject of data-bound controls using arrays as the data source. Most of the time a data-bound control will take its data from a `DataTable`. These controls save the programmer from having to map the data from the data source into the control explicitly.

Using Simple Data Binding

Simple data binding applies to controls such as combo boxes and list boxes. You must specify both the `DataTable` within the `DataSet` and the column within that `DataTable` to be used as the display value:

```
developersListBox.DataSource = ds.Tables[ "developers" ];
developersListBox.DisplayMember = "name";
```

Using Grid Controls

Both WinForms and WebForms have powerful grid controls that exploit data binding to display data.

WinForms DataGrid

WinForms has the `DataGrid` control to display a `DataTable`. This is the closest equivalent to a Swing `JTable` in WinForms, with the `DataTable` filling the role of the `TableModel`. Add a `DataGrid` to a `Form` in the usual way by dragging and drop-ping from the Toolbox. Then make a `DataTable` the `DataSource` for the `DataGrid`:

```
dataGrid1.DataSource = ds.Tables[ "developers" ];
```

The `DataGrid` supports multiple columns, so there is no need to specify a value for `DisplayMember`. Figure 6-17 shows how this would look.

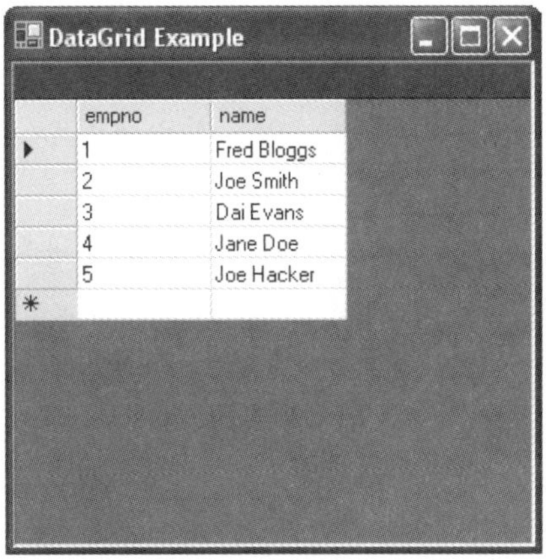

Figure 6-17. The WinForms `DataGrid` *control*

By default a `DataGrid` supports unrestricted editing of the data. All cells are editable and rows can be added and deleted freely. The `DataTable` is changed by these operations, but you must provide code to update the database to make the changes permanent.

If you only want to display the data, without supporting changes, set the `ReadOnly` property of the `DataGrid` to `true`. To set an individual column to read-only, you must locate the appropriate `DataGridColumnStyle` instance in the `TableStyles` property of the `DataGrid` and set its `ReadOnly` property to `true`.

A `DataGrid` can also display a `DataSet`, allowing traversal of any relationships that have been added between the tables. The initial table is established by set-ting the `DataMember` property. This is best suited to hierarchical data, where you want to allow *drill-down* traversal. The `DataSet` used earlier with a many-to-many relationship does not behave as you might expect.

Imagine you want to view the developers with an option to see their lan-guage skills. Create the following example:

1. Create a new Windows Application project called
    DataGridRelationExample.

2. Drag a `DataGrid` control from the Toolbox onto the form and set its `Dock` property to **Fill**. Set its `ReadOnly` property to **true**.

3.   Double-click the form to create a form load handler. Change the code to that shown in Listing 6-8.

Listing 6-8. Using Relationships in a DataSet *with a WinForms* DataGrid

```
const string connstr = @"Server=.\VSdotNET;"
    + @"Database=Chapter6;"
    + @"Integrated Security=SSPI";

private DataSet ds = null;

private void Form1_Load(object sender, System.EventArgs e)
{
    ds = new DataSet();

    using ( SqlConnection conn = new SqlConnection( connstr ) )
    {
        conn.Open();

        SqlDataAdapter da1
            = new SqlDataAdapter( "select * from developers", conn );
        da1.Fill( ds, "developers" );

        SqlDataAdapter da2
            = new SqlDataAdapter( "SELECT k.empno, l.name " +
                                  "FROM dotnetlanguages l " +
                                  "JOIN devlanglink k " +
                                  "ON l.id = k.langid",
                                  conn );
        da2.Fill( ds, "languages" );

        // create the relationship

        ds.Relations.Add( "language",
                ds.Tables[ "developers" ].Columns[ "empno" ],
                ds.Tables[ "languages" ].Columns[ "empno" ] );

        dataGrid1.DataSource = ds;
        dataGrid1.DataMember = "developers";
    }
}
```

4.   Build and run the application. The list of developers appears as in Figure 6-18. The DataGrid shows a plus sign (+) in the left margin that

you can expand (by clicking it) to follow the relation to the languages for that developer. The languages are shown with the context of the parent, as shown in Figure 6-19.

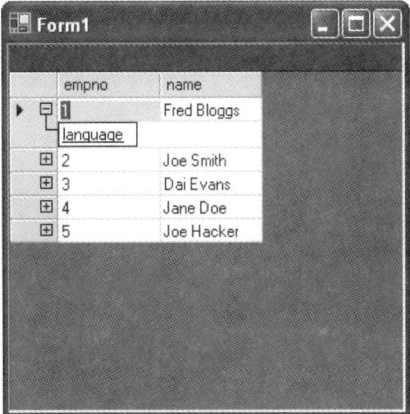

Figure 6-18. A DataGrid *showing a relationship*

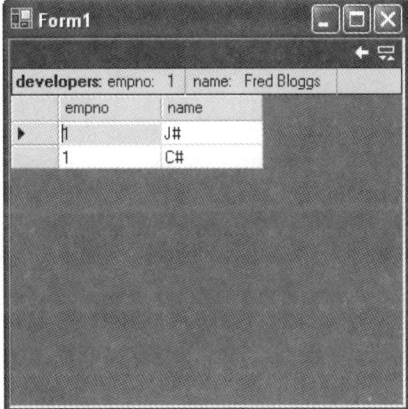

Figure 6-19. Displaying the child rows of a relationship in a WinForms DataGrid

WebForms DataGrid

ASP.NET WebForms also have a DataGrid control. Binding the control to a DataTable is much the same as in WinForms except that once the DataSource and DataMember properties have been set, you must invoke the DataBind method:

```
DataGrid1.DataSource = ds;
DataGrid1.DataMember = "developers";
DataGrid1.DataBind();
```

In contrast to the WinForms version, the WebForms DataGrid is read-only by default. It also does not seem to have any built-in support to traverse relationships. You can configure many visual aspects of the DataGrid. Figure 6-20 shows how it looks "out of the box" on a WebForms page.

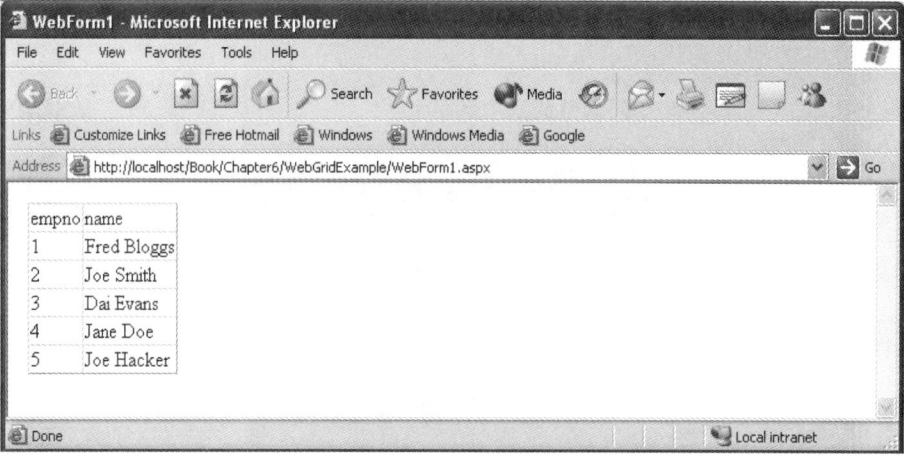

Figure 6-20. The WebForms DataGrid

Adding support for editing or even selecting the rows is not a matter of flipping a read-only flag. You must set up handlers for the events and register them with the control. There are no defaults that operate against the DataSet, so you must provide all the logic yourself. The following example shows how you achieve this:

1. Create a new ASP.NET Web Application project called **WebGridEditExample**.

2. Drag a DataGrid control from the Toolbox onto the Web form.

3. Switch to code view and add the code to populate the DataGrid, as shown in Listing 6-9. Notice that this includes changes to the Page_Load method.

Listing 6-9. Populating the DataSet *and Binding It to the WebForms* DataGrid

```
private const string connstr = @"Server=.\VSdotNET;"
    + @"Database=Chapter6;"
    + @"Integrated Security=SSPI";

private DataSet ds;

private void PopulateAndBind()
{
    ds = new DataSet();

    using ( SqlConnection conn = new SqlConnection( connstr ) )
    {
        conn.Open();

        SqlDataAdapter da1 =
            new SqlDataAdapter( "select * from developers", conn );
        da1.Fill( ds, "developers" );

        DataGrid1.DataSource = ds;
        DataGrid1.DataMember = "developers";
        DataGrid1.DataBind();
    }
}

private void Page_Load(object sender, System.EventArgs e)
{
    if ( !this.IsPostBack )
    {
        PopulateAndBind();
    }
}
```

4. Switch back to the designer and select the DataGrid. Open the Property Builder . . . link located on the Properties panel. Select the Columns pane and then expand the Button Column node in the Available columns tree-view. Select the Edit, Update, Cancel node and press the > button to add it to the selected columns list as shown in Figure 6-21. Click OK.

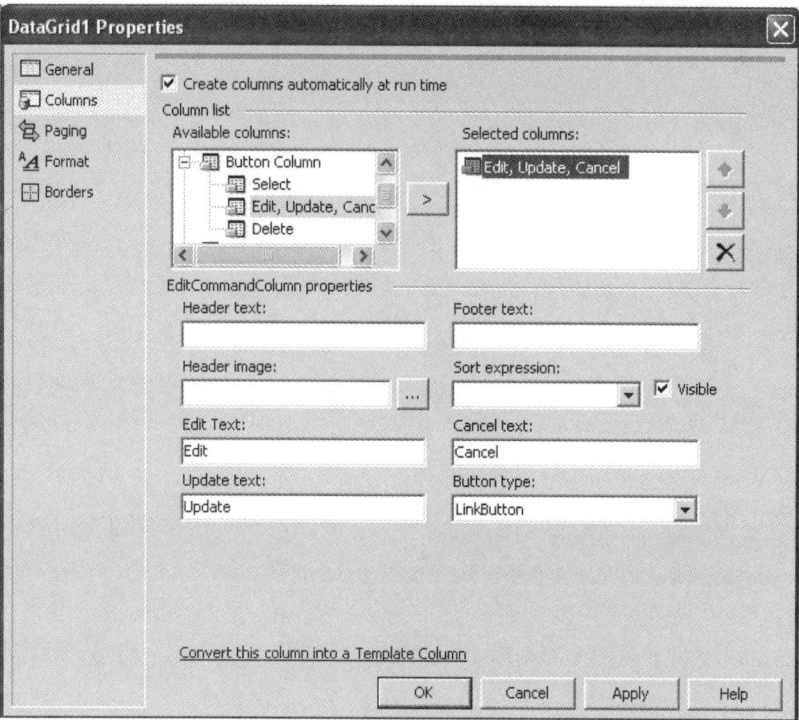

Figure 6-21. Adding the update commands column to the Web form

5. Now add the handlers for the Edit, Update, and Cancel events as shown in Listing 6-10. The Edit and Cancel handlers set the DataGrid object's EditItemIndex property to the selected row and –1, respectively. Unless you rebind to the DataSet after setting this value, it does not work correctly. Use the PopulateAndBind convenience function from Listing 6-9 to re-populate and rebind the DataSet. The Update handler must obtain the modified values from the DataGrid object's cell controls.

Listing 6-10. The Edit, Cancel, *and* Update *Handlers for the WebForms* DataGrid

```
public void DataGrid1_Edit(Object sender, DataGridCommandEventArgs E)
{
    DataGrid1.EditItemIndex = (int)E.Item.ItemIndex;
    PopulateAndBind();
}
```

```
public void DataGrid1_Cancel(Object sender, DataGridCommandEventArgs E)
{
    DataGrid1.EditItemIndex = -1;
    PopulateAndBind();
}

public void DataGrid1_Update(Object sender, DataGridCommandEventArgs E)
{
    int row = (int)E.Item.ItemIndex;

    int empno =
        Int32.Parse( ((TextBox)E.Item.Cells[1].Controls[0]).Text );
    String name = ((TextBox)E.Item.Cells[2].Controls[0]).Text;

    ds = new DataSet();

    using ( SqlConnection conn = new SqlConnection( connstr ) )
    {
        conn.Open();

        SqlDataAdapter da1
            = new SqlDataAdapter( "select * from developers",
                                    conn );
        da1.Fill( ds, "developers" );

        SqlCommandBuilder cb = new SqlCommandBuilder( da1 );

        DataRow dr = ds.Tables[ "developers" ].Rows[ row ];
        dr[ "empno" ] = empno;
        dr[ "name" ] = name;

        da1.Update( ds, "developers" );

        DataGrid1.EditItemIndex = -1;
        DataGrid1.DataSource = ds.Tables[ "developers" ];
        DataGrid1.DataBind();
    }
}
```

6. Then register the handlers with the control using the Events panel of the Properties window for the DataGrid control. Switch the Properties window to Events by selecting the Events icon (which looks like a lightning flash). Then connect the events to the methods, as shown in Figure 6-22.

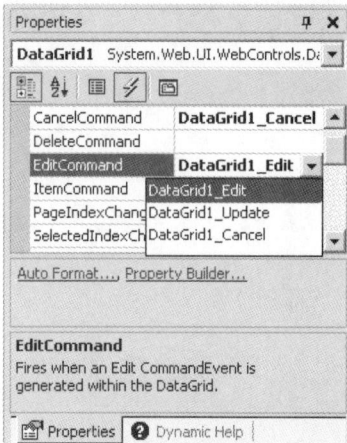

Figure 6-22. The Events panel of the Properties window

7. If you are connecting to a SQL Server database using a user ID and password in your connection string, you can build and run the application. If you need to use Windows authentication, there are a few additional steps.

8. Edit the project's web.config file to add `<identity impersonate="true" />` following the `<authentication>` element. This tells ASP.NET to impersonate the identity of the user connecting to the application so that you can authenticate to SQL Server/MSDE.

9. Open the Internet Information Services administrative tool from the Control Panel. Locate the virtual root for the project and open its Properties panel. Select the Directory Security tab. Uncheck the anonymous access box and ensure that the Windows-integrated authentication box is checked. This makes IIS require user authentication for the application.

10. Now you can build and run the application. Figure 6-23 shows this updatable version of the WebForms `DataGrid` on a Web page.

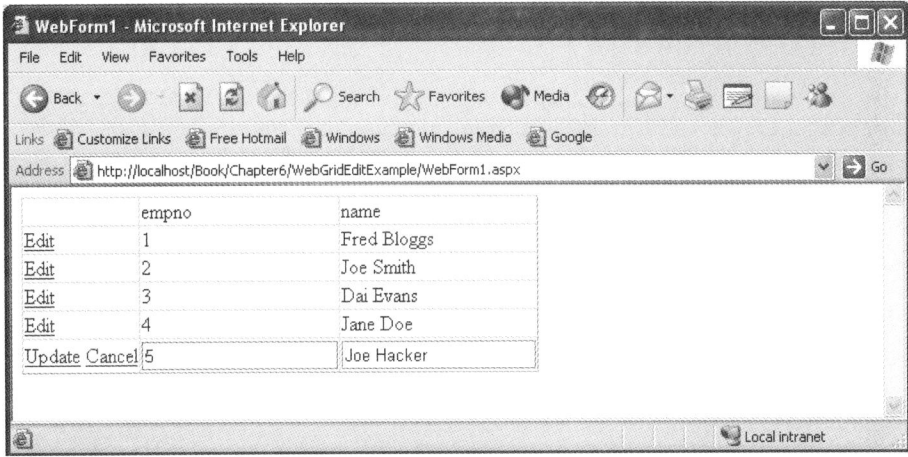

Figure 6-23. The updatable version of the DataGrid

The WebForms version of the DataGrid is not as powerful as the WinForms version, and it requires you to add a large amount of your own code to achieve what is basic functionality in the WinForms DataGrid.

Comparing ADO.NET to the Current ADO

The big difference from ADO is the same as that from JDBC: the disconnected DataSet model. ADO provides the disconnected RecordSet, which is much the same as the CachedRowSet, but neither provides the support for multiple tables that a DataSet does.

An ADO RecordSet is roughly analogous to a DataTable within a DataSet. It is marshaled by COM, which restricts it to Windows clients most of the time. A DataSet is marshaled as Extensible Markup Language (XML), which allows it to be used by non-Windows clients. Until the inner workings of a DataSet become well documented and client-side libraries appear on other platforms, I doubt you will see widespread use on non-Windows platforms.

The other big difference is the move away from the façade pattern to discrete providers with their own classes. ADO uses OLE DB providers and the façade pattern to hide the underlying implementation from developers. It remains to be seen if this is just expediency and if Microsoft will return to this in future incarnations of ADO.NET.

Summary

JDBC users will find it easy to transition to ADO.NET using the command and data reader classes following the patterns to which they have become accustomed. Anyone familiar with `CachedRowSet` will find the `DataSet` concept easy to grasp. Data binding will motivate interface developers to start using `DataSet` objects. Once you become comfortable with the disconnected model, you will start enjoying some of the other capabilities `DataSet` objects provide.

CHAPTER 7

Understanding Multithreading

THE JAVA LANGUAGE is inherently thread aware. The Java Language Specification defines behavior in multithreaded scenarios. There are Java language keywords that relate to multithreading. The same things can be said of C#. Your experience with this aspect of Java gives you an advantage over programmers moving to C# from other languages.

The .NET System.Threading namespace contains the classes that provide thread-related support. Unlike some Java platforms, all the platforms currently supported by .NET have native threading, so there is no equivalent to green threads.

This chapter describes how to start and control threads, the various synchronization mechanisms provided by the .NET Framework, and how they compare to their Java equivalents. It also discusses some of the issues and features specific to using threads in .NET.

Starting Threads

When you want to run code on a separate thread in Java, you typically create a class that implements Runnable and put the code in its run method. You can then create a Thread instance using your class and start the thread (see Listing 7-1).

Listing 7-1. Running Code on a Separate Thread in Java

```
public class Counter implements Runnable
{
    private int count;


    public Counter( int count )
    {
        this.count = count;
    }
```

```
        public void run()
        {
            for ( int i = 0; i < count; i++ )
            {
                System.out.println( "Reached " + i );
            }
        }

        public static void main( String[] args )
        {
            Counter c = new Counter( 10 );
            Thread t = new Thread( c );
            t.start();
        }
    }
```

In .NET, the pattern is similar. Instead of implementing an interface such as Runnable, use a ThreadStart delegate. The delegate is then used to instantiate the Thread object, which you then start explicitly. The ThreadStart delegate requires a void method, which takes no parameters, so define a method as follows:

```
public void DoCount()
{
    for ( int i = 0; i < count; i++ )
    {
        System.Console.WriteLine( "Reached {0}", i );
    }
}
```

Because you cannot pass parameters to the delegate, a good alternative is to set the parameters when you construct the delegate's object. Because the run method of Runnable accepts no parameters, you are probably using a similar technique in Java already. In this case, set the number of iterations:

```
private int count;

public Counter( int count )
{
    this.count = count;
}
```

Now instantiate the object and start the thread:

```
Counter c = new Counter( 10 );
Thread t = new Thread( new ThreadStart( c.DoCount ) );
t.Start();
```

One key thing to remember is that you need to add a using statement for System.Threading. Unlike the threading classes in Java, which reside in java.lang and are implicitly available, those in .NET have their own namespace.

The completed example, shown in Listing 7-2, looks similar to the preceding Java example.

Listing 7-2. Running Code on a Separate Thread in C#

```
using System;
using System.Threading;

namespace SimpleThreadExample
{
    class Counter
    {
        private int count;

        public Counter( int count )
        {
            this.count = count;
        }

        public void DoCount()
        {
            for ( int i = 0; i < count; i++ )
            {
                System.Console.WriteLine( "Reached {0}", i );
            }
        }

        [STAThread]
        static void Main(string[] args)
        {
            Counter c = new Counter( 10 );
            Thread t = new Thread( new ThreadStart( c.DoCount ) );
            t.Start();
        }
    }
}
```

Manipulating Threads

The System.Threading.Thread class contains most of the methods you have come to expect. Join, Suspend and Resume, and Sleep are the more interesting ones.

Using Join

After starting a thread, the second most common operation is to wait for a thread to complete. The Thread class in .NET has a Join method. In fact, it has three Join methods. The first is an unconditional Join, the second allows you to specify a number of milliseconds, and the third takes a TimeSpan object. Like the join in Java, these last two overloads of the Join method allow you to limit how long you will wait for a thread to complete. If you need resolution faster than a millisecond, you need to use a Timespan, but be aware that a TimeSpan has a maximum resolution of one tick, which is 100 nanoseconds.

In the following example a number of threads are created to perform a task. They must complete before the main thread can continue, so the unconditional form of Join is used against each one:

```
Thread[] t = new Thread[ threads ];

for( int k = 0; k < threads; k++ )
{
    t[ k ] = new Thread( new ThreadStart( DoCount ) );
    t[ k ].Name = "Thread " + k;
    t[ k ].Start();
}

// wait for all the threads to finish before continuing

for( int k = 0; k < threads; k++ )
{
    t[ k ].Join();
}
```

Using Suspend *and* Resume

The Thread class's suspend and resume methods are deprecated in Java because they can leave objects in inconsistent states. In .NET, this is not the case. If you invoke Suspend on a thread, it is not necessarily suspended immediately. The runtime allows the thread to run until it reaches a point where it may be safely suspended. Only then does the suspend operation take place. A single `Resume` call is needed to allow the thread to continue executing regardless of the number of Suspend calls.

The thread in the following example is repeatedly suspended and resumed for as long as it remains alive. Attempting to suspend a thread that has terminated will cause an exception. For example:

```
Thread t = new Thread( new ThreadStart( DoCount ) );
t.Start();
Thread.Sleep( sleepTime );

while ( t.IsAlive )
{
    t.Suspend();
    Thread.Sleep( sleepTime );
    t.Resume();
    Thread.Sleep( sleepTime );
}
```

But let's examine how safe this really is. Although to the runtime the thread is suspended at a "safe" point, there are no guarantees that the thread is not suspended in possession of a critical resource such as a lock. In the full version of the preceding example, I originally had the main loop writing to the console when it suspended the thread. The DoCount function was also writing to the console. If I happened to suspend the thread at the right point inside the IO library, I would become deadlocked. It is better design to choose points in the code where the threads do not hold any resources critical to your application and have the threads determine whether they need to wait at those points. Suspend may be attractive because it takes effect almost instantly, but designing in specific points where your threads wait will result in fewer customer reports of sporadic hangs that you can never reproduce in the test lab.

Using Yield and Sleep

In Java you can call `Thread.currentThread().yield()` to give up your remaining time slice and allow other threads to execute. To do this in .NET, call `Thread.Sleep` with a quantity of zero, which requests this special behavior:

```
// yield the time slice
Thread.Sleep( 0 );
```

When called with a parameter other than zero, the Sleep method behaves as it does in Java. The Sleep method makes the current thread wait for the specified time. It takes either a number of milliseconds or a TimeSpan instance:

```
Thread.Sleep( 1000 );
```

Using Foreground and Background Threads

A .NET process, like a Java process, remains alive as long as there are foreground threads running. In Java, daemon threads perform activity in the background and do not need to be explicitly stopped for the process to exit. The same concept exists in .NET. To create the equivalent of a daemon thread, set the Thread object's IsBackground property to true:

```
Thread t = new Thread( new ThreadStart( DoCount ) );
t.IsBackground = true;
t.Start();
```

Understanding Thread Pooling

Every managed process has a collection of threads called the *thread pool*. The framework uses threads from this collection to perform operations such as running asynchronous IO callbacks. However, you can also make use of the thread pool directly through the ThreadPool object.

Your first thought might be to look at the ThreadPool class and try to find a method to allocate a thread from the pool, but the thread pool does not work that way. Instead, you give the pool work to do and it allocates the work to its threads.

Imagine you are writing a server application that gets many short requests, say the TCP Daytime service described in RFC 867. You can service the requests serially or spawn a thread for each request; both strategies are often used. Launching separate threads also has the advantage of preventing one client from starving service to the others. However, when the work done to service each request is small, such as with Daytime, it often becomes expensive to spawn a thread per request. Assuming the traffic warrants it, this is a good candidate for a thread pool.

Work is queued to the thread pool by calling QueueUserWorkItem. Supply QueueUserWorkItem with a WaitCallback delegate and an object. When the delegate function is invoked to perform the work, the object will be passed as a parameter. This avoids the necessity of creating an object to hold parameters when there is only one parameter. In the case of the Daytime service it allows you to pass the client socket, which is all you need (see Listing 7-3).

Listing 7-3. Simple Multithreaded Daytime Server

```csharp
using System;
using System.IO;
using System.Net;
using System.Net.Sockets;
using System.Text;
using System.Threading;

namespace ThreadPoolExample
{
    class ThreadPoolExample
    {
        const int dayTimePort = 7777;

        static void ServiceClient( Object obj )
        {
            . . .
        }

        [STAThread]
        static void Main(string[] args)
        {
            using ( Socket svr = new Socket( AddressFamily.InterNetwork,
                SocketType.Stream,
                ProtocolType.Tcp ) )
            {
                svr.Bind( new IPEndPoint( IPAddress.Loopback, dayTimePort ) );
                svr.Listen( 5 );
                while ( true )
                {
                    Socket req = svr.Accept();
                    ThreadPool.QueueUserWorkItem(
                        new WaitCallback( ServiceClient ),
                        req );
                }
            }
        }
    }
}
```

The `WaitCallback` delegate function must take a single parameter, the object you supply in the call to `QueueUserWorkItem`. Because it is an `Object`, you must cast it to the true type to use it. In this case, cast it back to a `Socket`:

```
static void ServiceClient( Object obj )
{
    using ( Socket s = (Socket)obj )
    {
        string response = DateTime.Now.ToLongDateString()
                        + " "
                        + DateTime.Now.ToLongTimeString();

        Encoding enc = Encoding.GetEncoding( "ASCII" );
        Byte[] buff = enc.GetBytes( response );
        s.Send( buff );
        s.Shutdown( SocketShutdown.Both );
        s.Close();
    }
}
```

If you find yourself creating many short-lived threads, then you should be using the pool. It avoids the cost of creating and destroying threads for each piece of work. If your thread will be long lived, using the pool would not be a good idea because you will be depriving the pool of that thread and therefore reducing the number of threads available to service short requests. The documentation does not explicitly provide guidance on this matter, so you must use your own judgment.

Using `SynchronizationAttribute`

`SynchronizationAttribute` is a potential trap for the unwary! You have been looking around for something that looks like Java's synchronized method modifier and found `SynchronizationAttribute`. It appears to allow you to indicate that access to all methods and attributes be serialized.

The fact that `SynchronizationAttribute` comes from the `System.EnterpriseServices` namespace and not `System.Threading` should be a clue. The catch is that it only applies when the class is used as a COM+ component. It indicates that the component is not thread safe and that the COM+ runtime should ensure all access to the class is serialized.

If you are developing for COM+, this may be just what you wanted. With one attribute, you can serialize access to the entire class. If you are not using COM+, or if you need more fine-grained control, you need to use monitors, mutexes, or interlocked access (as described in the following sections).

Using Monitors

When you specify synchronized for a method in Java, behind the scenes, the object's monitor is taken on entry to the method and released on exit. Because there is no equivalent to the synchronized modifier in .NET, you have to explicitly obtain the monitor at the start of the method and release it on exit if you desire the same behavior.

A *monitor* is conceptually a token that may only be owned by a single thread at any given moment. Every object has one as a convenience for synchronization purposes.

Obtain a monitor by using Monitor.Enter and release it by using Monitor.Exit. The object whose monitor you want to use is given as the parameter to both calls. When calls are nested, be careful to invoke Exit as many times as you invoke Enter because a count is maintained:

```
public void SynchronizedMethod()
{
    try
    {
        Monitor.Enter( this );
        ....
    }
    finally
    {
        Monitor.Exit( this );
    }
}
```

In C# you can simplify this construct by using the lock statement:

```
public void SynchronizedMethod()
{
    lock ( this )
    {
        ....
    }
}
```

This is almost identical to Java's synchronized statement that is often used to lock an object with finer granularity than an entire method. If you need to attempt to obtain an object's monitor but not wait indefinitely, you can use the TryEnter method and specify a timeout:

```
public void SynchronizedMethod3()
{
    try
    {
        if ( Monitor.TryEnter( this, 250 ) )
        {
            . . . .
        }
    }
    finally
    {
        try
        {
            Monitor.Exit( this );
        }
        catch( SynchronizationLockException sle )
        {
            // it's okay if I didn't get the monitor
        }
    }
}
```

The other way monitors are used in Java is with the wait and notify methods of the Object class. This allows threads to block by calling wait until another thread signals that they have finished by calling notify. This same mechanism is available in .NET by calling the Wait and Pulse methods of the Monitor class.

Imagine you have written your own thread pool. In the worker threads, you need to wait for work. If locker is an object used specifically for signaling, you could write this:

```
lock( locker )
{
    Monitor.Wait( locker );
}
```

You must obtain the monitor before issuing Wait as in Java. In the dispatcher thread, you can wake up one of the threads when you have work for it by calling Pulse, like so:

```
lock( locker )
{
    Monitor.Pulse( locker );
}
```

or all of them by calling `PulseAll`. Again, you must obtain the monitor before calling these methods.

Using Mutexes

A *mutex* is similar to a monitor in that only one thread may own it at any given point in time. However, the set of threads that may own a mutex is not restricted to a single process—any thread in the system can own it. You can give a mutex a name when you create it to uniquely identify it within the system. A mutex is an operating system resource, and you can use it in both managed and unmanaged processes.

The other big difference between monitors and mutexes is that you can wait on multiple mutexes. If you need to acquire one of a number of mutexes, you can use `WaitHandle.WaitAny.` If you need to own all of a set of mutexes, you can use `WaitHandle.WaitAll`. There is no equivalent to these operations for monitors.

You can create a mutex as initially owned or not owned. If you do not already own the mutex, you can obtain it by calling `WaitOne`. Once finished with the mutex, you call `ReleaseMutex.`

One situation that is ideal for mutexes is when you have a small number of identical server threads with a large number of client threads. It does not matter which server thread services a client, but each server can only service one client at a time. If each server exposes a mutex, the clients can use `WaitAny` to get ownership:

```
int index = WaitHandle.WaitAny( m_muxArray );
```

Once the client has been served, the mutex can be released:

```
m_mutex.ReleaseMutex();
```

This would be difficult to achieve using monitors.

If you want to protect a critical section of code within a single process, the choice to use a mutex over a monitor may seem little more than a matter of style. Using mutexes comes into its own when you want to protect multiple resources as a collection or protect a resource across processes.

Applying Interlocked Access

The System.Threading.Interlocked class contains a set of static methods that provide simple atomic operations on variables. These operations are usually implemented in the instruction sets of modern processors.

A good example is incrementing an integer by one in a thread-safe fashion. You could do it using a monitor as follows:

```
private static Object locker = new Object();
private static int count = 0;

public int IncrementCount()
{
    int rc;

    lock( locker )
    {
        rc = ++count;
    }

    return rc;
}
```

The Java equivalent is much cleaner:

```
private static int count = 0;

public synchronized int IncrementCount()
{
    return ++count;
}
```

The potential problem with the monitor approach is that you lock the entire object each time you perform the increment operation. If there are many synchronized variables in the object, then you could end up with a lot of contention for the object's monitor.

Because the interlocked operations are typically atomic at the processor level, there is no need to obtain the object's monitor and thus no contention. Restating the previous example using the Interlocked class, you get the following:

```
private static int count = 0;

public int IncrementCount()
{
    return Interlocked.Increment( ref count );
}
```

The `Interlocked` class has functions for the `int`, `float`, and `object` reference types. If you need to protect another type, you will have to use its monitor.

What Is an Apartment?

Apartments are a COM concept. Every COM object lives in exactly one apartment. Calls between objects in different apartments typically require a proxy to be created and parameters marshaled even if they are in the same process. Calls between objects in the same apartment occur without the need to create proxies.

The oldest apartment model is the Single-Threaded Apartment (STA). In essence, this is a single thread. When a call is made to an object in an STA from another apartment, it goes through a proxy that ensures the appropriate synchronization occurs. Multiple COM objects can live in an STA, but they are served by a single thread.

COM objects can also live in a multithreaded apartment (MTA) that, as its name suggests, is served by a number of threads. Objects living in an MTA are required to provide their own synchronization. Typically there is only a single MTA per process, but this is not a requirement.

Windows 2000 introduced the Thread-Neutral Apartment (TNA) in which an object adapts to the threading model of its caller without the need for a proxy. Naturally such objects must be thread safe in case the caller is from the MTA.

As a .NET programmer your main concern with apartments occurs if you make a .NET object available as a COM component. Chapter 10, "Integrating Components," will cover how you do this, but you need to be aware of the threading models and use what you have learned in this chapter to make your objects thread safe. If you will be dealing with COM closely, there is no substitute for one of the classic books on the subject such as *Essential COM* by Don Box (Addison-Wesley, 1998).

Understanding Threads and Garbage Collection

Many people do not realize they have actually installed two versions of the .NET runtime. The version you use most of the time is optimized for client programs. This version, mscorwks, is used whenever you invoke a managed .exe file. The other version, mscorsvr, requires that you create the runtime using its COM interface, specifying the appropriate parameters to select the server version.

The only documented difference between the two is the way they handle garbage collection. The server version, mscorsvr, has garbage collection that is optimized for multithreaded server processes running on multiprocessor machines. The client version, mscorwks, is optimized for interactive processes on single-processor machines.

If you use ASP.NET, the server runtime will be launched if you are on a multi-processor machine. It remains to be seen if other environments will automatically use the server runtime..

Why did Microsoft make selecting the server runtime for your own programs so difficult? It would seem that an assembly attribute or linker flag would not be hard to implement. Maybe this will be forthcoming in future releases. For now, if you need the performance boost the server version provides, and your target environment does not provide it for you, please refer to Chapter 15, "Getting Outside the Box", for information on hosting the CLR.

Summary

If you used threads in Java, you will have seen many parallels with .NET and C#. It should be a relatively painless transition for you to make. The addition of the thread pool and mutexes make the environment richer but are not required for you to get started.

Understanding Networking

THIS CHAPTER EXAMINES network communication using the .NET Framework and compares it with the support provided by Java. It starts with the familiar Socket interface using both Transmission Control Protocol (TCP) and User Datagram Protocol (UDP). Then it explores .NET Remoting, which provides similar capabilities to Java's Remote Method Invocation (RMI). Finally, it examines the extensive support for Simple Object Access Protocol (SOAP) Web Services provided by ASP.NET and Visual Studio .NET.

Starting with Sockets

The Java socket classes provide a higher-level interface than those generally available to C and C++ programmers. Although the productivity gains benefit many, the inability to access low-level functions can be frustrating to programmers working on advanced projects. The designers of the System.Net.Sockets library have provided both a low-level interface that permits precise control and a high-level interface that is comparable to that available in Java.

Low-Level Socket Interface

The core of the low-level interface is the Socket class. Unlike Java where there are separate classes for TCP client, TCP server, UDP, and multicast, the .NET Socket class is configured much as a C programmer configures a socket connection. You establish a socket connection to the TCP echo service as follows:

```
using System;
using System.Net;
using System.Net.Sockets;
using System.Text;
```

```
namespace EchoClientLowExample
{
    class EchoClientLow
    {
        const int echoPort = 7;

        [STAThread]
        static void Main( string[] args )
        {
            Socket s = new Socket( AddressFamily.InterNetwork,
                                   SocketType.Stream,
                                   ProtocolType.Tcp );
            s.Connect( new IPEndPoint( IPAddress.Loopback, echoPort ) );
```

This is similar to what you would see in a C program using the Berkeley socket interface. The .NET System.Net.Sockets classes wrap that interface without taking anything away. If you use the SocketImpl class in Java, you get access to some of those features but are always constrained by the basic type you started with, TCP or UDP client or server.

When using the low-level interface, you must send and receive data using Byte arrays. As you turn your textual data into bytes you need to be conscious of how it is encoded. To use UTF8, write the following:

```
            UTF8Encoding enc = new UTF8Encoding();
            s.Send( enc.GetBytes( "test message" ) );
            Byte[] buff = new Byte[ 1024 ];
            s.Receive( buff );
            System.Console.WriteLine( enc.GetString( buff ) );
        }
    }
}
```

Working with the Socket class gives you all the flexibility a C programmer has. It comes at the price of exposing most of the details you have to contend with when using the C interface.

High-Level Socket Interface

The high-level interface is comparable to the java.net socket classes. TcpClient is roughly equivalent to Java's Socket class, and TcpListener compares well to the ServerSocket class. UdpClient combines the client-side functionality of the

DatagramSocket and MulticastSocket, but it does not support any server-side functionality.

You could rewrite the preceding TCP echo client example as Listing 8-1.

Listing 8-1. A TCP Echo Service Client Using the High-Level Socket Interface

```
using System;
using System.IO;
using System.Net.Sockets;

namespace EchoClientHighExample
{
    class EchoClientHigh
    {
        const int echoPort = 7;

        [STAThread]
        static void Main(string[] args)
        {
            using ( TcpClient tc
                        = new TcpClient( "localhost", echoPort ) )
            {
                NetworkStream ns = tc.GetStream();
                StreamWriter sw = new StreamWriter( ns );
                StreamReader sr = new StreamReader( ns );

                sw.WriteLine( "test message" );
                sw.Flush();
                System.Console.WriteLine( sr.ReadLine() );
            }
        }
    }
}
```

As with Java's Socket class, only the host and port are needed to establish the connection, and there is no separate Connect call. Instead of Send and Receive methods, TcpClient exposes a bidirectional NetworkStream. You can push StreamReader and StreamWriter classes onto the NetworkStream instance to deal with any encoding issues.

Even with such a trivial example as echo, the high-level interface is easier than using the Socket class. If you need access to the underlying Socket but do not want to give up the convenience of the high-level interface, access the Socket class through the Client property of TcpClient and UdpClient or the Server property of TcpListener.

If you are familiar with the java.net classes, you should be comfortable using the TcpClient, TcpListener, and UdpClient classes.

Using Pluggable Protocols

One of Java's much-publicized features is its ability to access Uniform Resource Locators (URLs) through an extensible transport framework. A similar extensible mechanism exists in .NET and is accessed by using the WebClient class in System.Net. The documentation refers to this as a *pluggable protocol*.

The following example demonstrates using WebClient to read a file URL. Notice that the URL cannot be specified in the WebClient constructor, but must be specified on the method that initiates the transfer. This is the opposite of using the URL class in Java. For example:

```
using ( WebClient cli = new WebClient() )
{
    Stream s = cli.OpenRead( "file:///C:/Test.txt" );
    StreamReader rdr = new StreamReader( s );
    System.Console.WriteLine( rdr.ReadToEnd() );
    rdr.Close();
}
```

The core libraries only support the http, https, and file URL schemes. To add support for additional transports, implement classes that inherit from the abstract classes WebRequest and WebResponse. Also provide a class that implements IWebRequestCreate. WebClient uses this as a factory for your WebRequest-derived class. The final step is to register the factory class using WebRequest.RegisterPrefix. You must do this in code and not in a configuration file. The ability to register a type in the configuration file and have all applications on the machine be able to exploit it is one of the features of the Java mechanism not available in .NET.

 **CAUTION** *Be careful, the* file *URL scheme refers to the file system only and is not a synonym for File Transfer Protocol (FTP).*

Understanding Remoting

Remoting is the .NET equivalent of Remote Method Invocation (RMI) in Java. It provides a mechanism for invoking methods on objects located in another process, usually on another machine. It works best between .NET applications. Remoting can be useful when the advanced capabilities of an Object Request Broker (ORB) such as CORBA, EJB, or COM+ are not required.

Overview

To use RMI, you begin by designing an interface that extends the `Remote` interface. In contrast, to use .NET remoting, begin by designing a class that inherits from the `MarshallByRefObject` class. (I am not confusing `Remote` with `UnicastRemoteObject`; this is an important difference between the two mechanisms.)

Any instance of a class that inherits from `MarshallByRefObject` will not be serialized and transmitted in an application using .NET remoting. Instead, a proxy will be created on the client end, and any calls will be forwarded to the real object in the server process.

RMI allows a choice of two transports: Java Remote Method Protocol (JRMP) and Internet Inter-ORB Protocol (IIOP). The main advantages of IIOP are interoperability with CORBA and thereby a limited ability to traverse firewalls. Remoting in .NET starts out with two transport protocols, HTTP and TCP, but provides a framework for the addition of others. The combination of a protocol and an encoding scheme is called a *channel,* and such classes all implement `IChannel`. The built-in channels are `HttpChannel` and `TcpChannel`. The HTTP channel uses SOAP and provides for interoperability with other SOAP implementations and the ability to traverse firewalls. The TCP channel uses a binary wire format and provides higher performance. Because of its proprietary nature, it is targeted at internal networks.

Remoting Client Development

In the client program, use the remote object as you would any other object. Generally the only hint that the program uses remoting is a call to initialize the remoting mechanism:

```
RemotingConfiguration.Configure( "RemotingClient.exe.config" );
```

In RMI you need to look up your well-known objects in the RMI registry or the COSNaming name server if you use IIOP. In .NET remoting, there is no root name server process. Instead, the application's configuration file describes any well-known objects and where their servers are located. In Listing 8-2, the `wellknown` element of the client section defines that any instances of class `RemotingLib.RemotingExample` from assembly `RemotingLib` are not local; they are located at the specified URL. In some configuration files you may see an `activated` element in place of `wellknown`. The "Activation Modes for Remote Objects" section later in this chapter covers the use of `activated`.

Listing 8-2. Sample Configuration File for a .NET Remoting Client

```
<configuration>
  <system.runtime.remoting>
    <application>

      <client>
        <wellknown type="RemotingLib.RemotingExample, RemotingLib"
url="tcp://localhost:7777/RemotingExample/RemotingExample.rem" />
      </client>

      <channels>
        <channel ref="tcp" />
      </channels>

    </application>
  </system.runtime.remoting>
</configuration>
```

Any objects you return that are not well known do not have to be listed in the configuration file. Simply inheriting from `MarshallByRefObject` ensures a reference is returned. Your client application will, however, need to reference assemblies for such classes.

The `channels` section of the configuration file defines the transports the client can use to contact the servers. In this case, it specifies the `TcpChannel` class, which is one of the two supplied in the core libraries. `TcpChannel` uses direct socket connections between the client and server and a binary encoding for the data. In this example, the URL scheme is `tcp` and the port is specified, as there is no default value.

This example specifies as much as possible in the configuration file. You can configure everything in code if you prefer, but obviously that is not as flexible. In ASP.NET applications, the web.config file is added to the project by the Visual Studio .NET project templates. For Windows console or WinForms applications, you need to add the configuration file yourself. Add an Extensible Markup

Language (XML) file to the project by right-clicking the project and selecting Add ➤ Add New Item . . . ➤ XML File, but name the file **app.config**. When you build the project, the file will be copied to the output directory and renamed correctly. If your executable is named RemotingClient.exe, the configuration file will be renamed to RemotingClient.exe.config.

Remoting Server Development

Writing a remoting server is straightforward because it initializes the environment in a similar fashion to the client:

```
static void Main(string[] args)
{
    RemotingConfiguration.Configure( "RemotingServer.exe.config" );

    System.Console.WriteLine( "Press enter to exit" );
    System.Console.ReadLine();
}
```

You might wonder where the objects that are being remoted are. In RMI the root objects would be instantiated and references published in the appropriate name server. In this case all the information about the well-known objects is contained in the configuration file as shown in Listing 8-3.

Listing 8-3. Sample Configuration File for a .NET Remoting Server

```
<configuration>
  <system.runtime.remoting>
    <application name="RemotingExample">

      <service>
        <wellknown mode="SingleCall"
          type="RemotingLib.RemotingExample, RemotingLib"
          objectUri="RemotingExample.rem" />
      </service>

      <channels>
        <channel port="7777" ref="tcp" />
      </channels>

    </application>
  </system.runtime.remoting>
</configuration>
```

This is similar to the client example; however, instead of the `client` section, there is a `service` section. Here, define the objects to be hosted by the server. In this case, it is an instance of `RemotingLib.RemotingExample`. Also, in the `wellknown` element, specify the name that will be used in the URL and how the objects will be instantiated.

The URL used in the client is scattered in pieces throughout the server configuration file. The last fragment is specified on the `objectUri` attribute of the `wellknown` element, and the preceding piece is the `name` attribute of the `application` element. The port and scheme are specified on the `channel` element. Knowing this you could deduce the URL of `tcp://servername:7777/RemotingExample/RemotingExample.rem` for use in a client of this server. A server is not restricted to one channel. If you added the following code to the `channels` section in the preceding configuration file, the server would allow access to the `RemotingExample` objects through either TCP on port 7777 or HTTP on port 7778:

```
<channel port="7778" ref="http" />
```

You can configure a server programmatically instead of specifying everything in the configuration file. When using advanced remoting functionality, it will be necessary to specify some things programmatically. For simple cases like that shown in the previous example, you could build a generic server and serve different objects by using different configuration files.

Using IIS as a .NET Remoting Host

An alternative to writing a server is to host your remote objects in Internet Information Services (IIS). This eliminates the need to manage additional server processes on your system. However, it only supports remoting using `HttpChannel`.

Create an IIS virtual root with the same name as the application. Your remoting configuration must be placed in the web.config file and not specify a port. The assemblies containing the remoted classes must be placed in the bin subdirectory of the virtual root.

A benefit of using IIS is that you can secure your objects by using any of the authentication mechanisms supported by IIS. Clients specify their credentials as properties on the `HttpChannel`. Although credentials can be specified in the configuration file, you will probably want to do so programmatically to keep the credentials secure.

If you are accustomed to using rmid to activate your RMI objects on demand and avoid keeping unnecessary server processes around, using IIS as a remoting host is the closest thing available.

Activation Modes for Remote Objects

The root remote objects in an RMI-based system are usually singletons. This model is necessary because an object reference is needed to make a call. In .NET remoting you have other alternatives.

CORBA and COM+ servers often use a model that activates an object for the life of a single method call. These objects usually keep all their state in a database, so there is no state to maintain in the server. This model is supported in .NET remoting by single call objects.

In RMI, the singleton locatable through the registry is often a factory for objects of another type that the clients are really interested in. If you could just invoke new on remote objects and have them created in the server, you would eliminate the need for the factory in some circumstances. Using .NET remoting, this is possible with objects known as *client-activated objects*. It is up to you to resolve issues arising from multiple clients instantiating identical objects.

Specify the activation mode for objects on the server in the configuration file or programmatically. In the preceding example, the mode attribute on the wellknown element specifies SingleCall. For a singleton, specify mode as Singleton. Client-activated objects are specified using an activated element instead of a wellknown element.

Using the soapsuds Tool to Generate Proxies

In Java, the only thing that needs to be shared between the client and server is the interface. You would use the rmic tool to generate stubs from the interface. The client has no knowledge of the implementation in the server. Up to this point I have talked about .NET remoting clients having access to the assemblies containing the remoted classes, but what if you do not want to share the implementation with the client?

You do not need to share the implementation. The client only needs a class that has the same method signature. You can supply your clients with a dummy class. Of course this has a maintenance cost if you cannot automate it. If your server uses HTTP and SOAP, you can use the soapsuds tool to generate an assembly containing proxy classes. This also allows clients to generate their own proxy classes without you needing to distribute anything.

The soapsuds tool can consume either the URL of a running server or the assembly containing the remoted classes. The output can be source code for proxies or a compiled assembly of those proxies.

The following command (which should be entered as a single line) extracts information from a running server and generates an assembly containing proxy classes:

```
soapsuds
    -url:http://localhost/RemotingExample/RemotingExample.soap?wsdl
    -oa:Prox.dll
```

Remoting Objects and Garbage Collection

Under normal circumstances, your objects stay alive as long as somebody holds a reference to them, but in a remoting situation, how is that achieved?

If you have used RMI you probably know that it uses a distributed reference counting mechanism in which the servers contact the clients to see if they are still using the objects to which they took references. Some criticize this scheme for generating traffic to check whether references are still being used. This technique is not used by .NET remoting. Instead a client takes a *lease* on an object for some period of time. Each time a call is made to an object, its lease is renewed. When the lease expires, the object is permitted to be garbage collected by normal means. This all occurs within the framework.

However, the lease is not a perfect solution. You might have a reference to a remote object that has been garbage collected because its lease has expired due to lack of use. The scheme used by RMI does not allow this to happen. The easy answer is to extend the default lease time for this object because it seems to be set too low. The time parameters for .NET remoting are all configurable in the application's configuration file, so this is easy to do and is application specific. Conversely, you might have objects that remain around too long after their clients have finished with them. If this occurs, consider reducing the default lease time for such objects.

Manipulating the lease renewal times is an imperfect solution. Should you need to take more control over the lease for an object, you can create a *sponsor*. When a sponsor is registered for a remote object and its lease expires, the lease manager in the object's application attempts to contact the sponsor to give it a chance to renew the lease. Multiple sponsors can be registered for an object, and the framework recognizes that it only takes one sponsor to extend the lease. To use a sponsor, create a class that implements the ISponsor interface and register it with a remote object's lease object. This will give you the ability to ensure objects are still around when you need them.

Security

RMI provides no intrinsic security mechanism and neither does .NET remoting. If you are using IIS to host your objects, then you can use one of the authentication mechanisms it supports to control access. In this case, configure the credentials on the HttpChannel in the client.

If you need anything more than this, you need to build it yourself or consider a more sophisticated ORB such as COM+ (see Chapter 10, "Creating Components"). You might also consider Web services.

Using ASP.NET Web Services

ASP.NET Web Services and Visual Studio .NET provide a productive environment for creating SOAP-based Web services. Much of the complexity you dealt with in Java is eliminated, and you can concentrate on the business logic.

There are a growing number of Java implementations for creating Web services. By far the most well known is Apache SOAP. Although other solutions may be more sophisticated, most people who use them have some familiarity with Apache SOAP, so I use it here as a baseline.

Writing a Web Service

Just as ASP.NET WebForms must be placed in .aspx files, ASP.NET Web services must be placed in .asmx files. Many examples will show you an .asmx file with inline code placed between script tags. Although this is perfectly valid, you will not see it too often in the real world because Visual Studio .NET uses code behind files for Web services just as it does with WebForms. The big difference is that WebForms still makes extensive use of the .aspx file and in most cases an .asmx file is reduced to something like the following:

```
<%@ WebService Language="c#" Codebehind="Service1.asmx.cs"
    Class="ExampleWebService.Service1" %>
```

The interesting part of the Web service is in the code behind file. Here you start by writing a class much as if it were to be invoked locally (just as you would for Apache SOAP). Instead of specifying information in something such as a deployment descriptor, you turn a class into a .NET Web service using inheritance and attributes. The class providing the Web Service inherits from System.Web.Services.WebService and usually has a WebService attribute specifying the namespace for the service. Each method that is accessible as a SOAP call is tagged with a WebMethod attribute. This enables you to have methods that are not accessible remotely if they make sense for the class.

Built using Visual Studio .NET, Listing 8-4 demonstrates the WebService attribute on the class and WebMethod attributes on the Web Service methods. It also contains methods generated by the designer that are for internal use; therefore, they do not have WebMethod attributes.

Listing 8-4. A Minimal Web Service Created Using Visual Studio .NET

```csharp
using System;
using System.Collections;
using System.ComponentModel;
using System.Data;
using System.Diagnostics;
using System.Web;
using System.Web.Services;


namespace ExampleWebService
{
    /// <summary>
    /// Summary description for Service1.
    /// </summary>
  [WebService(Namespace="http://www.csharpwebservices.com/dummy1")]
    public class Service1 : System.Web.Services.WebService
    {
        public Service1()
        {
            //CODEGEN: This call is required by the ASP.NET Web Se...
            InitializeComponent();
        }

        #region Component Designer generated code

        //Required by the Web Services Designer
        private IContainer components = null;

        /// <summary>
        /// Required method for Designer support - do not modify
        /// the contents of this method with the code editor.
        /// </summary>
        private void InitializeComponent()
        {
        }
```

```
/// <summary>
/// Clean up any resources being used.
/// </summary>
protected override void Dispose( bool disposing )
{
    if(disposing && components != null)
    {
        components.Dispose();
    }
    base.Dispose(disposing);
}


#endregion

[WebMethod]
public string SayHello( string who )
{
    return "Hello " + who + " from ASP.NET web services";
}
        }
    }
```

To create this Web Service, follow these steps:

1. Create a new ASP.NET Web Service project called **ExampleWebService**.

2. You will be placed in the design view for the code-behind file
    Service1.asmx.cs. Click the Click Here to Switch to Code View link. Much
    of the code shown in Listing 8-4 has been generated for you.

3. At the bottom of the file is a comment section describing a simple
    HelloWorld method. Replace this with the following:

    ```
    [WebMethod]
    public string SayHello( string who )
    {
        return "Hello " + who + " from ASP.NET web services";
    }
    ```

4. Build the application and then run it. Your browser will open and you
    will see the page shown in Figure 8-1.

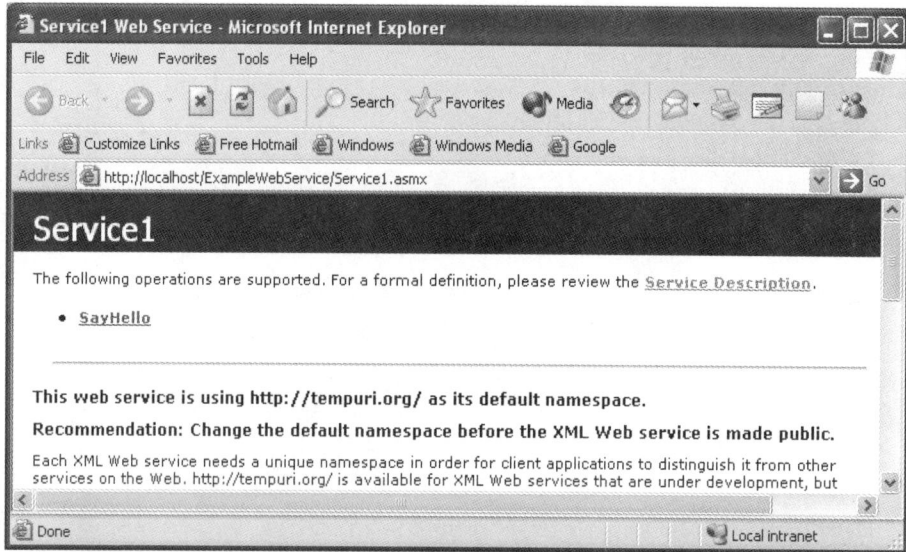

Figure 8-1. The browser window shown when a Web Service application is run in Visual Studio .NET

5. Click on the SayHello link. You are taken to the page shown in Figure 8-2 that describes how to invoke the method in terms of HTTP requests and responses. Of more interest are the set of controls at the top of the page that allow you to test your service. This feature is only available for simple services but is convenient when you can take advantage of it.

6. Enter your name and click the Invoke button. The XML response in Figure 8-3 will be shown. Close the browser windows and return to Visual Studio .NET.

7. Take another look at Figure 8-1. There is a warning about the XML namespace http://tempuri.org/, that ASP.NET uses if you do not specify your own. Close the browser windows and return to Visual Studio .NET. Add a WebService attribute to the Service1 class as follows:

```
[WebService(Namespace="http://www.csharpwebservices.com/dummy1")]
public class Service1 : System.Web.Services.WebService
{
```

8. Now rebuild the application and run it again. The namespace warning no longer appears.

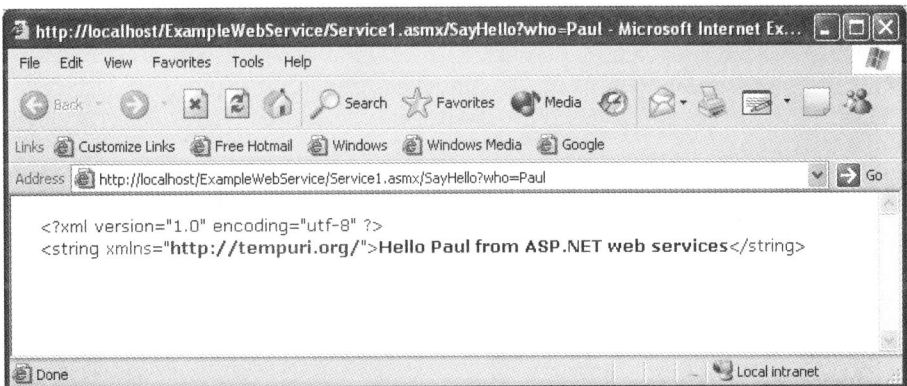

Figure 8-2. The Web page describing the SayHello *method*

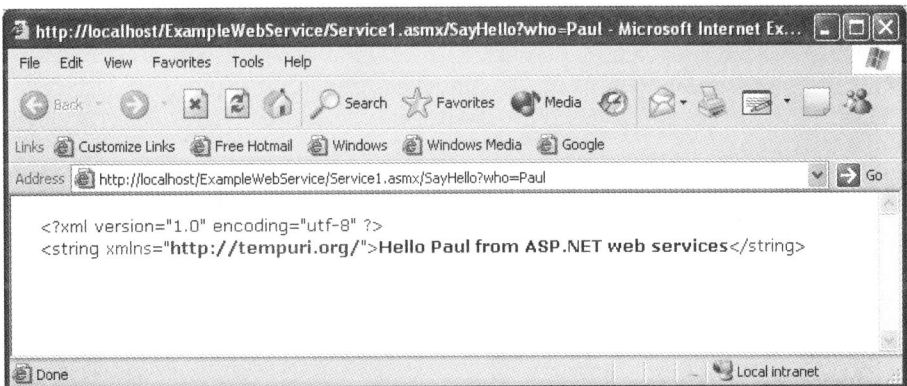

Figure 8-3. The response from the SayHello *method*

Writing a Web Service Client

Developing Web service clients in .NET can be straightforward or complex. If you are consuming an ASP.NET Web Service, it will be easy. If you are talking to anything else, it comes down to whether you have a Web Services Description Language (WSDL) file.

The WSDL file describes the Web Service according to an XML schema and allows Visual Studio .NET to generate a proxy class. This is similar to the way CORBA clients use Interface Definition Language (IDL) files. If you are consuming an ASP.NET Web service, you can view the WSDL file by appending **?WSDL** to the URL of the .asmx file:

```
http://localhost/ExampleWebService/Service1.asmx?WSDL
```

To consume a Web service in your application when developing in Visual Studio .NET, start by adding a Web reference as shown in Figure 8-4.

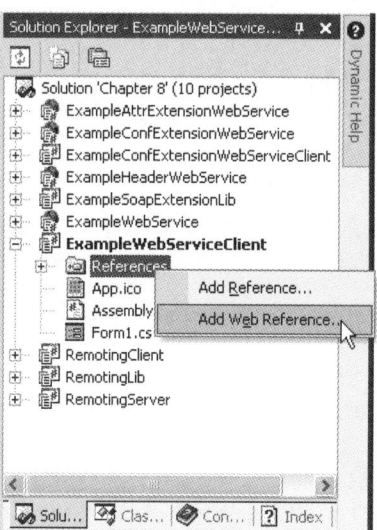

Figure 8-4. Adding a Web reference to a client application project

The Add Web Reference dialog box, shown in Figure 8-5, offers two ways to locate the server.

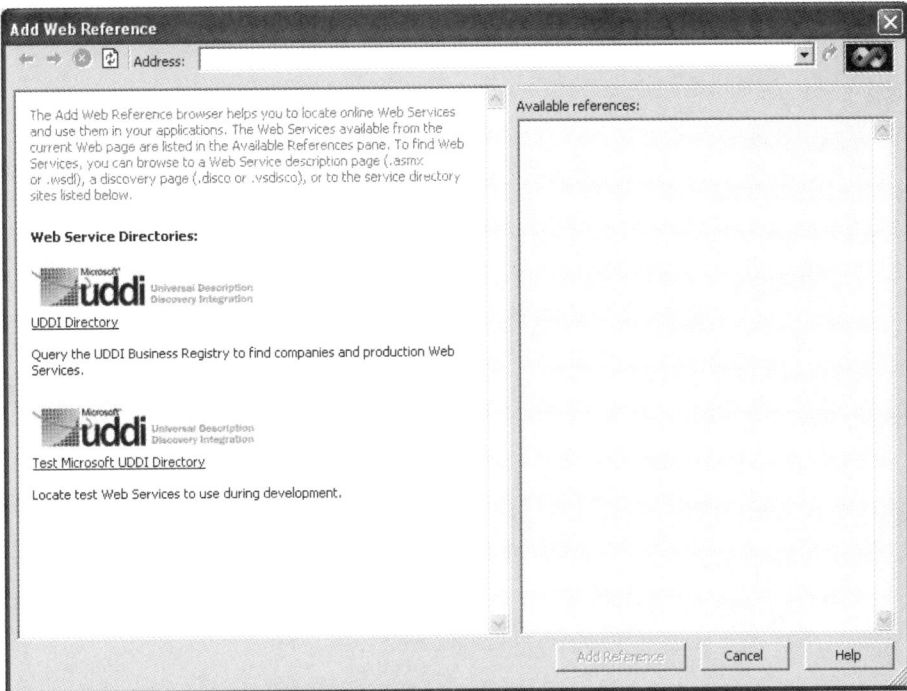

Figure 8-5. The Add Web Reference dialog box

If you know the URL of the service (the .asmx file), enter it into the box labeled Address, press Enter, and then click Add Reference.

The other option, to use Universal Description Discovery and Integration (UDDI), is more complex but important. UDDI is likely to become more heavily used in the future. UDDI is a federated directory of Web services you can interrogate to locate services provided by other organizations. It is not restricted to .NET or even Microsoft, although Microsoft provides a UDDI server node that may be used by the Add Web Reference dialog box. Locate a Web service by entering the name of the company that provides the service. You are then presented with a list of product offerings comprised of individual Web services termed *tModels*, as shown in Figure 8-6. To complete the process, select the desired tModel and click Add Reference.

NOTE *UDDI is a Web service itself with a complex interface. It is so complex in fact that many toolkit providers supply a library to simplify access. You may have come across this in Java. Microsoft's UDDI team provides a downloadable Software Development Kit (SDK) that includes a .NET interface.*

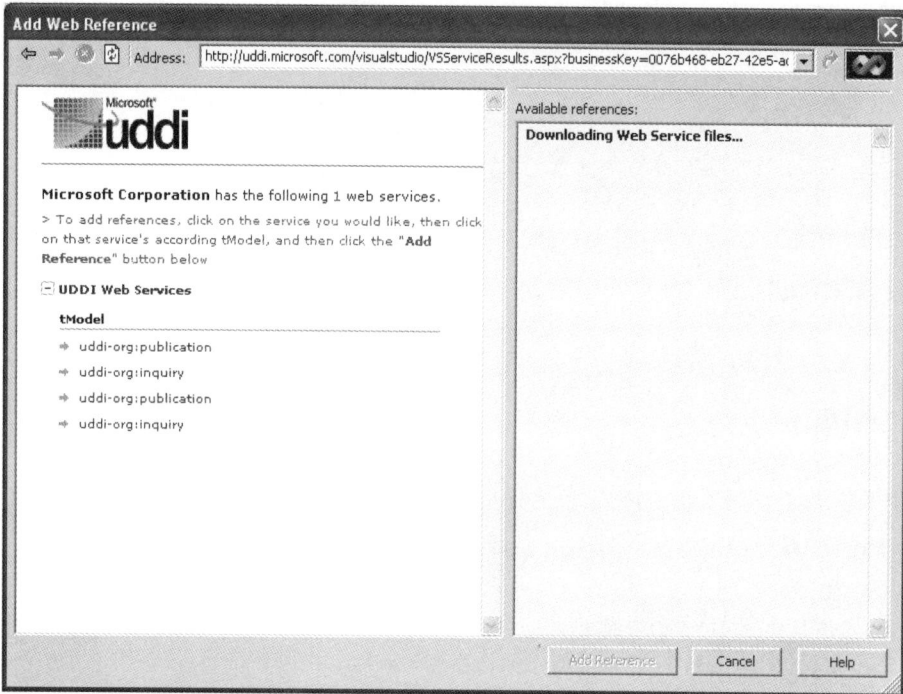

Figure 8-6. Adding a Web reference from UDDI

However you get there, Visual Studio finally consumes the WSDL description of the service you want to access and generates a proxy class that looks externally to have all the public methods of the Web service. You create an instance of the class and call the methods just as if it were a local class.

To create a WinForms client for the Web Service you just created, follow these steps:

1. Create a new Windows Application project called **ExampleWebServiceClient**.

2. Drag Label, TextBox, and Button controls to the form and create the interface shown in Figure 8-7. Rename the TextBox to **nameTextBox** and the Button to **helloButton**.

3. Right-click the project and select Add Web Reference . . . (as shown previously in Figure 8-4). When the Add Web Reference dialog box appears, enter the URL of your Web Service. This will probably be **http://localhost/ExampleWebService/Service1.asmx** unless you

Figure 8-7. The user interface for ExampleWebServiceClient

modified the default location. Press Enter and you will see the dialog box shown in Figure 8-8. Click Add Reference, and the proxy will be added to your project.

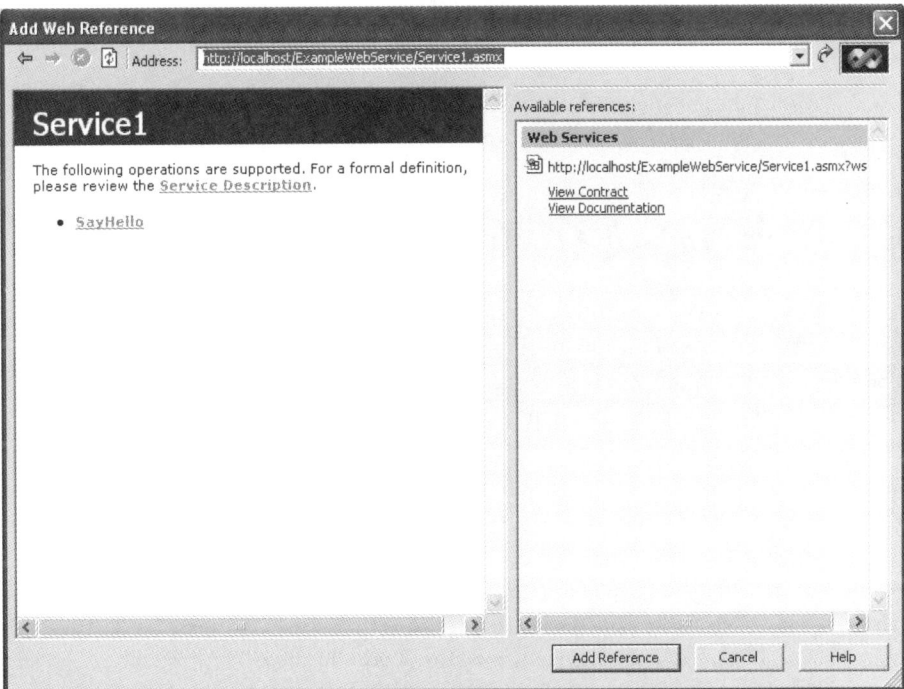

Figure 8-8. The Add Web Reference dialog box upon entering the URL of ExampleWebService

189

4. Now double-click the button to create a button click handler. Enter the following code, which creates an instance of the proxy and invokes the SayHello method as normal. Notice that the proxy class was created in a namespace based on the name of the server, in this case localhost:

```
private void helloButton_Click(object sender, System.EventArgs e)
{
    localhost.Service1 svc = new localhost.Service1();

    String resp = svc.SayHello( nameTextBox.Text );

    MessageBox.Show( this,
        resp,
        "Web Service Response",
        MessageBoxButtons.OK,
        MessageBoxIcon.Information );
}
```

5. Build the project and run it. When you enter your name you should see the response in a message box.

Exceptions in Web Services

As you may already know from Java, SOAP passes failure information in the fault element of the SOAP document. Apache SOAP enables you to throw a SOAPException on the server side that is used to populate the fault. On the client side you must interrogate the Response object to see if a fault was sent.

Things are a little easier in .NET Web Services. On the server side any exception that percolates out of the Web service is mapped into a fault. Any fault arriving on the client side is thrown as a SoapException or SoapHeaderException.

To distinguish between different classes of exceptions on the client, you would be best throwing SoapExceptions yourself for those that pass across the wire. This gives you an opportunity to populate the Detail property with information your client program can interrogate. If you let the exceptions be mapped automatically, you are stuck displaying the text provided by the server program. As you can see in Figure 8-9, this is not always user friendly.

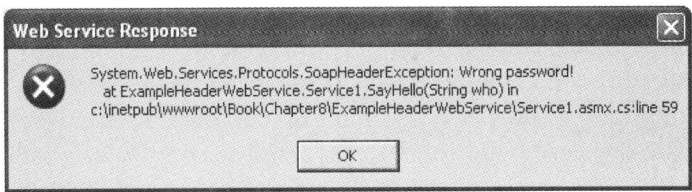

Figure 8-9. Displaying the text of an exception thrown in a Web service

Serializing and Deserializing Parameters

When you pass a class as a parameter or return value for an Apache SOAP call, you provide a serializer/deserializer to perform the XML encoding and decoding. In the simple case, you typically rely on `BeanSerializer`, which, as its name implies, is able to encode and decode any JavaBean. In ASP.NET, you can rely on the standard XML encoding rules to encode and decode your classes and structs. In both cases, the fun begins when you want to go beyond the default behavior.

In Apache SOAP when you need a non-default encoding and decoding you have to learn how to implement a serializer and deserializer. You must then register them in the deployment descriptor type mappings for each service that uses them.

In ASP.NET you can use XML or SOAP *shaping* attributes to control how your classes are mapped into XML. (Chapter 9, "Working with XML," will cover the XML shaping attributes.) The SOAP shaping attributes are more limited but follow the same pattern as the XML shaping attributes for people using Section 5 encoding (described next).

Encoding Parameter Values

If you try to get an Apache SOAP application to talk to a .NET application, you will soon discover the first big difference between them. Apache SOAP defaults to creating the XML representation of the data according to the rules in Section 5 of the SOAP specification, called *Section 5 encoding*. ASP.NET defaults to encoding the data as pure XML, called *literal encoding*. There is nothing wrong with this; there is no single correct default.

The Section 5 encoding rules, often referred to simply as Section 5, were devised to provide a standard way to identify common types used in RPC calls so that toolkits could map the data in a manner appropriate to the languages used at either end. It passes the type information with the parameter values in every message. At that time WSDL did not exist, so there was no recognized mechanism to define the types ahead of time.

Most toolkits default to Section 5 encoding. Many do not yet support literal XML encoding but most intend to do so. If you need to communicate with servers written in another toolkit, the generated proxy will use the correct encoding style as long as they provide a WSDL file. If your server needs to accommodate clients who only support Section 5, specify the `SoapRpcService` attribute on the class implementing the Web Service to switch to this encoding:

```
[SoapRpcService]
[WebService(Namespace="http://www.csharpwebservices.com/dummy ")]
public class Service1 : System.Web.Services.WebService
{
    ...
}
```

No other changes are required. It is also possible to override the encoding per method using similar attributes, but I would strongly discourage this.

Making the change to literal encoding in Apache SOAP is not trivial. The toolkit simply passes the parameters as XML nodes to your method. It is up to you to deserialize the XML. You will probably decide that it is much easier to switch to Section 5 encoding in your .NET programs if you need to interoperate with older toolkits. Newer toolkits, including Sun's Web Services Developer Pack (WSDP) and Axis, the successor to Apache SOAP, support literal encoding and WSDL, so this is not a concern. Should you decide to switch your Web Service to use literal encoding once all your clients support it, you can do so by removing the `SoapRpcService` attribute.

SOAP Headers

SOAP headers were envisioned to carry context and control information for consumption by components outside the Web service methods. The arrival of the Global XML Architecture (GXA) specifications, such as WS-Routing, with their reliance on headers has done much to reinforce that concept.

In an Apache SOAP client you must pass the header objects to the `Call` constructor or add the headers to the `Envelope`'s header collection, prior to calling `invoke`. On the server side, it gets ugly quickly. There is no stock interception point at which to process the headers unless you write an envelope editor transport hook. The problem with this is that it has to parse the XML itself if it needs to access the headers; only the raw stream is available. The Web Service method itself has no context to use to get access to the headers. The only solution that seems to make sense is to take a copy of `RPCRouterServlet` and customize it to suit your needs.

Handling headers in ASP.NET Web Services is easier. You can use attributes to make headers accessible to the Web Service methods. If you want to process headers at an application level, you can write a SOAP extension and add it to the processing chain by using attributes or configuration files.

Let's create a Web Service that uses a simple authentication header. This is not one that would stand up to scrutiny in the real world, but it is sufficient for an example:

1. First, create a new ASP.NET Web Service project called **ExampleHeaderWebService**.

2. Add a class to the project called **SimpleAuthenticationSoapHeader**. This will be serialized as the SOAP header so it must inherit from SoapHeader. Modify the class as follows:

```
using System;
using System.Web.Services.Protocols;

namespace ExampleHeaderWebService
{
    public class SimpleAuthenticationSoapHeader : SoapHeader
    {
        private string m_password;

        public string Password
        {
            get
            {
                return m_password;
            }
            set
            {
                m_password = value;
            }
        }
    }
}
```

3. Next, open Service1 and switch to the code view. The Web Service class must contain a public member of the header type. Add a `SimpleAuthenticationSoapHeader` instance as follows:

```
public class Service1 : System.Web.Services.WebService
{
    ...
    public SimpleAuthenticationSoapHeader header;
    ...
}
```

4. Each method that needs to process the header must have a `SoapHeaderAttribute` that specifies the name of the SOAP header class member to be populated. In these methods you can access the header through the member variable. Headers processed this way are considered understood by the framework and will not raise faults if marked `mustUnderstand='1'`. Add a `SayHello` method, which accesses the header as follows:

```
[WebMethod]
[ SoapHeader( "header" ) ]
public string SayHello( string who )
{
    if ( header.Password != "password" )
    {
        throw new SoapHeaderException( "Wrong password!",
            SoapException.ClientFaultCode,
            this.Context.Request.Url.ToString() );
    }
    return "Hello " + who + " from ASP.NET web services";
}
```

5. You cannot test Web Services that use headers from your browser. If you run the project the pages describing the service still appear but the forms for testing the methods are omitted. You must create a client to test them.

6. From the client's perspective, using headers is easy. The SOAP headers are described by the WSDL and get generated in the proxy as member variables of the service. Create header instances to populate the member variables prior to making a call. Listing 8-5 shows the button click handler from a WinForms application that uses the service you have just created.

Listing 8-5. Adding SOAP Headers in a Client Application

```
private void button1_Click(object sender, System.EventArgs e)
{
    localhost.Service1 svc = new localhost.Service1();
    svc.SimpleAuthenticationSoapHeaderValue
        = new localhost.SimpleAuthenticationSoapHeader();
    svc.SimpleAuthenticationSoapHeaderValue.Password
        = passwordTextBox.Text;
    try
    {
        String resp = svc.SayHello( nameTextBox.Text );
        MessageBox.Show( this,
            resp,
            "Web Service Response",
            MessageBoxButtons.OK,
            MessageBoxIcon.Information );
    }
    catch( SoapHeaderException she)
    {
        MessageBox.Show( this,
            she.Message,
            "Web Service Response",
            MessageBoxButtons.OK,
            MessageBoxIcon.Error );
    }
}
```

SOAP headers can be part of the response as well as part of the request. The `SoapHeaderAttribute` has a property `Direction`, which as its name implies, specifies if a header is input, output, or both.

SOAP Extensions

An ASP.NET *SOAP extension* allows you to perform preprocessing and postprocessing of the request and response (similar to an envelope editor transport hook in Apache SOAP). Use SOAP extensions to perform processing when you want to apply it to multiple methods or services before or after the Web Service method itself.

Writing a SOAP Extension

A SOAP extension inherits from `System.Web.Services.Protocols.SoapExtension`. It gets control at four points in the processing of a request. From the server's perspective, these are as follows:

- Before the request is deserialized

- After it is deserialized

- Before the response is serialized

- After the response is serialized

An Apache SOAP envelope editor is only given access to the messages in serialized form and therefore has to crack open the XML somehow if it needs to manipulate it. This is equivalent to the before deserialization and after serialization points in a .NET SOAP extension. The after deserialization and before serialization points have access to the message's object model including the envelope and any headers.

The `ProcessMessage` method of `SoapExtension` is invoked at each of the four interception points. To determine which one caused a given invocation, examine the `Stage` property. The `SoapMessageStage` enumeration's names are self-explanatory. A typical `ProcessMessage` implementation looks like Listing 8-6.

Listing 8-6. A Skeleton `ProcessMessage` *Implementation for a SOAP Extension Class*

```
public override void ProcessMessage( SoapMessage message )
{
    switch ( message.Stage )
    {
        case SoapMessageStage.BeforeSerialize:
            ...
            break;

        case SoapMessageStage.AfterSerialize:
            ...
            break;

        case SoapMessageStage.BeforeDeserialize:
            ...
            break;
```

```
    case SoapMessageStage.AfterDeserialize:

      ...
      break;

    default: // should never happen
      throw new Exception( "Unrecognized SoapMessageStage "
                            + message.Stage.ToString() );
    }
}
```

The other methods you need to implement depend on how your extension is applied to the Web Service methods and how they relate to the initialization of your extension. An extension can be specified on a per-method basis either by using an attribute (in which case initialization data can be provided) or per application in the web.config file. The extension's constructor is typically used to initialize members that are independent of the initialization context.

Using Attributes to Apply an Extension

You can apply extensions on a per-method basis by creating an attribute for your extension. This has the advantage that only the methods you specify use the extension and that you can provide method specific initialization values to customize the extension's behavior.

Create the attribute by inheriting from SoapExtensionAttribute. A minimal attribute would look like Listing 8-7.

Listing 8-7. A Typical SoapExtensionAttribute *Implementation*
```
[ AttributeUsage( AttributeTargets.Method ) ]
public class ExampleSoapExtensionAttribute : SoapExtensionAttribute
{
    public override Type ExtensionType
    {
        get
        {
            return typeof( ExampleSoapExtension );
        }
    }

    private int m_priority;
```

```
        public override int Priority
        {
            get
            {
                return m_priority;
            }
            set
            {
                m_priority = value;
            }
        }
    }
}
```

The extension will be invoked for any methods tagged with the attribute. The ExtensionType property must return the Type of the extension. The "Setting the Execution Order of Extensions" section covers the purpose of the Priority property.

Attributes become more powerful when they have some additional properties, which the extension can use to customize its behavior for the specific method. If you add a property Password to ExampleSoapExtensionAttribute, you can modify the preceding SOAP header example to have per-method passwords validated in an extension instead of duplicating the code in each method:

```
[WebMethod]
[ SoapHeader( "header" ) ]
[ ExampleSoapExtension( Password = "password" ) ]
public string SayHello( string who )
{
    return "Hello " + who + " from ASP.NET web services";
}

[WebMethod]
[ SoapHeader( "header" ) ]
[ ExampleSoapExtension( Password = "drowssap" ) ]
public string SayGoodbye( string who )
{
    return "Goodbye " + who + " from ASP.NET web services";
}
```

Initialization of the extension is complex enough that you may want to reread the following a couple of times to make sure you have it straight in your mind. When an extension is specified using attributes, an instance is created for each method that specifies the attribute on its first call. At that point, the default constructor is run. It has no context and can only do initialization that is context independent. The extension's `GetInitializer` is then called—in this case, the version that takes a `LogicalMethodInfo` and a `SoapExtensionAttribute`. This enables you to extract method-specific information and construct an object to contain the initialization information:

```
public override object GetInitializer(
    LogicalMethodInfo methodInfo,
    SoapExtensionAttribute attribute )
{
    return ( ( ExampleSoapExtensionAttribute)attribute ).Password;
}
```

On each call to the Web service method, the extension's `Initialize` method is called with the initialization object to allow you to set up the extension for processing the call:

```
private string m_password;

public override void Initialize( object initializer )
{
    m_password = (string)initializer;
}
```

In this example, you use the password value specified in the attribute in these methods. Now when `ProcessMessage` is called for each stage, the initialization data is available for use (see Listing 8-8).

Listing 8-8. The `ProcessMessage` *Method of the Authentication SOAP Extension*

```
public override void ProcessMessage( SoapMessage message )
{
    switch ( message.Stage )
    {
        ...
        case SoapMessageStage.AfterDeserialize:
            {
                bool found = false;

                foreach ( SoapHeader header in message.Headers )
                {
                    if ( header is SimpleAuthenticationSoapHeader )
                    {
```

```
                if (
        ((SimpleAuthenticationSoapHeader)header).Password
                                    == m_password )
            {
                found = true;
            }
            else
            {
                throw new SoapHeaderException(
                    "Wrong password!",
                    SoapException.ClientFaultCode,
                    message.Url.ToString() );
            }
        }
    }
    if ( !found )
    {
        throw new SoapHeaderException(
            "Missing password!",
            SoapException.ClientFaultCode,
            message.Url.ToString() );
    }
}
break;

    ...
    }
}
```

The advantages of using an attribute are that you can be selective about which methods the extension applies to and you can supply method specific initialization parameters.

Using a Configuration File Entry to Apply an Extension

To apply your extension to all methods in an application, make an entry in the web.config file. This avoids the need to modify the code to tag all the methods and eliminates the risk that somebody forgets to do so at some point in the future.

In the configuration file, web.config, you must add a soapExtensionTypes element inside the webServices element. The soapExtensionTypes element in turn contains add elements that specify the extensions:

```
<configuration>
    <system.web>
        ...
        <webServices>
            <soapExtensionTypes>
                <add
                type="ExampleSoapExtensionLib.ExampleSoapExtension,
                        ExampleSoapExtensionLib"
                    priority="0"
                    group="0" />
            </soapExtensionTypes>
        </webServices>
        ...
    </system.web>
</configuration>
```

The key attribute is type, which like many configuration file attributes, specifies the class to use by its fully qualified name and assembly.

Initialization is slightly different in this case. The GetInitializer variant that accepts a Type is used. Because there is no provision for specifying initialization data in the element, you must extract it from elsewhere (although it could be from custom elements in web.config). In the example, you can hard-code the password:

```
public override object GetInitializer( Type wsType )
{
    return "one4all";
}
```

The rest of the sequence is as described previously for attributes.

Setting the Execution Order of Extensions

If you are using multiple extensions, how do you ensure they are invoked in a particular order? For example, imagine you have an extension that performs custom authentication of the requests and another that logs all requests. You probably have a requirement that states whether you should log requests that fail authentication. Let's say you do not want to log them, so that means the authentication extension must get control first.

One of the things you specify for every extension is a priority. The lowest priority value is invoked first. So in this example, the authentication extension should have a lower priority value than the logging extension.

There is another dimension to this, however. Extensions defined in a configuration file have a group specified that can take the value 0 or 1. Extensions in group 0 are invoked first in ascending priority order. Then extensions defined using attributes are invoked in ascending priority order. Finally, extensions defined in group 1 are invoked in ascending priority order.

The one thing you cannot do is insert an extension using the configuration file between extensions defined using attributes.

Using Extensions on the Client

Most of the discussion so far has focused on using SOAP extensions on the server. You can also use them on the client, but there are issues that can make this more complex.

Interception of the request occurs at the same points as on the server, but of course the request and response roles are reversed. If your extension is going to be used on both the client and server, as might occur with an encryption extension, you might need to consider this. The most common way of determining if you are running on the client or the server is to test the type of the SoapMessage to see if it is a SoapServerMessage. If it is, you are running in the server. For example:

```
if ( message is SoapServerMessage )
{
    // server logic
    ...
}
else
{
    // client logic
    ...
}
```

Extensions are not specified in WSDL, so the proxy generated for you by Visual Studio .NET does not contain your custom attribute. You must add the attribute yourself by opening the proxy and editing it. It is a nuisance to do this every time you update the Web reference to reflect changes to the service. That is right! Every time you update the Web reference, your changes are lost and you have to remember to change the proxy code. This is annoying during initial development but consider the potential for errors during the maintenance phase of the application's life.

The other option is to specify the extension in the client application's configuration file. This is only viable if the extension applies to all the Web Service methods the client invokes. If the client uses Web Services other than yours, this is unlikely to work correctly.

Summary

The networking capabilities in .NET are at least equal to those in Java. Many people working at the socket level will welcome the greater control available in .NET. There are tradeoffs to be made between .NET Remoting and RMI although the basic functionality is the same. SOAP Web Services are becoming more important and the ease with which they can be created in Visual Studio .NET is the envy of developers using other tools.

CHAPTER 9

Working with XML

THERE IS NO GETTING AWAY from Extensible Markup Language (XML) in the .NET Framework. All configuration files are XML documents, ASP.NET Web Services use XML in the Simple Object Access Protocol (SOAP), and ADO.NET datasets are based on XML. Naturally, the framework contains rich support to enable you to employ XML specifications in your own programs.

This chapter examines the XML support in the .NET Framework including the Document Object Model (DOM), XML Schema, Extensible Stylesheet Language Transformation (XSLT), and XPath support. It also looks at command-line tools of Visual Studio .NET, which assist XML development.

In the Java world, Java API for XML Processing (JAXP) is the latest specification for XML support, but most of us learned XML using Xerces and Xalan from the Apache project. I will therefore use those as the basis for comparison in this chapter.

Introducing the `System.XML` Classes

The `System.XML` assembly contains the namespaces `System.Xml`, `System.Xml.Schema`, `System.Xml.Serialization`, `System.Xml.XPath`, and `System.Xml.Xsl`:

- `System.XML` contains the DOM support you would turn to Xerces for in Java. There is no Simple API for XML (SAX) support in the .NET Framework, although there are classes that provide similar functionality.

- `System.Xml.Schema` contains classes that allow you to manipulate a schema. There is no equivalent in Xerces.

- `System.Xml.Serialization` contains classes, mostly attributes, which support mapping between XML documents and object structures. This is a useful feature that you have already seen used by ASP.NET Web Services.

- `System.Xml.XPath` contains classes that provide XML Path Language (XPath) support. Java programmers would turn to Xalan for this functionality.

- `System.Xml.Xsl` contains classes that provide XSLT support similar in functionality to those in Xalan.

Using XML DOM

The Document Object Model (DOM) provided by `System.Xml` in the .NET Framework is comparable to that provided by Xerces.

Manipulating the DOM

Creating a DOM document in .NET is similar to creating a document using Xerces. However, because the underlying implementation is not pluggable, you do not have to create equivalents to `DocumentBuilderFactory` and `DocumentBuilder` before you can instantiate a document as you would in Xerces. You should find most of the classes and methods you know from Xerces in the .NET DOM, although some of the methods from Xerces may well be properties in .NET.

To manipulate the DOM, follow these steps:

1. Create a new Windows Application project called **SimpleDomExample**. Add controls to the form to create the interface shown in Figure 9-1.

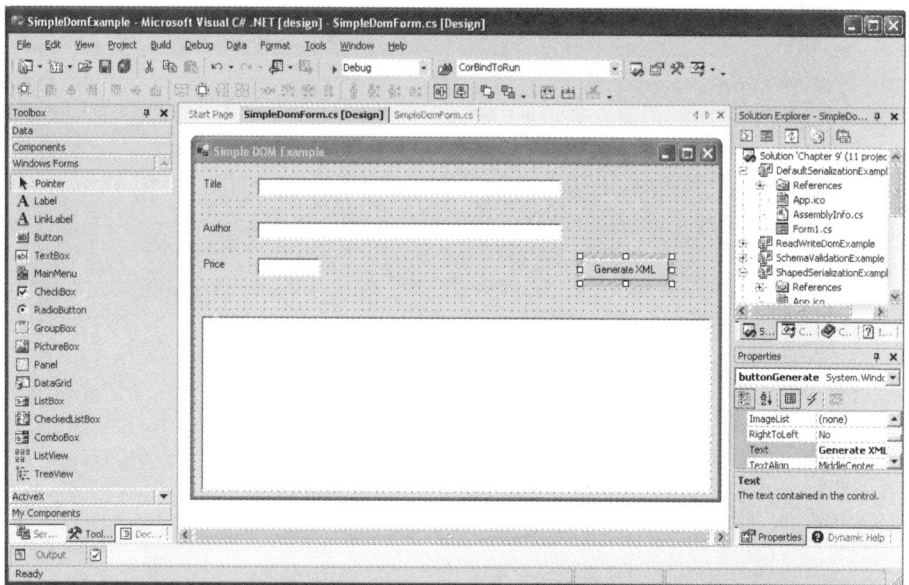

Figure 9-1. The user interface for the SimpleDomExample application

2. Name the appropriate textboxes **textBoxTitle**, **textBoxAuthor**, **textBoxPrice**, and **textBoxResult**. Name the button **buttonGenerate**.

3. Now double-click buttonGenerate to add a button click handler.

4. Finally, add a using statement for System.Xml and then modify the button click handler as shown in Listing 9-1.

Listing 9-1. Building an XML Document Using the DOM Classes in .NET

```
private void buttonGenerate_Click(object sender,
                                  System.EventArgs e)
{
    XmlDocument doc = new XmlDocument();

    XmlElement root = doc.CreateElement( "books" );
    doc.AppendChild( root );

    XmlElement eltBook = doc.CreateElement( "book" );
    root.AppendChild( eltBook );

    XmlElement eltTitle = doc.CreateElement( "title" );
    eltTitle.AppendChild(
        doc.CreateTextNode( textBoxTitle.Text ) );
    eltBook.AppendChild( eltTitle );

    XmlElement eltAuthor = doc.CreateElement( "author" );
    eltAuthor.AppendChild(
        doc.CreateTextNode(  textBoxAuthor.Text ) );
    eltBook.AppendChild( eltAuthor );

    XmlElement eltPrice = doc.CreateElement( "price" );
    eltPrice.AppendChild(
        doc.CreateTextNode(  textBoxPrice.Text ) );
    eltBook.AppendChild( eltPrice );

    textBoxResult.Text = doc.OuterXml;
}
```

Build and run this example. You can enter values that are used to construct an XML document. The document is then displayed in textBoxResult, as shown in Figure 9-2.

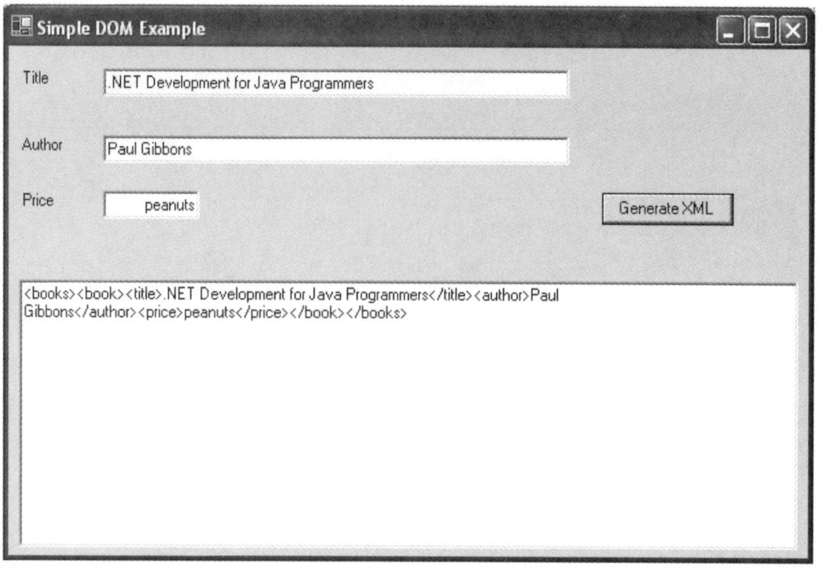

Figure 9-2. SimpleDomExample in action

Reading and Writing XML

Reading XML into a DOM and writing it out is simpler than with Xerces. The XmlDocument class contains Load and Save methods that allow you to directly access files or URLs. They also support other sources such as streams.

The following demonstrates how easily a document can be loaded from a file:

```
doc.Load( "inputFile.xml" );
```

Saving a document is equally straightforward:

```
doc.Save( "outputFile.xml" );
```

These methods use the XML declaration, such as the following, to determine what encoding to use:

```
<?xml version="1.0" encoding="ISO-8859-1"?>
```

Microsoft added an XmlDeclaration class to the DOM to allow this to be maintained as part of the document. The Save method uses the encoding set in this node if it is present.

The InnerXml *and* OuterXml *Methods*

One useful feature of the .NET DOM is the ability to get the textual representation of a document fragment from any node using the InnerXml and OuterXml properties of XmlNode. InnerXml returns the XML for the contents of an XmlNode instance excluding the node itself. OuterXml includes the XmlNode.

Implementing XmlReader **and** XmlWriter **Instead of SAX**

There is no SAX support in the .NET libraries. There is, however, a high-performance, forward-only parser that provides similar capabilities. The base class for accessing this functionality is XmlReader, and the primary concrete implementation is XmlTextReader. There are corresponding XmlWriter and XmlTextWriter classes.

Whereas SAX raises events to your code to handle arriving nodes (a push model), XmlReader places the onus on you to request the nodes and process them much as you would records in a conventional data file (a pull model).

The XmlDocument Load and Save methods allow you to use an XmlTextReader or XmlTextWriter, respectively, as sources for data. This is primarily for validation with XmlValidatingReader. However, it also permits processing some fragments in a DOM while using XmlReader for the bulk of the document.

Using an XmlWriter in XmlDocument.Save is useful for formatting XML documents. The XmlTextWriter supports "pretty printing" through the Formatting property. When set to Indented, each level is indented according to the number of characters specified in the Indentation property. This is much the same as using the setIndenting and setIndent methods of OutputFormat in Xerces:

```
XmlTextWriter tw = new XmlTextWriter( "outputFile.xml", null );
tw.Formatting = Formatting.Indented;
tw.Indentation = 4;
doc.Save( tw );
tw.Close();
```

Understanding XML Schema Validation

.NET supports XML Schemas just as Xerces does. You can validate a document against any schemas it specifies using XmlValidatingReader. In addition to XSD schemas, .NET supports validation against XDR schemas and DTDs.

In Xerces you set a property to the file system location where copies of the schemas are kept or rely on the document to specify a schemaLocation attribute for all the schemas it references.

In .NET you can rely on the schemaLocation attribute or provide an XmlSchemaCollection instance containing the schemas to avoid fetching them for each transform. The XmlSchemaCollection also provides performance benefits when you are validating multiple documents against the same set of schemas because the cost of loading the schema into memory is only incurred once:

```
XmlSchemaCollection xsc = new XmlSchemaCollection();
xsc.Add( "urn:schema-1", "s1.xsd" );
xsc.Add( "urn:scheam-2", "s2.xsd" );
```

Once the schema collection has been built, use it in a given validation by adding it to the Schemas property of the XmlValidatingReader instance.

XmlValidatingReader raises ValidationEvents to notify your code when a validation failure occurs. Field these by registering a ValidationEventHandler (see Listing 9-2).

Listing 9-2. Validating an XML Document Using XmlValidatingReader

```
private int m_errors = 0;

private void ValidationCallBack( object sender,
                                     ValidationEventArgs args )
{
    m_errors++;
}

   ...
    XmlDocument doc = new XmlDocument();
    XmlTextReader tr = new XmlTextReader("inputFile.xml" );
    XmlValidatingReader vr = new XmlValidatingReader( tr );
    vr.Schemas.Add( xsc );
    vr.ValidationEventHandler +=
            new ValidationEventHandler( ValidationCallBack );
    doc.Load( vr );
    vr.Close();
    tr.Close();
    System.Console.WriteLine( "There were {0} validation errors",
                                 m_errors );
```

This is not dissimilar to registering an error handler in Xerces but, because the ValidationEventHandler is restricted to validation errors, is more convenient.

Implementing XSLT Transforms

XSLT process XML documents into other XML documents according to specifications written in Extensible Stylesheet Language (XSL). XSL is a functional language that is itself expressed as a XML document.

In Java you would normally use Xalan to process XSLT transforms. The .NET Framework support is contained in the `System.Xml.Xsl` namespace.

Processing an XML document using an XSLT transform follows a similar pattern in .NET to that you are used to from Java. There is no need to create a factory, but you instantiate an `XslTransform`, load the XSL stylesheet, and invoke `Transform` on the input file. `Transform` has several overloads to make it convenient under most conditions.

To implement XSLT transforms, follow these steps:

1. Create a new Windows Application project called
    SimpleTransformExample. Make the form look like Figure 9-3.

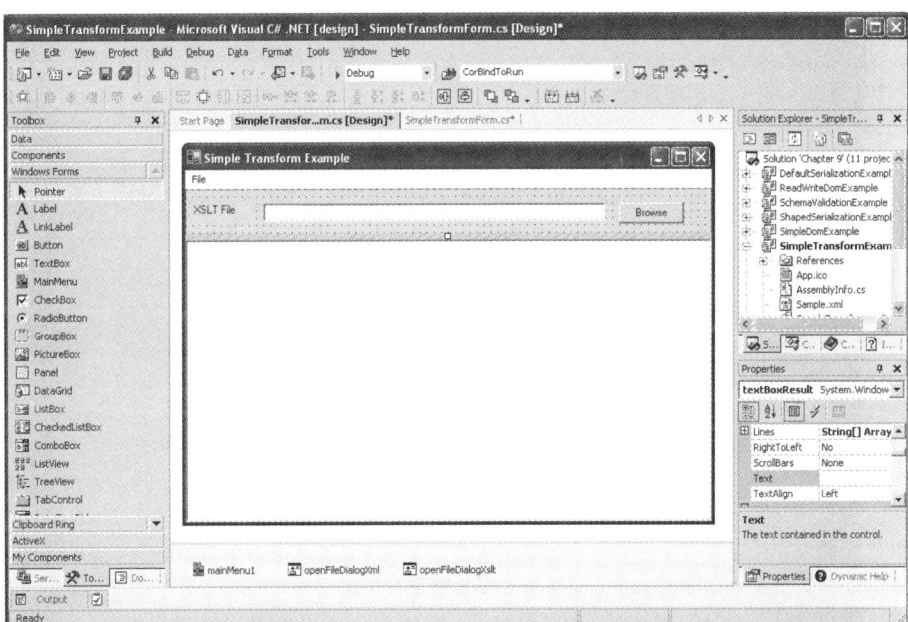

Figure 9-3. The interface for the transform example

2. Rename the `TextBox` controls `textBoxXslt` and `textBoxResult`, then the
    `Button` control `buttonBrowse`.

3. Add a `MainMenu` control, and construct the menu shown in Figure 9-4. Rename the `MenuItem` controls to **menuItemOpen** and **menuItemExit**.

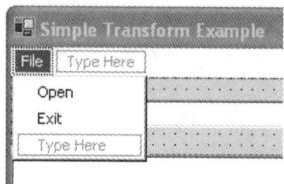

Figure 9-4. The menu for the transform example

4. Add two `OpenFileDialog` controls named **openFileDialogXml** and **openFileDialogXslt**.

5. Add the following using statements to those provided by Visual Studio .NET:

```
using System.IO;
using System.Xml;
using System.Xml.XPath;
using System.Xml.Xsl;
```

6. Implement the button click handler for `buttonBrowse` to populate `textBoxXslt` as follows:

```
private void buttonBrowse_Click(object sender, System.EventArgs e)
{
    if ( openFileDialogXslt.ShowDialog( this ) == DialogResult.OK )
    {
        textBoxXslt.Text = openFileDialogXslt.FileName;
    }
}
```

7. Implement the file exit menu selection handler as follows:

```
private void menuItemExit_Click(object sender, System.EventArgs e)
{
    Close();
}
```

8. Finally, implement the file open menu selection handler to perform the transform, as shown in Listing 9-3.

Listing 9-3. Running an XSL Transform on an XML Document

```
private void menuItemOpen_Click(object sender, System.EventArgs e)
{
    try
    {
        if ( openFileDialogXml.ShowDialog( this ) == DialogResult.OK )
        {
            XPathDocument doc =
                new XPathDocument( openFileDialogXml.OpenFile() );
            StringWriter sw = new StringWriter();
            XmlTextWriter tw = new XmlTextWriter( sw );
            tw.Formatting = Formatting.Indented;
            tw.Indentation = 4;

            XslTransform tr = new XslTransform();
            tr.Load( textBoxXslt.Text );

            tr.Transform( doc.CreateNavigator(), null, tw );

            tw.Close();
            sw.Close();

            textBoxResult.Text = sw.ToString();
        }
    }
    catch( Exception exc )
    {
        MessageBox.Show( this, exc.Message );
    }
}
```

If you are reading in an XML document purely for the purpose of processing it with an XSLT transform, you can use an XPathDocument in place of an XmlDocument. An XPathDocument is a read-only document optimized for XPath processing as used in XSLT.

You can now build and run the application. When you provide a transform and an XML file, you will see the result in the large textbox, as shown in Figure 9-5.

There are no command-line tools to invoke a transform equivalent to those in Xalan. However, writing one would not be difficult.

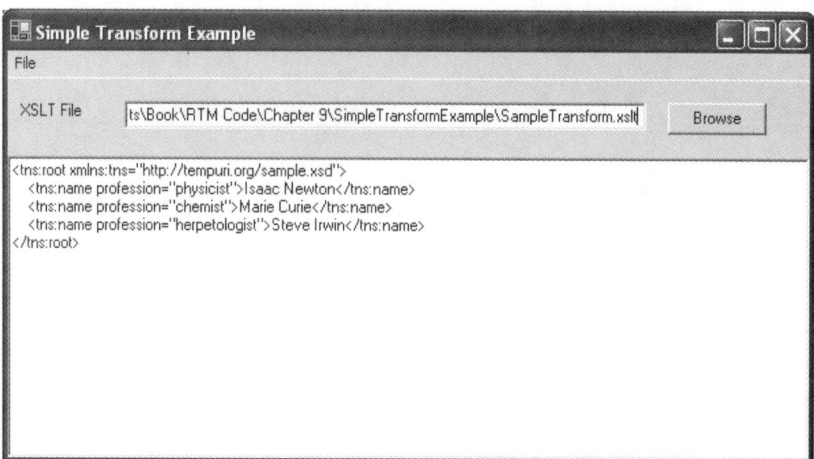

Figure 9-5. The completed transform example

Passing Parameters to the Transform

You can set parameters on the XslTranform object for use in the XSL transform as you can in Xalan. However, instead of setting the parameters on the XslTransform, you create an XsltArgumentList object and set the parameter values on that. The XsltArgumentList instance is passed as a parameter to the Transform method of XslTransform.

Although XsltArgumentList.AddParam takes an Object type for the value, unlike Xalan you are restricted in the types you can use as parameters. Of the simple types, you can pass a string, bool, or double. The other two possibilities are an XPathNavigator or an XPathNodeIterator, which allow you to introduce parts of other XML documents to the transformation process.

The actual code for passing parameters is quite straightforward. You create the XsltArgumentList, add the parameters using its AddParam method, and then use the XsltArgumentList instance on the Transform method call. For example:

```
XsltArgumentList arg = new XsltArgumentList();
arg.AddParam( "arg", "", textBoxValue.Text );
tr.Transform( doc.CreateNavigator(), arg, tw );
```

Embedding Extensions in the Transform

You can embed extensions in your XSL document in a similar fashion to that provided by Xalan. However, you are not restricted to scripting languages and can even embed C# code.

In Xalan you embed a script extension as the contents of a `script` element within a `component` element. In .NET it is all achieved with a `script` element:

```
<msxsl:script language="C#" implements-prefix="myext">
    <![CDATA[
        public string doit()
        {
            return "you would do something useful here of course";
        }
    ]]>
</msxsl:script>
```

You must declare the `msxsl` and `myext` namespaces. Using the extension in your XSL is as simple as the following:

```
<value-of select="myext:doit()"/>
```

Using XPath Expressions

The expressions you use in XSL are not part of the XSLT specification. They actually come from the XML Path Language (XPath) specification. You can use these to navigate your document more readily than the primitive traversal mechanisms provided by the DOM. You may have already used the XPath support in Xalan outside a transform for exactly this reason.

The .NET classes to support this are in the `System.Xml.XPath` namespace. You start by obtaining an `XPathNavigator` instance, usually from the document. You can use an `XmlDocument` or an `XPathDocument` depending on your other needs. The `CreateNavigator` method returns the `XPathNavigator`. Once you have the navigator, you can use it to evaluate XPath expressions. The two most useful methods for this are `Select` and `Evaluate`.

`Select` allows you to obtain the set of nodes matching your expression. For instance, given the following document:

```
<scientists>
    <physicist>
        <name>Isaac Newton</name>
        <discovery>gravity</discovery>
    </physicist>
    <chemist>
        <name>Marie Curie</name>
        <discovery>radioactivity</discovery>
    </chemist>
```

```
    <herpetologist>
        <name>Steve Irwin</name>
        <discovery>they bite!</discovery>
    </herpetologist>
</scientists>...
```

If you wanted to list all the names, you could write the following:

```
XPathNavigator nav = doc.CreateNavigator();
XPathNodeIterator ni = nav.Select( "//name" );
textBoxResult.Text = "";
while ( ni.MoveNext() )
{
    textBoxResult.Text += ni.Current.Value + "\r\n";
}
```

Evaluate is similar but allows you to obtain the results of expressions that do not necessarily return a node set. Although the signature says it returns an object, the possible return types are an XPathNodeIterator, a bool, a double, or a string. The actual type depends on the expression. If you wanted to count the number of name elements in the preceding document, you could write:

```
XPathNavigator nav = doc.CreateNavigator();
double ct = (double)nav.Evaluate( "count(//name)" );
textBoxResult.Text = "There are "+ ct + " names";
```

If you are going to use the same expression repeatedly, you can compile it into an XPathExpression and pass that in place of the string to improve performance. Compile the expression using the Compile method of XPathNavigator. The preceding Select example would become this:

```
XPathNavigator nav = doc.CreateNavigator();
XPathExpression xpe = nav.Compile( "//name" );
XPathNodeIterator ni = nav.Select( xpe );
textBoxResult.Text = "";
while ( ni.MoveNext() )
{
    textBoxResult.Text += ni.Current.Value + "\r\n";
}
```

Using XML Serialization

This is a useful feature of XML support in the .NET Framework. It allows you to process XML in the form of an object structure, which on many occasions is more natural than manipulating a DOM. It also provides a convenient way to serialize an object structure in a readily understood textual form.

There is no equivalent to this in Xerces, although it is hard to imagine that something similar does not exist for Java somewhere.

Understanding Basic Serialization

The default serialization of an object uses an element form. The primitive types are mapped to equivalent XML Schema types. If you just want to serialize and deserialize objects, this is usually quite sufficient and easily manipulated by a human with a simple text editor. You have already seen this in action in Chapter 8, "Understanding Networking," when you used ASP.NET Web Services.

To serialize object structures yourself you need to use `XmlSerializer` from the `System.Xml.Serialization` namespace. The `Serialize` method enables you to write out the XML serialized form and `Deserialize` reads in XML and constructs the object tree.

Imagine you need to write out the structure created by the code in Listing 9-4 as XML.

Listing 9-4. A Simple Object Structure for Demonstrating XML Serialization

```
public class XGroup
{
    public XGroup()
    {
        members = new XMember[5];
    }
    public XGroup( string name ) : this()
    {
        m_name = name;
    }
    public string m_name;
    public XMember[] members;
}
public class XMember
{
    public XMember()
    {
    }
```

```
        public XMember( string name ) :this()
        {
            m_name = name;
        }

        public string m_name;
    }
.........
        XGroup g = new XGroup( "group name" );
        g.members[0] = new XMember( "mem 1" );
        g.members[1] = new XMember( "mem 2" );
        g.members[2] = new XMember( "mem 3" );
```

Create an XmlSerializer for the XGroup type and invoke Serialize as follows:

```
XmlSerializer ser = new XmlSerializer( typeof( XGroup ) );
ser.Serialize( tw, g );
```

This would result in the following XML being written to the text writer tw:

```
<XGroup xmlns:xsd=".....">
    <m_name>group name</m_name>
    <members>
        <XMember>
            <m_name>mem 1</m_name>
        </XMember>
        <XMember>
            <m_name>mem 2</m_name>
        </XMember>
        <XMember>
            <m_name>mem 3</m_name>
        </XMember>
        <XMember xsi:nil="true" />
        <XMember xsi:nil="true" />
    </members>
</XGroup>
```

You could read the file back in later using Deserialize as in the following:

```
g = (XGroup)ser.Deserialize( instream );
```

 **NOTE** *Only public member variables and public properties are serialized by this mechanism.*

Using Shaping Attributes

The serialization mechanism is much more powerful than just the default mapping. Most of the classes in the System.Xml.Serialization namespace are attributes. These attributes allow you to tag the classes, properties, and member variables to control how they map into the resulting XML document. This is referred to as *XML shaping*.

The simplest change is to specify that a property or variable be serialized as an attribute instead of as an element. You do this by applying an XmlAttributeAttribute as follows:

```
[XmlAttribute]
public string s1;
```

By default the name of the property or variable is used as the element or attribute name in the XML document. You can override this by specifying the appropriate ElementName or AttributeName properties of the attribute:

```
[XmlElement( ElementName = "string2" )]
public string s2;
```

To specify the XML Schema type of the element or attribute, set the DataType property of the attribute:

```
[XmlElement( DataType = "anyURI" )]
public string s3;
```

If the document you are processing uses namespaces, you can specify them on the member attributes using the Namespace property, or you can specify the namespace for a given type by tagging the type with an XmlTypeAttribute and specifying its Namespace property:

```
[XmlType( Namespace="urn:my-examples:shaping" )]
public class Shaped
{
    ...
}
```

The Type that will be used as the root of the document may be tagged with an XmlRootAttribute rather than an XmlTypeAttribute. This allows you to specify the name of the root element. If you do not override the root element name, the Type name is used by default:

```
[XmlRoot( ElementName="sroot",
          Namespace="urn:my-examples:shaping" )]
public class ShapedRoot
{
    ...
}
```

Using XML shaping should allow you to use a convenient object model even when the schema specifies a form that does not fit the default serialization rules.

Working with the XML Schema Definition Tool

The .NET Framework SDK contains the XML Schema Definition Tool, xsd, which you can use to generate XML schema files (.xsd files) from a variety of sources.

When you are prototyping, you will often create a representative data file to refine your design. When you then want to create the schema based on that file, you can use the xsd command to generate a schema from that XML file:

```
xsd theirnew.xml
```

The result will probably require some refinement before it is perfect, but it can save you valuable time and is less error prone than the average developer.

You can also generate an assembly from a type compiled into an assembly. This allows you to generate the schema for a set of types you use with XML serialization:

```
xsd mynew.dll /type:Scientists
```

The most useful feature of xsd is its ability to generate a set of types for use with XML serialization from a schema. So if you need to process some XML files and want to use the serialization model instead of a DOM, you are not forced to create the classes by hand.

So given the following schema:

```
<xs:schema id="cars" targetNamespace=...>
    <xs:element name="cars">
        <xs:complexType>
            <xs:choice maxOccurs="unbounded">
                <xs:element name="car">
                    <xs:complexType>
                        <xs:attribute name="make"
                                      form="unqualified"
                                      type="xs:string" />
                        <xs:attribute name="model"
                                      form="unqualified"
                                      type="xs:string" />
                    </xs:complexType>
                </xs:element>
            </xs:choice>
        </xs:complexType>
    </xs:element>
</xs:schema>...
```

running the xsd tool against it with this command:

```
xsd simple.xsd /classes
```

would generate the classes shown in Listing 9-5.

Listing 9-5. Classes Generated from an XML Schema by xsd *to Support Serialization*

```
//
// This source code was auto-generated by xsd, Version=1.0.3705.0.
//
using System.Xml.Serialization;

/// <remarks/>
[System.Xml.Serialization.XmlTypeAttribute(
        Namespace="http://tempuri.org/simple.xsd")]
[System.Xml.Serialization.XmlRootAttribute("cars",
        Namespace="http://tempuri.org/simple.xsd", IsNullable=false)]
public class cars {
```

```
        /// <remarks/>
        [System.Xml.Serialization.XmlElementAttribute("car")]
        public carsCar[] Items;
}


/// <remarks/>
[System.Xml.Serialization.XmlTypeAttribute(
        Namespace="http://tempuri.org/simple.xsd")]
public class carsCar {

        /// <remarks/>      [System.Xml.Serialization.XmlAttributeAttribute(
            Form=System.Xml.Schema.XmlSchemaForm.Unqualified)]
        public string make;

        /// <remarks/>      [System.Xml.Serialization.XmlAttributeAttribute(
            Form=System.Xml.Schema.XmlSchemaForm.Unqualified)]
        public string model;
}
```

Creating instances of these classes and serializing them would result in an XML file similar to the following:

```
<?xml version="1.0" encoding="utf-8"?>
<cars xmlns="http://tempuri.org/simple.xsd">
    <car make="ford" model="windstar" />
    <car make="jeep" model="wrangler" />
</cars>
```

Using Visual Studio .NET and XML

Visual Studio .NET has a reasonable XML editor to assist in creating XML data files. You can validate a document from within the editor if the schemas and their locations are specified. Like the xsd tool, you can generate a schema from a data document.

The schema editor is where things get interesting. It allows you to use either raw XML or a visual mode where you drag elements from the toolbox to build up the types and the relationships between them. The visual mode can be useful for roughing out or visualizing a schema—although I prefer to switch back to the XML mode for finishing the details.

Summary

Both the .NET Framework and Visual Studio .NET provide extensive support for manipulating XML data in your applications. In the framework you have XML DOM, XSLT, and XPath support. The `XmlReader` and `XmlWriter` classes provide a high-performance streaming parser (although some will be disappointed at the lack of a SAX parser). XML serialization provides an easy way to store your data structures as XML documents. Visual Studio .NET complements these features with editors that facilitate the creation of XML documents and schemas.

CHAPTER 10

Creating Components

THE .NET EQUIVALENT of a JavaBean is a *component*, and the .NET equivalent of a Java component is a *control*. Prior to .NET, the component framework of choice for Windows was Component Object Model (COM). Naturally, .NET provides good interoperability with COM, and in this chapter you will discover how to make .NET components become COM objects and how to use legacy COM objects in .NET applications.

You may also have heard of COM+, which sounds like it is the successor to COM. The relationship between COM and COM+ is more like that between JavaBeans and Enterprise JavaBeans; however, as you will see, COM+ and Enterprise JavaBeans are not equivalent. The ServicedComponent class is the base for .NET components that participate in COM+.

Introducing .NET Components

Any Java class may be a JavaBean as long as it follows the conventions in the JavaBean specification. A .NET component must implement the IComponent interface. The IComponent interface is not too demanding to implement; however, most programmers will choose to inherit from Component, which provides a convenient base class.

The Component class implements the IComponent interface and inherits from MarshallByRefObject. This means the object will be accessed through a proxy should it be passed out of the appdomain by remoting. This is the most common scenario for a component. Should you need a component that is marshaled by value, use the MarshallByValueComponent class as a base for your component.

Creating a .NET Component

In this next example you will create a component. Start by creating a new Class Library project called **BareBonesComponentLibrary**. Replace the code in Class1.cs with Listing 10-1. This is a simple component that has a single property Message.

Listing 10-1. A Minimal .NET Component

```
using System;
using System.ComponentModel;

namespace BareBonesComponentLibrary
{
    public class BareBonesComponent : Component
    {
        public BareBonesComponent()
        {
        }

        private string m_message;

        public string Message
        {
            get
            {
                return m_message;
            }
            set
            {
                m_message = value;
            }
        }
    }
}
```

Using the Component

To demonstrate that the component you just created is a real component, usable from the designer, create a new Windows Application project called **BareBonesComponentDemo**. Once the project is created and the form is displayed in the designer, add the component to the Toolbox. I prefer to create my own Toolbox tab to keep my components separate from the ones Microsoft supplies. Add a new Toolbox tab by right-clicking on the Toolbox and selecting Add Tab, as shown in Figure 10-1.

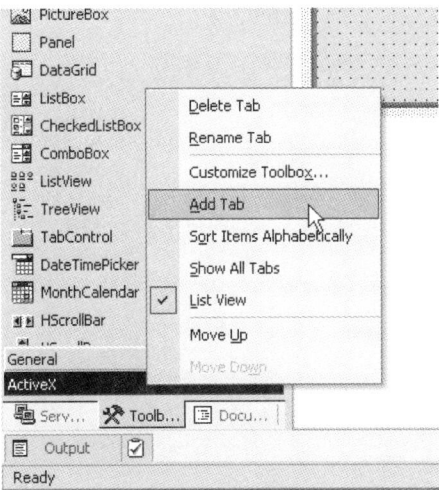

Figure 10-1. Adding a new tab to the Toolbox

A new tab will be added to the bottom of the Toolbox and you can enter its name as shown in Figure 10-2.

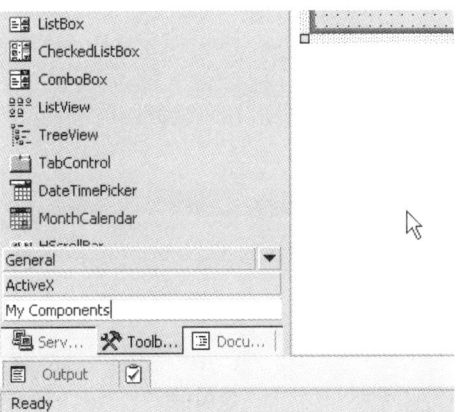

Figure 10-2. Naming the new Toolbox tab

Once the tab has been added, select it. Now you want to add the component to this tab. Right-click the Toolbox and select Customize Toolbox . . . , as shown in Figure 10-3.

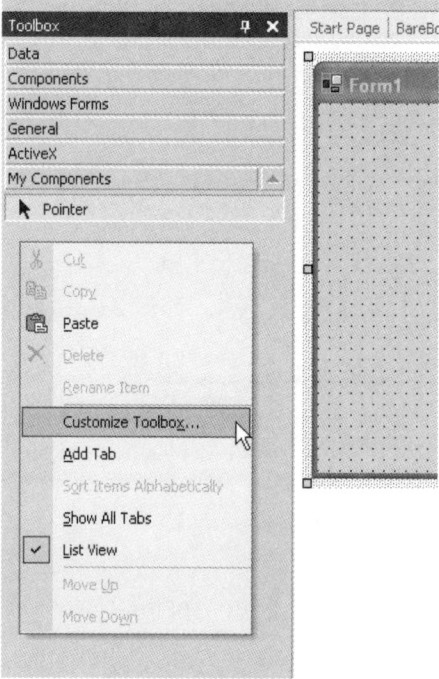

Figure 10-3. Starting to add a component to the Toolbox

When the dialog box appears, select the .NET Framework Components tab and then click Browse . . . , as shown in Figure 10-4.

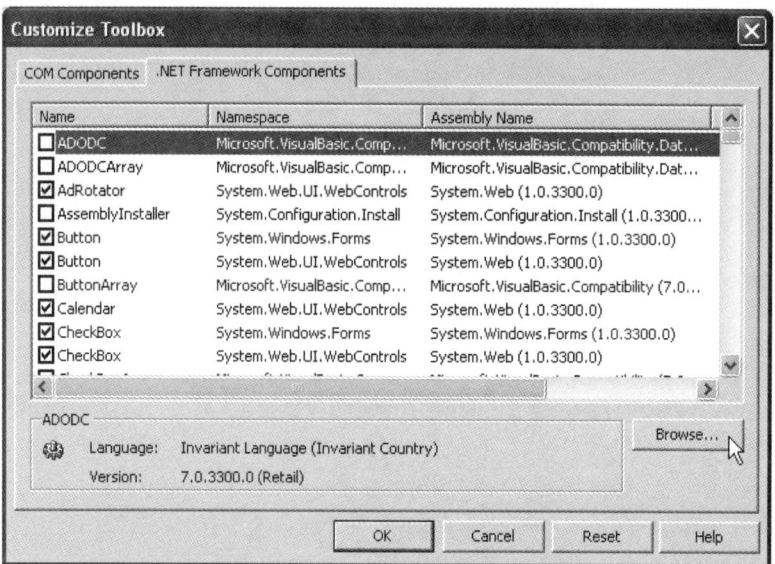

Figure 10-4. Browsing for a .NET component

This will open the standard file open dialog box that allows you to navigate to the correct folder and to select BareBonesLibrary.dll. You will then be returned to the Customize Toolbox dialog box with the `BareBonesComponent` listed, as shown in Figure 10-5.

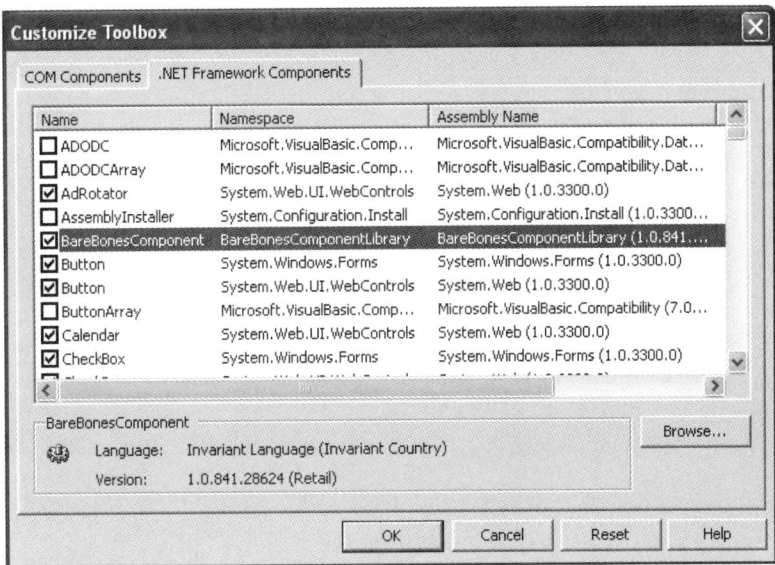

Figure 10-5. The component selected ready for adding to the Toolbox

Now click OK and the component will be added to the Toolbox tab, as shown in Figure 10-6.

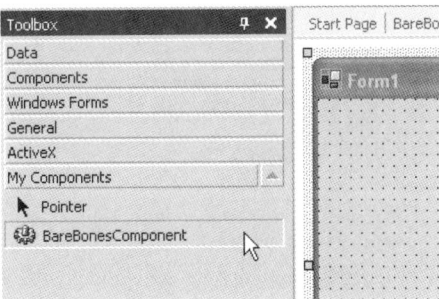

Figure 10-6. The component added to the new Toolbox tab

Now you are ready to add the component to the form. Drag it from the Toolbox onto the form as you would any other component. Because it is a nonvisual component it will appear below the form as shown in Figure 10-7.

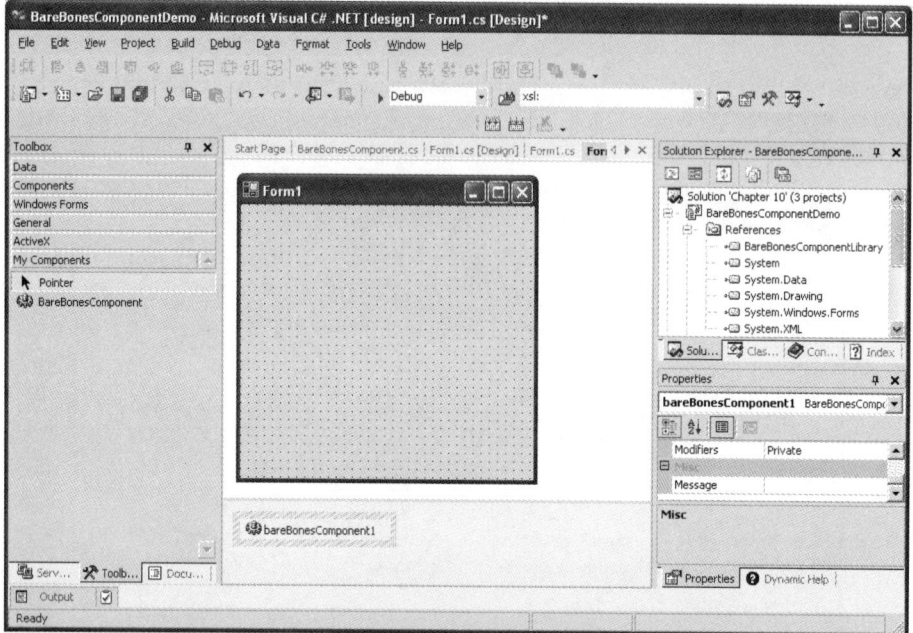

Figure 10-7. The component added to the form as a nonvisual component

You can select the component and edit the Message property in the Properties pane, as shown in Figure 10-8.

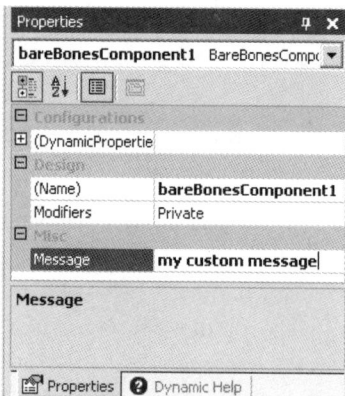

Figure 10-8. Setting properties of the component

Writing Designer-Friendly Components

As written, the component has one potential flaw. The Visual Studio .NET designer makes an assumption about calling `Dispose` on components. If the component does not have a constructor that takes an `IContainer` and adds itself to that `IContainer`, it will not call the component's `Dispose` method when the container (in this case, the form) is disposed.

If you had to modify each component to comply with this convention, it would soon get tedious. Instead, use Visual Studio .NET to provide a basic component with this functionality. In the Solution Explorer, select the BareBonesComponentLibrary project and right-click to open its context menu. Select Add ➢ Add Component . . . and then name the component **VsBareBonesComponent**. The only change you need to make is to add the `Message` property exactly as it appears in `BareBonesComponent`.

If you look closely at `VsBareBonesComponent`, you will soon see that it contains more code than the version you wrote by hand. The key piece is the constructor that takes a container:

```
public VsBareBonesComponent(
    System.ComponentModel.IContainer container)
{
    /// <summary>
    /// Required for Windows.Forms Class Composition Designer supp...
    /// </summary>
    container.Add(this);
    InitializeComponent();

    //
    // TODO: Add any constructor code after InitializeComponent ca...
    //
}
```

Add this component to the Toolbox and place it on a form like the previous version. If you create your components this way, the designer will take care of adding your components to a container, which in turn will ensure that your `Dispose` method gets called.

Using `Dispose` in Components

The `Dispose` method for `Component` has two overloads. The first form matches that specified by `IDisposable` and takes no parameters. The second form takes a bool called disposing. When disposing is true, it indicates that it is being called by the regular Dispose; when false, it is being called by the finalizer.

To code Dispose, override the form that takes the disposing bool and ensure that you call the base class implementation. Your implementation should tolerate being called multiple times. For an example, take a look at Form1.cs in BareBonesComponentDemo:

```
/// <summary>
/// Clean up any resources being used.
/// </summary>
protected override void Dispose( bool disposing )
{
    if( disposing )
    {
        if (components != null)
        {
            components.Dispose();
        }
    }
    base.Dispose( disposing );
}
```

Using Containers

Containers are the other part of the equation that allows you to build up applications in the designer. Containers provide a convenient way to maintain a collection of components and are used by many components that support creation in the Visual Studio .NET designer. Calling Dispose on a container in turn calls Dispose on each of the components it contains.

If you examine the code of any component or form generated by Visual Studio .NET, you will find that it includes a variable called components, which is an instance of Container. This container keeps track of any components added by the designer provided they implement the constructor discussed previously.

Just as Component is an implementation of the IComponent interface, Container is an implementation of the IContainer interface. Most people are content to use the stock Container class as is. Should you decide you need to derive your own container class from Container, the overloads of Dispose behave in the same way as they do for Component.

Using Controls

A WinForms control is a special type of component that has a user interface. There are two types of controls. Controls that inherit from UserControl are compositions of other controls. Controls that inherit from Control draw their own user interface.

Starting from UserControl

A UserControl control is appropriate when you can create the desired behavior by composing some of the existing WinForms controls.

To create a user control, follow these steps:

1. Start by creating a new Windows Control Library project called **UserControlExampleLibrary**. Rename the UserControl1 class to **UserControlExample**, so you have a unique name when you add it to the Toolbox later. User controls are built up by dragging existing controls onto the canvas in the designer. For this example, you are going to build a simple version of the NumericUpDown control.

2. Drag a TextBox and a VScrollBar onto the UserControl from the Toolbox. Make the TextBox blank and read-only. Arrange the controls as shown in Figure 10-9.

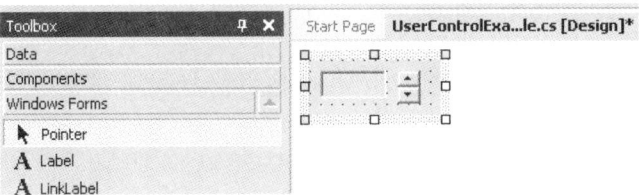

Figure 10-9. Arranging the textbox and vertical scrollbar on the user control

3. This user control has three properties: Min, Max, and Current, which will all be integers. To do this, add the code in Listing 10-2.

Listing 10-2. The Properties of UserControlExample

```
private int m_min = int.MinValue;
private int m_max = int.MaxValue;
private int m_current = 0;
```

```csharp
public int Min
{
    get
    {
        return m_min;
    }
    set
    {
        m_min = value;
    }
}

public int Max
{
    get
    {
        return m_max;
    }
    set
    {
        m_max = value;
    }
}

public int Current
{
    get
    {
        return m_current;
    }
    set
    {
        if ( ( value > m_max ) || ( value < m_min ) )
        {
            throw new ArgumentOutOfRangeException( "Current" );
        }
        m_current = value;
        textBox1.Text = m_current.ToString();
    }
}
```

4. Now make the VScrollBar update the value of the Current property and thereby the value displayed in the TextBox. Double-click the VScrollBar to add a scroll event handler, then modify it to read as shown in Listing 10-3.

Listing 10-3. The Scroll Event Handler for the VScrollBar of the UserControl

```
private void vScrollBar1_Scroll(object sender,
    System.Windows.Forms.ScrollEventArgs e)
{
    if ( e.Type == ScrollEventType.SmallIncrement )
    {
        try
        {
            Current -= 1;
        }
        catch
        {
        }
    }
    else
    {
        if ( e.Type == ScrollEventType.SmallDecrement )
        {
            try
            {
                Current += 1;
            }
            catch
            {
            }
        }
    }
    vScrollBar1.Value = 50;
}
```

5. Add the control to the Toolbox and create a new Windows Application project called **UserControlExampleDemo** to test it. Drag the UserControlExample control to the form, as shown in Figure 10-10.

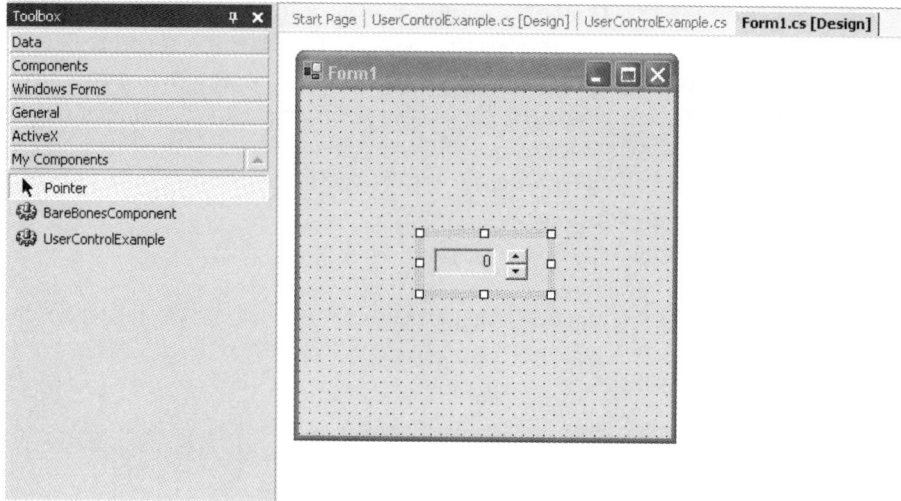

Figure 10-10. The user control hosted on a WinForms form

6. You can also set the Min, Max and Current properties of the control in the Properties pane, as shown in Figure 10-11.

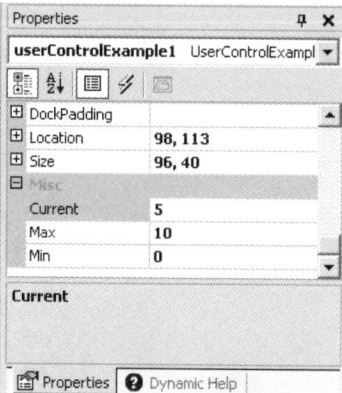

Figure 10-11. Setting properties of the user control

When you run this program, you can use the scrollbar buttons to modify the value within the range specified by the Min and Max properties.

Starting from `Control`

If the control you want to create cannot be built up from existing WinForms controls by composition or subclassing, you must start from `Control` itself. Follow these steps:

1. To create a control, start by adding a new Windows Control Library project called **ControlExampleLibrary**.

2. In the Solution Explorer, right-click `UserControl1` in this project and delete it.

3. Now right-click the project and select Add ➤ Add Inherited Control. . . . When the dialog box appears, select Custom Control, as shown in Figure 10-12, and name the file **ControlExample.cs**.

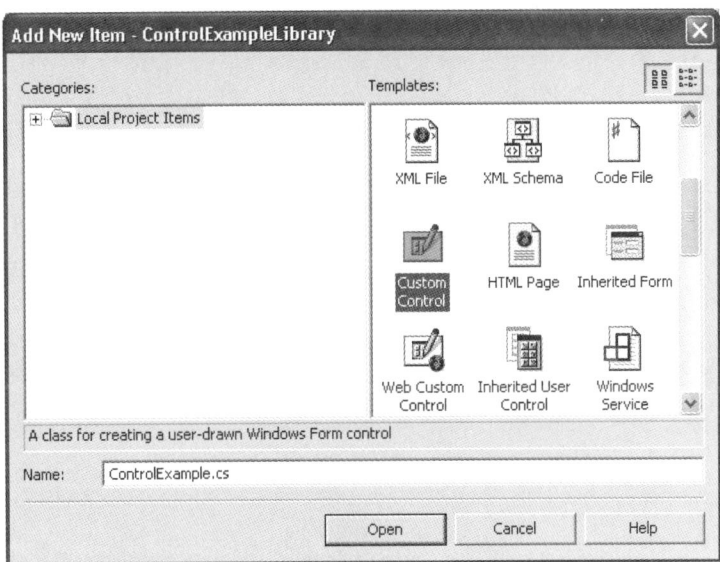

Figure 10-12. Adding the custom control

4. Next, modify the file to read as shown in Listing 10-4. The key method is `OnPaint`, which uses classes from `System.Drawing` to draw the user interface of the control. In this case it does nothing more than draw a blue ellipse in the bounding rectangle of the control.

Listing 10-4. A Simple WinForms Control

```csharp
using System;
using System.Collections;
using System.ComponentModel;
using System.Drawing;
using System.Data;
using System.Windows.Forms;

namespace ControlExampleLibrary
{
    /// <summary>
    /// Summary description for ControlExample.
    /// </summary>
    public class ControlExample : System.Windows.Forms.Control
    {
        public ControlExample()
        {
            ResizeRedraw = true;
        }

        protected override void OnPaint(PaintEventArgs pe)
        {
            // TODO: Add custom paint code here
            using ( SolidBrush b
                            = new SolidBrush( Color.SteelBlue ) )
            {
                pe.Graphics.FillEllipse( b, DisplayRectangle );
            }

            // Calling the base class OnPaint
            base.OnPaint(pe);
        }
    }
}
```

5. Now compile the control and add it to the Toolbox.

6. To demonstrate the control, create a new Windows Application project called **ControlExampleDemo** and drag the control onto the form. Compile the application and run it to see that the control displays the blue ellipse.

7. Modify the Dock property of the control to **Fill** and recompile the application. The control now resizes with the window, as shown in Figure 10-13.

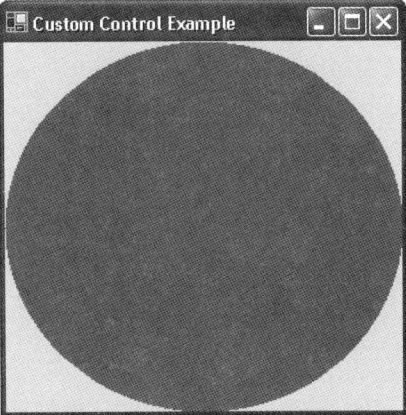

Figure 10-13. The custom control in action

Although this control does nothing spectacular, it demonstrates the basics of writing your own control. By adding event handlers and drawing code you can create more sophisticated controls.

Addressing Multithreading Issues

Java has the restriction that all user interface (UI) operations must occur on the Abstract Windowing Toolkit (AWT) event processing thread. To support multithreaded applications, the SwingUtilities class has the invokeAndWait and invokeLater methods, which allow you to schedule update logic to run on the correct thread.

.NET has a similar restriction that UI operations must occur on the thread that created the Control. Again support is provided to schedule update logic on the correct thread in the form of static methods on the Control-Invoke and BeginInvoke.

There are two forms of the Invoke method. The first takes a delegate instance, and the second takes a delegate and an array of objects that are passed as parameters to the method contained in the delegate.

Follow these steps to create an example that demonstrates the use of Invoke:

1. Create a new Windows Application project called **ControlInvokeExample**. Drag two Label controls onto the form. Change

the Text property of label1 to **Now you see me**. Change the Text property of label2 to **Now you don't** and set its Visible property to **false**.

2. Now double-click the form's background. This will create an OnLoad han-
    dler like the following:

```
private void Form1_Load(object sender, System.EventArgs e)
{
}
```

3. Add a using statement to the start of the file as follows:

```
using System.Threading;
```

4. Next, modify the handler to start a new thread, which runs the
    DemoInvoke method:

```
private void Form1_Load(object sender, System.EventArgs e)
{
    Thread t = new Thread( new ThreadStart( this.DemoInvoke ) );
    t.IsBackground = true;
    t.Start();
}
```

5. The DemoInvoke method should be written as follows:

```
private delegate void ShowHideDelegate();

private void DemoInvoke()
{
    ShowHideDelegate l1h = new ShowHideDelegate( label1.Hide );
    ShowHideDelegate l2h = new ShowHideDelegate( label2.Hide );
    ShowHideDelegate l1s = new ShowHideDelegate( label1.Show );
    ShowHideDelegate l2s = new ShowHideDelegate( label2.Show );

    while ( true )
    {
        Thread.Sleep( 3000 );
        label1.Invoke( l1h );
        label2.Invoke( l2s );

        Thread.Sleep( 3000 );
        label1.Invoke( l1s );
```

```
            label2.Invoke( l2h );
        }
    }
```

6. Build the example and run it. The label will change every three seconds. There was no need to create any anonymous inner classes. This is an example of the power of delegates.

The equivalent of Java's invokeLater is BeginInvoke, which has the same two overloads as Invoke. It also follows the standard asynchronous pattern in .NET, which means you can optionally test when the operation has completed and obtain its return value using the EndInvoke method. To demonstrate BeginInvoke, modify Form1_Load to start a thread using DemoBeginInvoke as shown in Listing 10-5.

Listing 10-5. An Example of using BeginInvoke

```
private void Form1_Load(object sender, System.EventArgs e)
{
    Thread t
        = new Thread( new ThreadStart( this.DemoBeginInvoke ) );
    t.IsBackground = true;
    t.Start();
}
private Color SetBackColor( Color c )
{
    Color old = BackColor;
    BackColor = c;

    return old;
}

private delegate Color BackColorDelegate( Color c );

private void DemoBeginInvoke()
{
    ShowHideDelegate l1h = new ShowHideDelegate( label1.Hide );
    ShowHideDelegate l2h = new ShowHideDelegate( label2.Hide );
    ShowHideDelegate l1s = new ShowHideDelegate( label1.Show );
    ShowHideDelegate l2s = new ShowHideDelegate( label2.Show );
    BackColorDelegate bcd
        = new BackColorDelegate( this.SetBackColor );

    while ( true )
```

```
        {
            Thread.Sleep( 3000 );
            IAsyncResult ar
                = BeginInvoke( bcd, new Object[] { Color.Red, } );
            label1.BeginInvoke( l1h );
            label2.BeginInvoke( l2s );

            Thread.Sleep( 3000 );

            Color oldColor = (Color)EndInvoke( ar );

            BeginInvoke( bcd, new Object[] { oldColor, } );
            label1.BeginInvoke( l1s );
            label2.BeginInvoke( l2h );
        }
    }
```

This example shows how to use EndInvoke to obtain the return value from the method at the point it is needed. It also demonstrates how to use the form of BeginInvoke that takes an array of parameters for the method contained by the delegate.

In Java you can optimize out the call to invokeAndWait or invokeLater by using the SwingUtilities isEventDispatchThread method. In .NET you can use the Control class's InvokeRequired method to perform the same test.

Versioning

When you create your applications from scratch and create an assembly that results in a single .exe file, you do not need to worry about having the correct version of anything other than the .NET runtime. When creating applications that use third-party components, make sure you use the correct version for the application because other applications may have installed a different version.

The .NET Framework supports specifying versions for assemblies and controlling how they are checked at runtime. This check hinges on the component author following the rules for specifying a version in the component's assembly.

Creating an Assembly with a Version Number

To create an assembly with a version number, follow these steps:

1. Create a new Class Library project called
    VersionedComponentExampleLibrary. Delete the default file Class1.cs
    and then add a component called **VersionedComponent**.

2. Add a `Message` property exactly as you did in `BareBonesComponent` at the start of this chapter. Now open AssemblyInfo.cs and look at the version attribute:

```
[assembly: AssemblyVersion("1.0.*")]
```

3. There are actually four components to the version number. The first two, which read as 1 and 0 in the default, are the major and minor version. The third component is the build number and the fourth is the revision number. As specified, the build and revision are generated for you. The build will be set to the number of days since Jan. 1, 2000, and the revision is the number of seconds since midnight modulo 2. You need more precise control for this example, so set the version number to 1.0.0.0 to begin with:

```
[assembly: AssemblyVersion("1.0.0.0")]
```

4. Setting the version attribute is not sufficient to trigger version checking in applications that use your assembly. You have to strong name sign the assembly. This is not the same as signing the assembly with a code-signing certificate, although there are similarities. Creating a strong name-key pair does not involve a third party such as VeriSign and does not carry the same guarantee of origin. It does, however, provide a unique identity for your assembly and confidence that it has not been tampered with. Open the Visual Studio .NET command prompt by selecting Start ➤ All Programs ➤ Microsoft Visual Studio .NET ➤ Visual Studio .NET Tools ➤ Visual Studio .NET Command Prompt.

5. Change directory to the library project. Create a strong name key using the `sn` command as follows:

```
sn -k example.snk
```

6. Now make the assembly use this key file by modifying the `AssemblyKeyFile` attribute:

```
[assembly: AssemblyKeyFile(@"..\..\example.snk")]
```

7. Notice that the location of the .snk file is specified relative to the build output directory. You can now build your component project.

8. To test the behavior of an application, create a project that uses your component. Keep this in a separate solution or it may get accidentally

rebuilt. Create a new Windows Application project called **VersionedComponentExampleClient.** Add `VersionedComponent` to the Toolbox and add an instance to the form. Set the `Message` property to **Hello Versioned World.** Add a `Label` to the form, and then double-click the form background and create the following handler:

```
private void Form1_Load(object sender, System.EventArgs e)
{
    label1.Text = versionedComponent1.Message;
}
```

9. Compile and run the application.

Now take a look at the properties of the assembly reference for the library that was added when you placed the component on the form. As you can see in Figure 10-14, it specifies version 1.0.0.0.

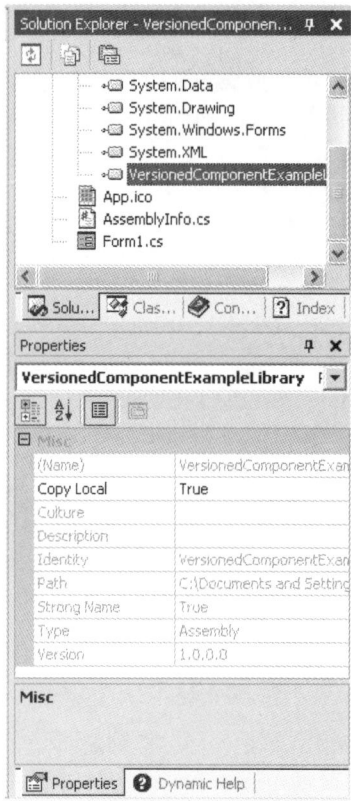

Figure 10-14. The version number property of the library reference

Checking the Version at Runtime

When using a versioned component in your application, it is not necessary to write any special code to test the version. When you added the reference to the assembly, the version and strong name were part of the information recorded.

Now imagine that you fix a bug in VersionedComponent. You would typically change the version to 1.0.0.1 and then use that version in newer applications. Your older applications will continue to use the older version of the library until you replace it. But when you do replace it, older applications will recognize the version mismatch and throw an exception. To demonstrate this, change the version of VersionedComponent to 1.0.0.1 and rebuild the library. Now copy VersionComponentExampleLibrary.dll to the output directory of VersionedComponentExampleClient. Run the application, but do not use Visual Studio .NET, because as it automatically rebuilds the project. Use Windows Explorer or the command line instead. The program throws an exception and you are offered a chance to debug as shown in Figure 10-15. Your customers would only see an exception dialog box.

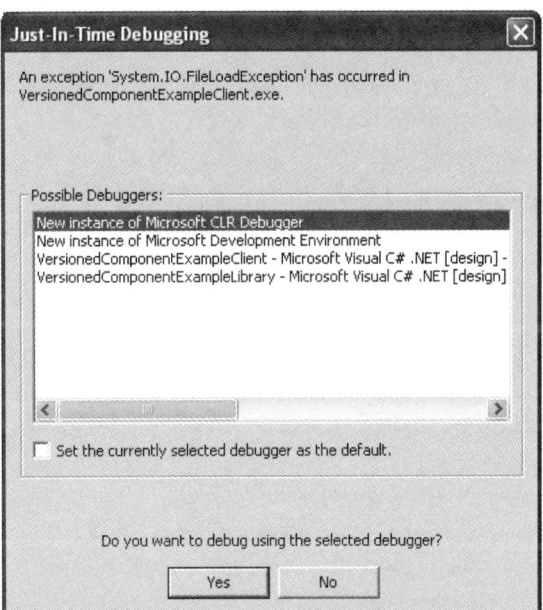

Figure 10-15. FileLoadException *thrown because of a version mismatch*

What if your updated component is backward compatible with the original, contains a bug fix, and you want the new version to be used? You can specify in

the application's configuration file that the new version be used by using the
bindingRedirect element:

1. In the Server Explorer, right-click VersionedComponentExampleClient and
    select Add ➤ Add New Item. . . .

2. Then select XML File and name it
    VersionedComponentExampleClient.exe.config. Do not attempt to use
    the configuration file name of app.config as that requires the project to
    be rebuilt and would invalidate the example.

3. Next, enter the following into the file:

```xml
<?xml version="1.0" encoding="utf-8" ?>
<configuration>
    <runtime>
        <assemblyBinding xmlns="urn:schemas-microsoft-com:asm.v1">
            <dependentAssembly>
                <assemblyIdentity
                    name="VersionedComponentExampleLibrary"
                    publicKeyToken="e3b5d33ca9933100" />
                <bindingRedirect
                    oldVersion="1.0.0.0"
                    newVersion="1.0.0.1" />
            </dependentAssembly>
        </assemblyBinding>
    </runtime>
</configuration>
```

4. You will need to determine the correct value of publicKeyToken for your
    library assembly. To do this, use the sn command again:

```
sn -T versionedcomponentexamplelibrary.dll
```

5. Finally, save this file and copy it to the output directory without rebuild-
    ing the project. Now when you run the application (still do not use Visual
    Studio .NET), the new version of the library is used and no exception is
    thrown.

Understanding COM

COM is the current component framework for unmanaged code. As you will
recall, unmanaged code compiles to native machine language and runs outside

the CLR. The name Object Linking and Embedding (OLE) was used originally and is still used by some today. ActiveX controls are also specialized COM objects in the same way that WinForms controls are .NET components.

Fortunately for all the development shops that have an existing investment in COM components, .NET has good interoperability with COM. You can use COM components from .NET and a .NET component can be exposed as a COM component. There are straightforward ways to do this that cover most cases, although .NET goes the extra mile to let you handle the problematic cases. Using these advanced features comes at a cost.

Creating a Quick and Dirty COM Component

Every .NET component can be exposed as a COM component by following a few additional steps:

1. Create a new Class Library project called **ManagedComComponentExample**.

2. In the Solution Explorer, right-click Class1.cs and select Delete. Then right-click the project and select Add ➤ Add Component . . . to add a new .NET component called **ManagedComComponent**.

3. Add the now familiar Message property. The assembly must be strong named, so follow the steps described in the earlier "Versioning" section to add an .snk file to the project and then update AssemblyInfo.cs to refer to it and specify a version number.

4. All COM components have entries in the Windows Registry. Register your .NET component using the regasm tool as follows:

   ```
   regasm .\ManagedComComponentExample.dll /codebase
   ```

5. Your component is now usable as a COM component. Create a new JScript file called VerifyComInstall.js that contains the following:

   ```
   mcc = new ActiveXObject( "ManagedComComponentExample.ManagedComComponent"
   );
   mcc.Message = "Hello COM component";
   WScript.Echo( mcc.Message );
   ```

When you run this it uses COM to access your component. The runtime creates a *COM Callable Wrapper* (CCW), which acts as a proxy to your class.

Creating a Real-World COM Component

Although the preceding example exposed your component through COM, it does not reflect how to do this in a real project. Reusable components should be accessed through interfaces that are the contract between the component writer and the component user. This is intrinsic to COM, where all access is through interfaces. When you registered ManagedComComponentExample.dll using regasm, it created a COM interface for your class automatically. Unfortunately, this means any change made to your class violates the contract. To remedy this, define an interface and implement it in your class, but only register the interface. You can achieve all of this by applying the appropriate attributes:

1. Start by defining the interface, IMessage. Create a new Class Library project called **RealManagedComExampleLibrary**, then rename Class1.cs to **IMessage.cs** and make it read as follows:

```
using System;

namespace RealManagedComComponentExample
{
    public interface IMessage
    {
        string Message
        {
            get;
            set;
        }
    }
}
```

2. Next add a new component called **RealManagedComExample**. Modify it to implement IMessage. Change the class declaration to read as follows:

```
public class RealManagedComComponent :
    System.ComponentModel.Component,
    IMessage
```

3. Then add the usual Message attribute implementation.

4. Finally, add the strong name in AssemblyInfo.cs as before.

5. This is a basic component with an interface. Now you need to make it COM friendly. The first step is to prevent generation of the COM interface for the component class. To do this add the ClassInterface attribute to RealManagedComComponent and specify that none should be generated. You will need to add a using statement for System.Runtime.InteropServices:

```
[ ClassInterface( ClassInterfaceType.None ) ]
public class RealManagedComComponent :
    System.ComponentModel.Component,
    IMessage
```

6. The other attribute you will commonly use is the Guid attribute. The framework generates these, but it is often desirable to codify Guid attributes so they do not accidentally get changed. Visual Studio .NET provides a convenient tool for generating GUIDs on the menu at Tools ➤ Create GUID. The dialog box that appears provides convenient ways to create GUIDs, as shown in Figure 10-16.

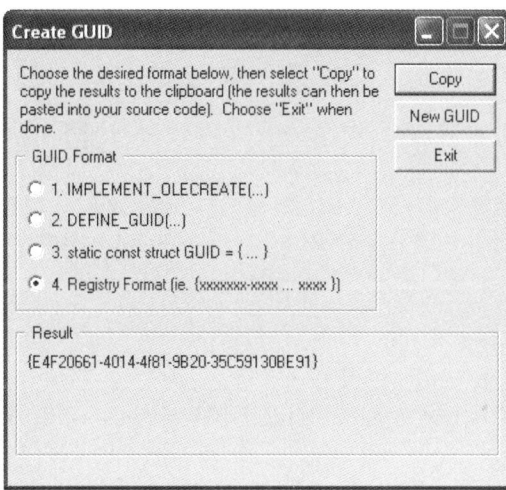

Figure 10-16. The Create GUID dialog box

7. Specify the Guid attribute for IMessage:

```
[ Guid ( "248B4080-D2AF-4af2-A541-F64A3949DED5" ) ]
public interface IMessage
```

8. Then for RealManagedComComponent:

```
[ ClassInterface( ClassInterfaceType.None ) ]
[ Guid ( "7E57BBE7-66AA-478d-8CA1-9DCE901CB8A5" ) ]
public class RealManagedComComponent :
    System.ComponentModel.Component,
    IMessage
```

9. You can now build and use the RealManagedComComponent component.

Other attributes allow further control over the COM characteristics of your class. These are essential if you want to replace an existing COM component with managed code. Refer to the documentation if you need to know more.

Using a COM Component from Managed Code

Just as COM Callable Wrappers provide a proxy for COM clients to access your managed classes, Runtime Callable Wrappers (RCWs) provide a proxy for managed clients to access COM classes. CCWs are generated dynamically, but RCWs need to be generated and built into assemblies.

Generating the RCW Using Visual Studio .NET

The most straightforward way to use a COM component from managed code is to generate the RCW using Visual Studio .NET. The following example uses this technique to access the COM interface of Excel 2002:

1. Create a new ConsoleApplication project called **ExcelInteropExample**.

2. Now open the context menu for References ➤ Add Reference . . . but change to the COM tab in the Add Reference dialog box.

3. Find Microsoft Excel 10 Object Library in the list, highlight it, click Select, and then click OK. This will generate the RCW for Excel and add it to the project.

4. Now change Class1 to read as follows:

```
using System;
using System.Runtime.InteropServices;
```

```
namespace ExcelInteropExample
{
    class Class1
    {
        [STAThread]
        static void Main(string[] args)
        {
            Excel.Application app = new Excel.ApplicationClass();
            app.Visible = true;
            app.Workbooks.Add( VarEnum.VT_NULL );
            app.ActiveCell.set_Value(
                    Excel.XlRangeValueDataType.xlRangeValueDefault,
                    "Hello Excel" );
        }
    }
}
```

This uses the RCW to open a new Excel workbook and writes to the top left cell.

NOTE   *If you have a different version of Excel you will need to add a reference to the appropriate COM library and may need to modify the code.*

Generating the RCW Using `tlbimp`

If you want to resort to the command line, use the `tlbimp` tool to accomplish the same RCW generation you performed with Visual Studio .NET. This can be useful in build tools. To generate the RCW for Excel, use the following:

```
tlbimp "c:\Program Files\Microsoft Office\Office10\EXCEL.EXE"
```

CAUTION   *You may have to adjust this path to reflect the location where you have Excel installed.*

Hand-Coding RCWs

In some cases, `tlbimp` cannot map the native COM type to a .NET type, and it is necessary to resort to marshalling in code. It can be done when necessary, but it is quite complex and beyond the scope of this book.

Using `ildasm` and `ilasm` to Modify the RCW

Rather than write the mashalling code in C#, some people prefer to take the output of `tlbimp` and modify the MSIL by hand. They run `ildasm` on the RCW generated by `tlbimp`, edit the resulting MSIL, and then use `ilasm` to compile the MSIL into an assembly.

Taking this path requires that you understand not just MSIL but how to write marshalling code at that level. How this is done is beyond the scope of this book, but it is a technique you will hear about in discussions related to COM interoperability. Unfortunately, at this time, there are no tutorials or references that will help you learn this technique.

Dealing with Exceptions

COM does not have an exception model. COM methods always return a value called a HRESULT, which indicates any error conditions. The .NET Framework maps these error codes to exceptions, which allow COM objects to be used like any other object. Many HRESULT values map readily to exceptions defined by the framework. Those that do not are thrown using COMException.

Be wary of COM components intended to be used only from C++. Modern versions of such components may throw C++ exceptions assuming the C++ runtime is there to catch them.

Understanding COM+

When Microsoft first announced COM+, it billed the technology as the successor to COM. Those plans were scaled back before its release, and COM+ as it stands today provides enterprise application services for COM objects. The relationship between COM and COM+ has many similarities to the relationship between JavaBeans and Enterprise JavaBeans. COM+ also provides enterprise application services for .NET objects.

Comparing COM+ and Enterprise JavaBeans

When you first compare the functionality of Enterprise JavaBeans to COM+, you may be confused. There is no easy recipe for switching between the technologies, although they fill much the same role.

COM+ makes no distinction between different types of business objects. There is no formal separation equivalent to session and entity beans. No special object-relational mapping support equivalent to entity beans exists in COM+, so no such distinction is necessary. Your objects must manage all interaction with your data store themselves.

There is good support for distributed transactions in COM+. Users of .NET can take advantage of declarative transactions using attributes. You can also control transactions procedurally. The concept of stateful and stateless session beans exists in EJB. A *stateful* session bean can hold a transaction open over multiple method calls by a client application. This is not supported by COM+; a transaction is logically contained by a single client call into the application.

Security in COM+ is role-based much like in Enterprise JavaBeans. You can create roles and configure which roles have access to a given method without having to modify the code.

EJB containers can employ object pooling to improve performance. COM+ also supports object pooling but allows pooled objects to be aware of the fact. COM+ pooling is often combined with Just In Time Activation (JITA), which avoids allocating copies of stateless objects until they are actually used.

Enterprise JavaBeans have *message-driven beans* that consume a message queue. COM+ queued components provide a more abstract face to using message queuing. Chapter 12, "Communicating via Message Queuing," discusses this in more detail.

Using ServicedComponent

The base class for COM+ objects in .NET is ServicedComponent. You can think of it as equivalent to javax.ejb.SessionBean or javax.ejbEntityBean. ServicedComponent does not inherit from either Component or IComponent. This seems odd at first, but because you do not build up a COM+ application in the Visual Studio .NET designer, it does not appear to create any difficulties.

Using Distributed Transactions

Because most people's interest in COM+ will revolve around distributed transactions, I will use that as the basis for an example. In this example, the FirstServicedComponent class provides a business method, NewAccount, which uses two other classes, `Person` and `Account`, to create entries in separate data-bases:

1. Create a new Class Library project called **FirstServicedComponentExample**.

2. Add a reference to `System.EnterpriseServices` by right-clicking the project's References folder in the Server Explorer and selecting Add Reference..

3. When the Add Reference dialog box appears, select the .NET tab and scroll the list until you see `System.EnterpriseServices`. Select that entry, click Select, and then click OK.

4. Create three classes: `FirstServicedComponent`, `Person`, and `Account`, each of which inherits from `ServicedComponent`. The `FirstServicedComponent` class should look like Listing 10-6.

Listing 10-6. The `FirstServicedComponent` *Class*

```
using System;
using System.EnterpriseServices;
using System.Runtime.InteropServices;

namespace FirstServicedComponentExample
{
    [ Transaction ]
    public class FirstServicedComponent : ServicedComponent
    {
        public FirstServicedComponent()
        {
        }

        [ AutoComplete ]
        public void NewAccount( string name )
        {
            using ( Person p = new Person() )
            {
                p.Name = name;
                p.Save();
                using ( Account a = new Account() )
                {
                    a.PersonId = p.Id;
```

```
            a.Save();
        }
    }
}
}
}
```

The Transaction attribute on the class specifies that a transaction is required for all methods in this class. If no transaction is in force when a method in this class is invoked, one will be created.

The AutoComplete attribute on the NewAccount method specifies that on exit from the method the transaction should be committed unless an exception is thrown out of the method. In the latter case, the transaction should be rolled back.

5. The FirstServicedComponent uses the two other classes to update tables in two separate databases. The databases are created by right-clicking the MSDE/SQL Server instance in Server Explorer and selecting New Database, as shown in Figure 10-17.

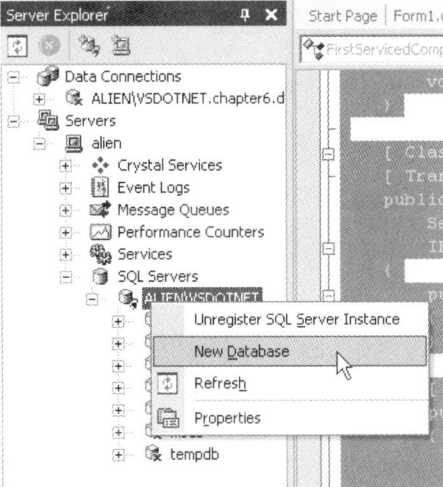

Figure 10-17. Creating a new database

6. Create database Chapter10a to hold the people table, which should match Figure 10-18.

dbo.people : T...ET.Chapter10a)			
Column Name	Data Type	Length	Allow Nulls
⚷ id	uniqueidentifier	16	
name	char	30	

Figure 10-18. The people table

7. Create a second database, Chapter10b, to hold the accounts table, which should match Figure 10-19.

dbo.accounts :...ET.Chapter10b)			
Column Name	Data Type	Length	Allow Nulls
▶⚷ id	uniqueidentifier	16	
pid	uniqueidentifier	16	

Figure 10-19. The accounts table

8. The Person class updates the people table and should look like Listing 10-7.

Listing 10-7. The Person Class

```
using System;
using System.EnterpriseServices;
using System.Data;
using System.Data.SqlClient;
using System.Data.SqlTypes;
using System.Runtime.InteropServices;

namespace FirstServicedComponentExample
{
    [ Transaction ]
    public class Person : ServicedComponent
    {
        public Person()
        {
        }

        protected Guid m_id;

        public Guid Id
        {
            get
```

```
            {
                return m_id;
            }
        }

    protected string m_name;

    public string Name
    {
        get
        {
            return m_name;
        }
        set
        {
            m_name = value;
        }
    }

    public void Save()
    {
        m_id = Guid.NewGuid();

        string cstr = @"Server=.\VSdotNET;"
            + @"Database=Chapter10a;"
            + @"Integrated Security=SSPI";
        using ( SqlConnection conn = new SqlConnection( cstr ))
        {
            conn.Open();
            SqlCommand cmd = new SqlCommand(
        "insert into people ( id, name ) values ( @id, @name )",
                conn );
            SqlParameter id = cmd.Parameters.Add( "@id",
                                    SqlDbType.UniqueIdentifier );
            id.Value = m_id;
            SqlParameter name = cmd.Parameters.Add( "@name",
                                    SqlDbType.NVarChar, 30 );
            name.Value = m_name;
            cmd.ExecuteNonQuery();
        }
    }
    }
}
```

9. In this case the Transaction attribute causes the class to enlist in the transaction started by the NewAccount method. Because you want the NewAccount method to bracket the transaction, none of the methods in Person use the AutoComplete attribute.

10. The Account class is similar to the Person class but uses a different database and a separate database connection. It should look like Listing 10-8.

Listing 10-8. The Account *Class*

```
using System;
using System.EnterpriseServices;
using System.Data;
using System.Data.SqlClient;
using System.Data.SqlTypes;
using System.Runtime.InteropServices;

namespace FirstServicedComponentExample
{
    [ Transaction ]
    public class Account : ServicedComponent
    {
        public Account()
        {
        }

        protected Guid m_id;

        public Guid Id
        {
            get
            {
                return m_id;
            }
        }

        protected Guid m_personId;

        public Guid PersonId
        {
            set
            {
                m_personId = value;
```

```
        }
        get
        {
            return m_personId;
        }
    }

    public void Save()
    {
        m_id = Guid.NewGuid();

        string cstr = @"Server=.\VSdotNET;"
            + @"Database=Chapter10b;"
            + @"Integrated Security=SSPI";
        using ( SqlConnection conn = new SqlConnection( cstr ))
        {
            conn.Open();
            SqlCommand cmd = new SqlCommand(
        "insert into accounts ( id, pid ) values ( @id, @pid )",
                    conn );
            SqlParameter id = cmd.Parameters.Add( "@id",
                                    SqlDbType.UniqueIdentifier );
            id.Value = m_id;
            SqlParameter pid = cmd.Parameters.Add( "@pid",
                                    SqlDbType.UniqueIdentifier );
            pid.Value = m_personId;
            cmd.ExecuteNonQuery();
        }
    }
}
```

 **NOTE**   *Ensure that you update the database connection strings in both the* Person *and* Account *classes to refer to the SQL Server or MSDE running on your system. Refer to Chapter 6, "Using ADO.NET," for details of how to do this.*

11. Before the library can be built, it needs to be strong named. You already know how this is done. The other assembly level attribute that needs to be specified is the COM+ application name. This is necessary to avoid manually registering the assembly. This is quite useful during development but is not usually practical in production. For automatic registration to function the user running the application must have Administrator privilege for the system. Specify the COM+ application name for the assembly by adding the ApplicationName attribute to Assembly.cs:

```
[ assembly: ApplicationName( "FirstServicedComponent" ) ]
```

12. The assembly should build at this point.

13. Now you need an application to use the COM+ application you created so add a new Windows Application project called **FirstServicedComponentDemo**.

14. Add a TextBox to enter the person's name and a Button labeled **Create Account**, as shown in Figure 10-20.

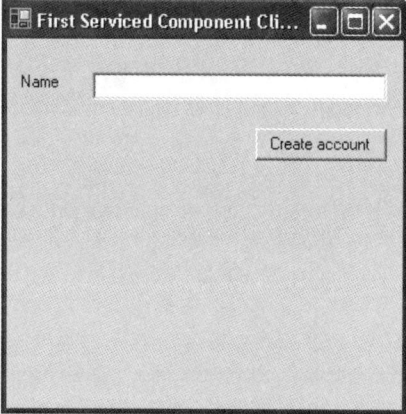

Figure 10-20. The form to test the COM+ application

15. The button click handler should read as follows:

```
private void button1_Click(object sender, System.EventArgs e)
{
    try
    {
```

```
            using ( FirstServicedComponent fsc = new
    FirstServicedComponent() )
            {
                fsc.NewAccount( textBox1.Text );
                MessageBox.Show( this, "Account created" );
            }
        }
        catch( Exception exc )
        {
            MessageBox.Show( this, exc.ToString() );
        }
    }
```

16. When you run this application, the tables in both databases get updated.

17. To demonstrate that the distributed transaction is working, add the following to the Save method of Account:

```
public void Save()
{
    // fail 50% of the time

     if ( new Random().NextDouble() > 0.5 )
    {
        throw new Exception( "random error" );
    }
```

This throws an exception 50 percent of the time. You can verify that the names were not added to the people table even though that part of the process has completed at the point the exception is thrown.

Setting Security

You can configure security for a COM+ application entirely using the Component Services tool located in the Control Panel under Administrative Tools. In .NET you can specify almost all of these options in the application source using attributes. Take the attribute path for the FirstServicedComponentExample application:

1. First you must turn on security checking for the application. Specify the ApplicationAccessControl attribute for the application's assembly:

```
[ assembly: ApplicationAccessControl( true ) ]
```

2. Next you need to turn it on for the individual components where access checking must occur using the `ComponentAccessControl` attribute as follows:

```
[ Transaction ]
[ ComponentAccessControl]
public class FirstServicedComponent : ServicedComponent
```

3. You can use the `PrivateComponent` attribute to remove access to classes from outside the application. Use this to eliminate internal classes from the set of classes you need to secure, in this case `Person` and `Account`. Applying this to `Person`:

```
[ Transaction ]
[ PrivateComponent ]
public class Person : ServicedComponent
```

4. COM+ security is based on roles. Define roles for the application and then add users to the appropriate roles. You can specify the roles using the `SecurityRole` attribute in a number of places. If specified for the application's assembly, it defines the role for the application but does not apply it to any components or methods:

```
[ assembly: SecurityRole( "FSCUser" ) ]
```

5. When specified for a method or class, the role is added to the application and applied to the individual method or all methods in the class, respectively:

```
[ Transaction ]
[ ComponentAccessControl]
[ SecurityRole( "FSCUser" ) ]
public class FirstServicedComponent : ServicedComponent
```

The one thing you cannot specify using attributes is which users are members of a role. For that you need to use the Component Services tool:

1. Before you do that, try running `FirstServicedClient` and verify that you get an `UnauthorizedAccessException`.

2. Now you need to add yourself to the FSCUser role in the FirstServicedComponent application. In Windows XP, you get to Component Services through Start ➤ Control Panel ➤ Performance and Maintenance ➤ Administrative Tools ➤ Component Services. You should see the window shown in Figure 10-21.

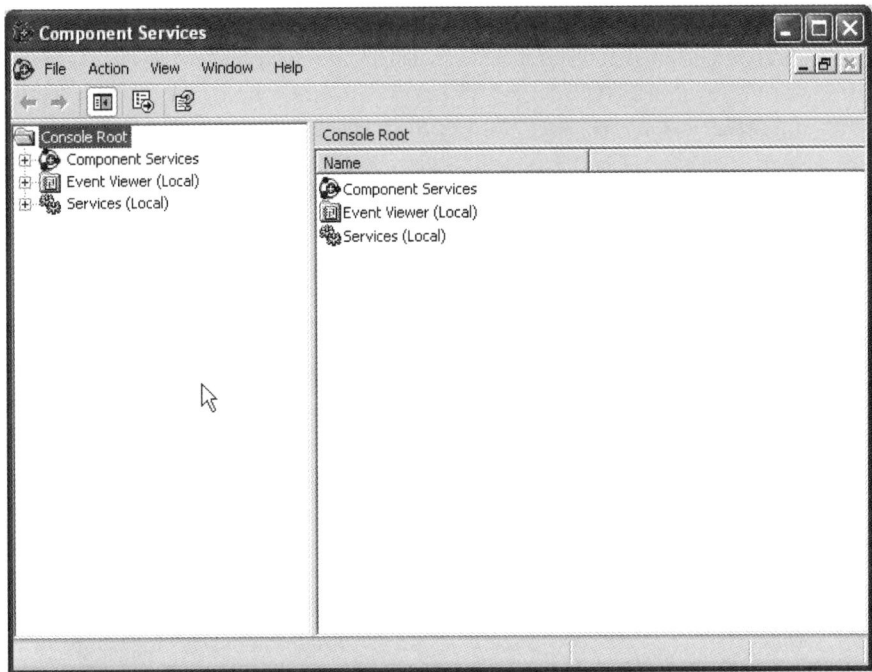

Figure 10-21. The Component Services tool

3. Expand the Component Services node down through COM+ Applications and FirstServicedComponent to the role FSCUser, as shown in Figure 10-22.

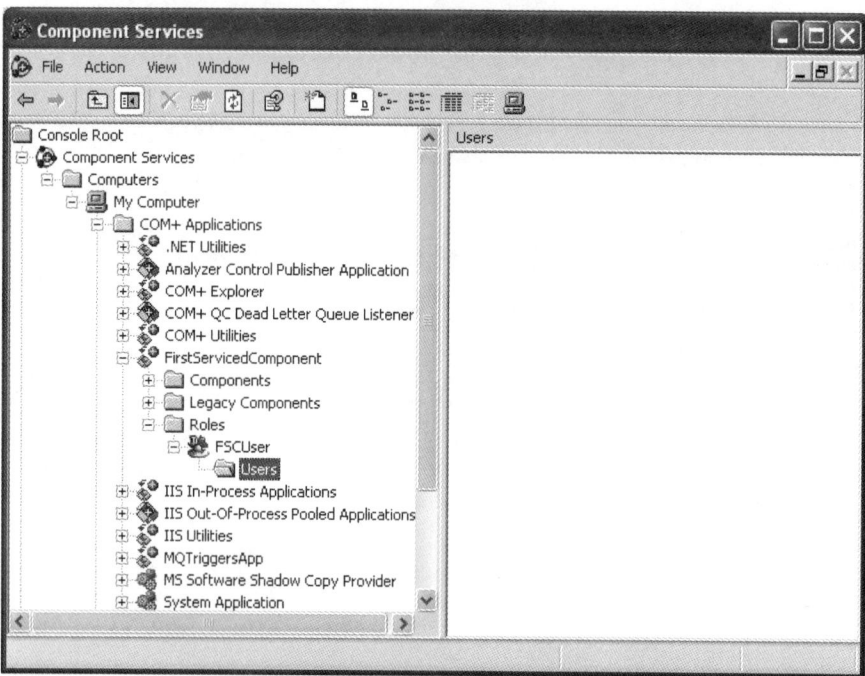

Figure 10-22. The tree expanded down to the roles in `FirstServicedComponent`

4. You can see that there are no users currently in the FSCUser role. Right-click the Users node under FSCUser and select New ➤ User. You will be placed in a dialog box where you can enter user accounts to be added to the role, as shown in Figure 10-23.

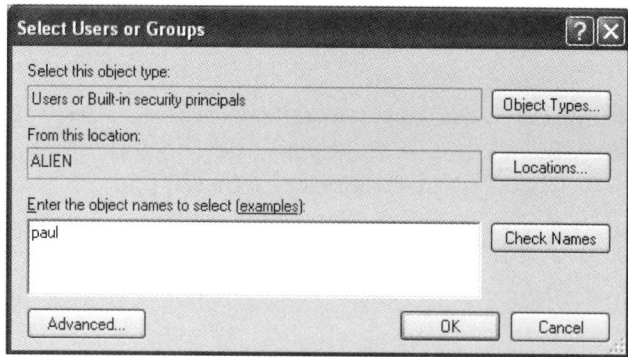

Figure 10-23. Adding a user to the `FSCUser` *role*

5. Add yourself to the role and then rerun `FirstServicedClient`. You should no longer get the `UnauthorizedAccessException`.

Registering via the Command Line

You have relied on automatic registration of your components so far. This is convenient for development but has limited value for production. Automatic registration only works when the user running the application is a member of the Administrators group. Although this is typically true for developers, most end users do not have such privileges. If your application will be used by ASP.NET, the ASPNET account is definitely not part of the Administrators group.

The `regsvcs` tool allows you to register your assemblies with COM+ from the command line. Open a command prompt and switch to the output directory of `FirstServicedComponentExample`. Issue the following to register your application:

```
regsvcs FirstServicedComponentExample.dll
```

Looking to `ObjectSpaces`

So, `ServicedComponent` seems to equate somewhat to an Enterprise JavaBeans session bean; what about entity beans? At the 2001 Professional Developers Conference, Microsoft previewed a .NET technology called *ObjectSpaces* that provides an object-relational mapping solution far superior to `DataSet` and its related classes. All that has been heard since is that the team is working hard on the product. No release schedule has been announced.

Summary

Components in .NET provide a framework for code reuse that should look familiar to a Java programmer. The COM support makes interoperating with legacy components relatively easy. COM+ `ServicedComponents` provide enterprise application features that have parallels in Enterprise JavaBeans. Once again, your knowledge and experience gives you a framework for understanding and exploiting this new technology.

CHAPTER 11

Packaging and Installing Applications

PACKAGING IN JAVA is usually a matter of creating the appropriate JAR or WAR file. Installation consists of placing that file in the appropriate directory. Things are quite different in Windows where users expect easy-to-use installation programs.

Another Look at Assemblies

You have been using assemblies throughout this book. In all cases, those assemblies have been single-file assemblies. This is the easiest model with which to deal. However, an assembly is not restricted to a single file. It may be composed of multiple files.

Building Multifile Assemblies

The main reason to create a multifile assembly is to combine code written in different languages into a single .exe or .dll. Visual Studio .NET does not support creating such files because it does not allow mixing languages within a project.

You can also attach resource files to an assembly rather than embedding them. The only reason to do this would be to avoid unnecessary file transfers in an application deployed on the Web (not an ASP.NET application—usually a WinForms application).

Comparing Assemblies to JAR Files

A *Java Archive* (JAR) file contains multiple compiled types all packaged into a single file like an assembly. Are they really the same concept, though?

The unit of execution in Java is a .class file. JAR files were created to overcome packaging problems created by the limitation that each Java type results in an independent .class file. JAR files support an internal directory structure and can contain files other than .class files. In many cases, you can extract and execute the contents of a JAR file from the file system with no change in the behavior of the application.

Assemblies are the unit of execution in .NET. They can contain multiple types, but you cannot pull them apart and store the types in individual files in the file system unless they were built that way. There is no internal directory structure. You can include arbitrary files in assemblies as resources. An assembly more closely resembles a group of .class files bound together than a JAR file.

Using xcopy Deployment

Much fuss has been made of xcopy deployment. xcopy is the Windows command-line tool for performing a recursive copy of a directory tree. For Windows developers used to COM development, it is a big improvement. Deploying a COM component requires updating the Registry and therefore needs an installation program.

xcopy is the simplest deployment strategy, but it is also the most limited. It cannot register a COM component or a COM+ application. It also cannot make provisions to remove any COM+ applications that self-register. xcopy cannot install any assemblies into the Global Assembly Cache (GAC), create an Internet Information Services (IIS) virtual root for an ASP.NET application, or set any permissions.

Applications deployed this way will not appear in the control panel's Add or Remove Programs tool and can only be de-installed by remembering where they were put and deleting the directory tree.

Using CAB Files

Cabinet (CAB) files were used to package applications for installation at one time. Now they remain only for packaging ActiveX controls. CAB files support an internal directory structure similar to a JAR file. You can use them to hold a single .NET assembly, although there seems little point unless it is being exposed as an ActiveX control.

Using Windows Installer

This is the conventional Windows install process. The end result is an .msi file that the user can double-click to install. After installation it appears in the Control Panel's Add or Remove Programs tool and can be uninstalled if necessary.

Visual Studio .NET supports building a Windows installer project using the output of your other projects, which makes this far easier than it was in the past.

These *setup projects* can be made quite powerful in a short time and are likely to become your first choice for installing your applications.

Building an Installer Package

To build an installer package for a simple WinForms application, follow these steps:

1. Create a new solution called **InstallerExample**. A solution is a way to group related projects. You create solutions using the same dialog you use for projects but select the Visual Studio Solutions project type and the Blank Solution template as shown in Figure 11-1. Solutions make creating installer packages easier because the setup project is aware of the other projects in the solution.

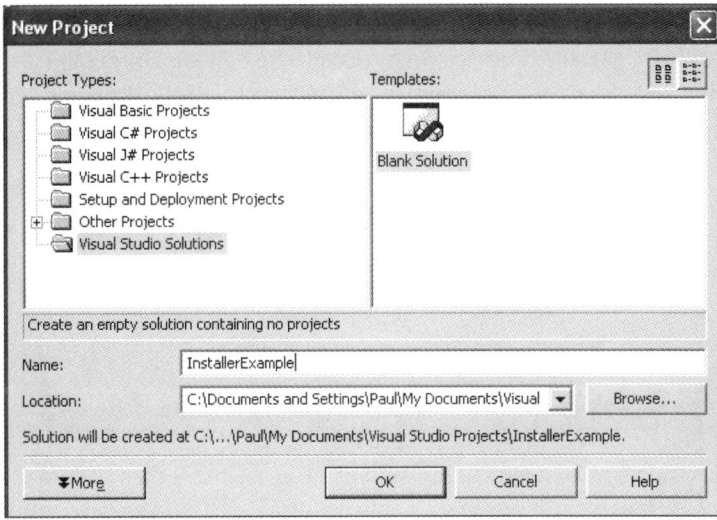

Figure 11-1. Creating a new solution

2. Add a Windows Application project to the solution called HelloForInstall by selecting File ➤ Add Project ➤ New Project . . . and completing the familiar project creation dialog box. Go ahead and re-create the classic HelloWorld example and build the project.

3. Now add a setup project to the solution called **HelloSetup**. Choose the Setup Wizard, as shown in Figure 11-2.

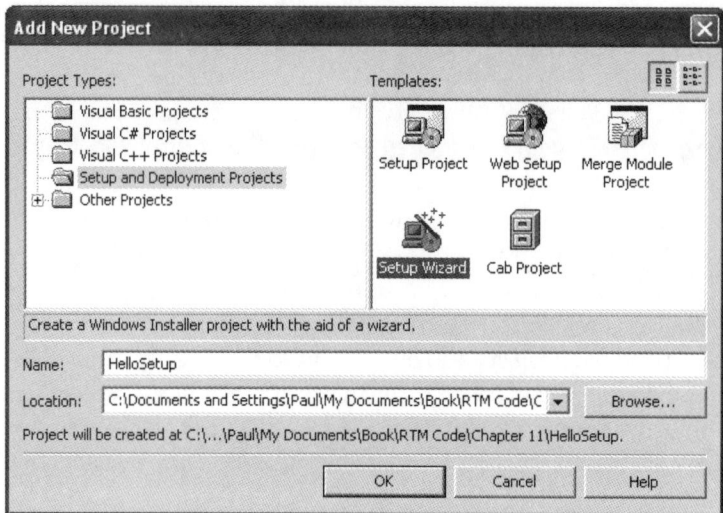

Figure 11-2. Creating a Setup Wizard project

4. Take the defaults for all screens except the one shown in Figure 11-3. On that screen select the primary output from the HelloForInstall project you just created.

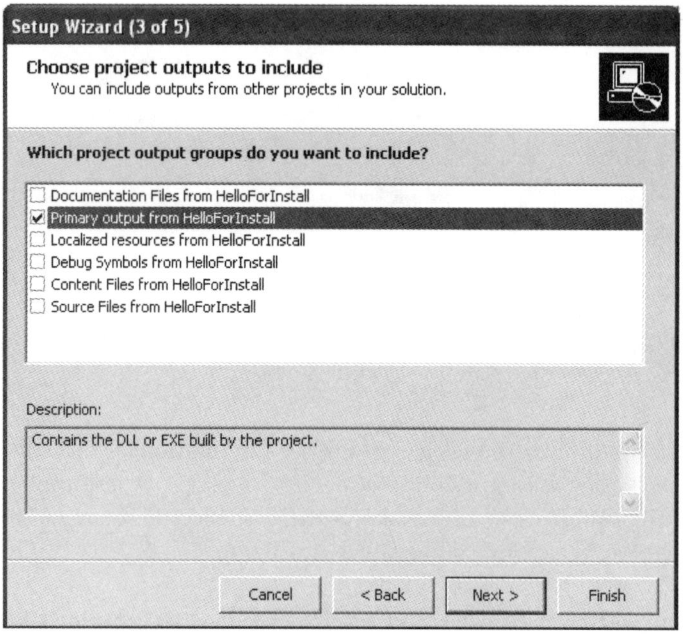

Figure 11-3. Selecting what to include in the setup project

5. Once you have completed the wizard, build the setup project. This will create the .msi file to install your WinForms application. You can run the installation by double-clicking the .msi file or by selecting Project ➤ Install, as shown in Figure 11-4. You can uninstall the project by selecting Project ➤ Uninstall or from the Control Panel's Add or Remove Programs tool.

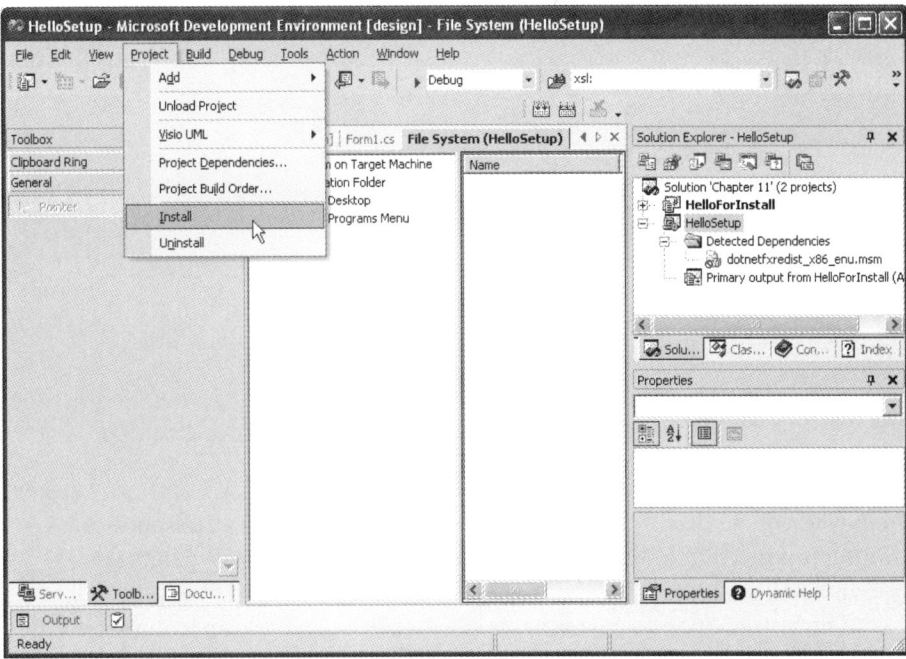

Figure 11-4. Installing the setup project from Visual Studio .NET

Including .NET in the Installation Package

You may have noticed that the installer package you just created detected the need for the .NET Redistributable Components merge module but then excluded it from the setup project.

Including the .NET Redistributable Components merge module bloats the install by several megabytes, so the wizard creates a project that does not include the merge module but checks for the presence of the runtime before it allows the install to proceed. You can see this check if you open the project's context menu and select View ➤ Launch Conditions.

To include the runtime in your installer module, you must uncheck the Exclude option on the merge module, as shown in Figure 11-5, and then delete the launch condition that checks for the presence of the runtime.

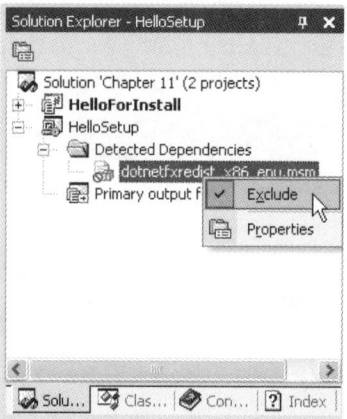

Figure 11-5. Removing the Exclude option on the .NET Redistributable Components merge module

Customizing the Installation Steps

The installer package you created is straightforward; however, you can customize it to add additional options and steps.

This install does not ask the user for an unlock code (serial number), register them with you, or modify its behavior based on the presence or absence of another product. Refer to the documentation for details on how to add such steps to the installation.

As an introduction to customizing the install, add a desktop icon that is only installed if the user selects a checkbox on an optional panel that will be added to the package. Follow these steps:

1. On the File System view of the setup project, select the User's Desktop folder and choose Add ➢ File . . . , as shown in Figure 11-6. Then browse to the HelloForInstall project and select App.ico.

2. Once the file is in the setup project add the panel with the checkboxes to the interface. Open the setup project's context menu and select View ➢ User Interface. You will see the panels arranged as in Figure 11-7.

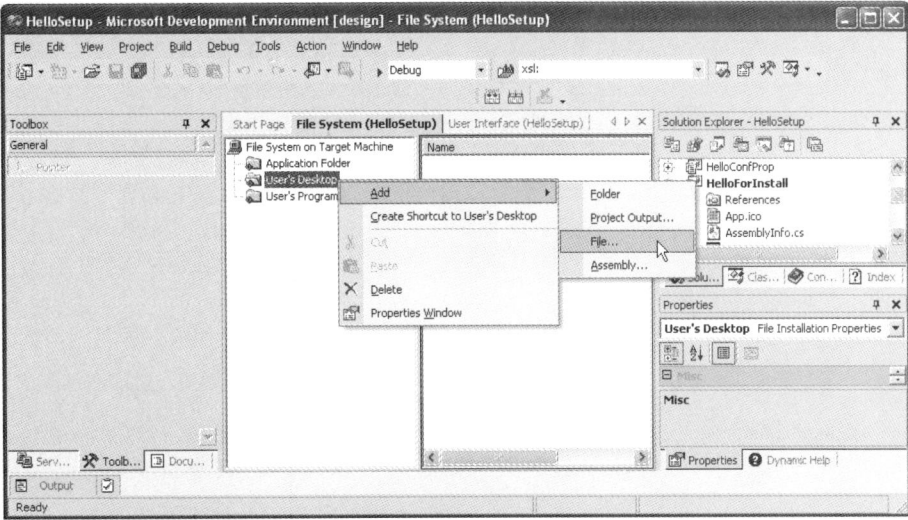

Figure 11-6. Adding the icon file to the install

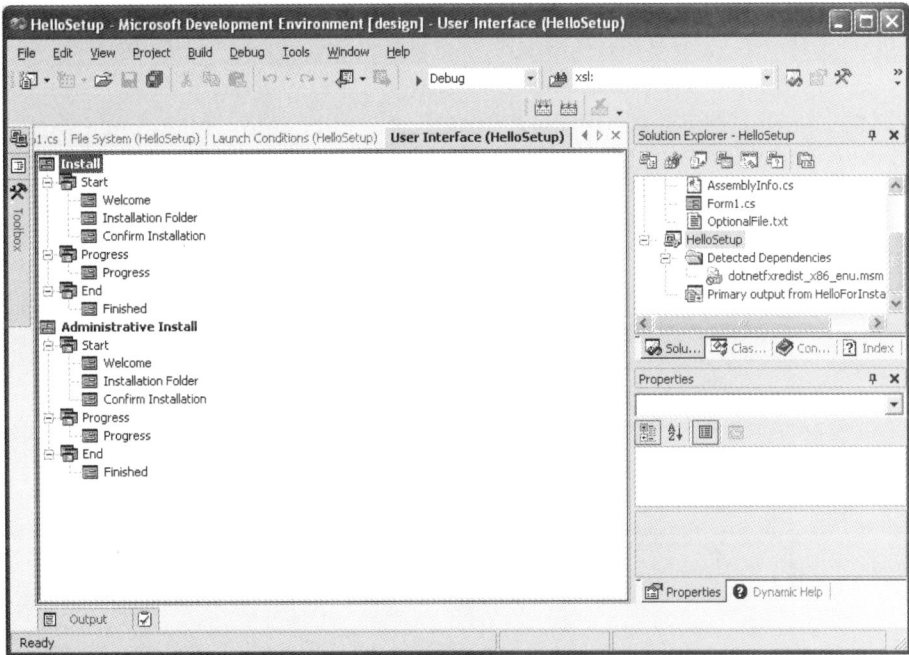

Figure 11-7. The panels in the setup project

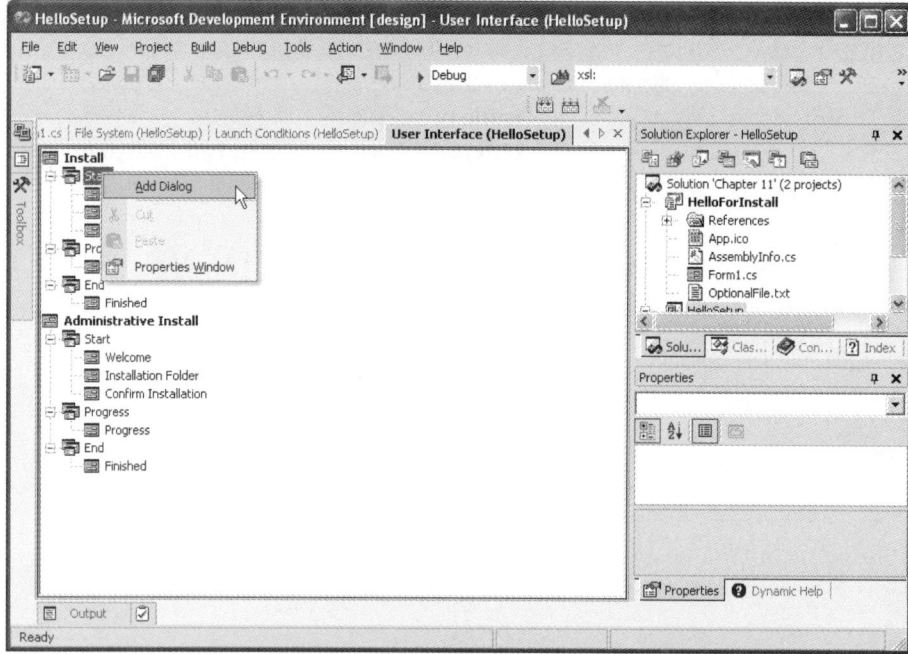

Figure 11-8. The context menu item for adding a dialog box to the install

3. Now, add a checkbox panel, so open the Start group's context menu and select Add Dialog, as shown in Figure 11-8.

4. Choose the Checkboxes (A) panel, as shown in Figure 11-9.

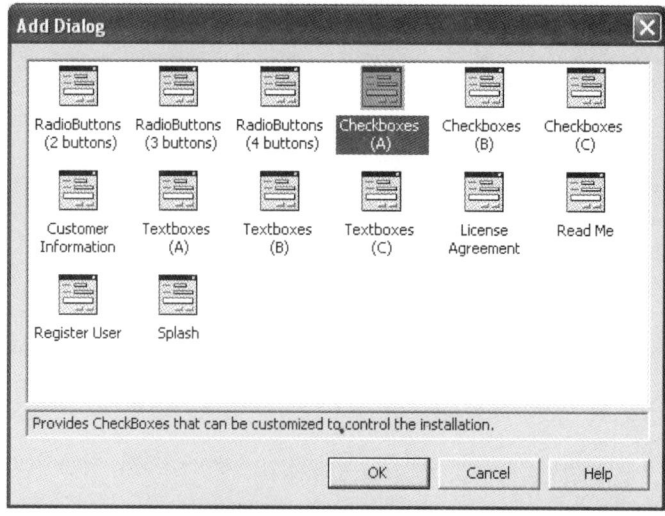

Figure 11-9. Selecting the panel to add

5. The A or B or C exists because there are only three panels of checkboxes you can add to your setup. Customize the checkboxes displayed on your panel by setting the properties for the panel. Because you only need one of the checkboxes, set the visible property for checkboxes 2 through 4 to **false**. Now change the CheckBox1Label property to **Add an icon to my desktop**.

6. To make the installation of the icon onto the desktop depend on the checkbox, open the Properties window for the file and make the Condition property **CHECKBOXA1=1**, as shown in Figure 11-10.

Figure 11-10. Setting the install condition for the desktop icon

7. Now when you run the install, you are presented with the panel in Figure 11-11, which allows you to choose whether an icon will be placed on your desktop.

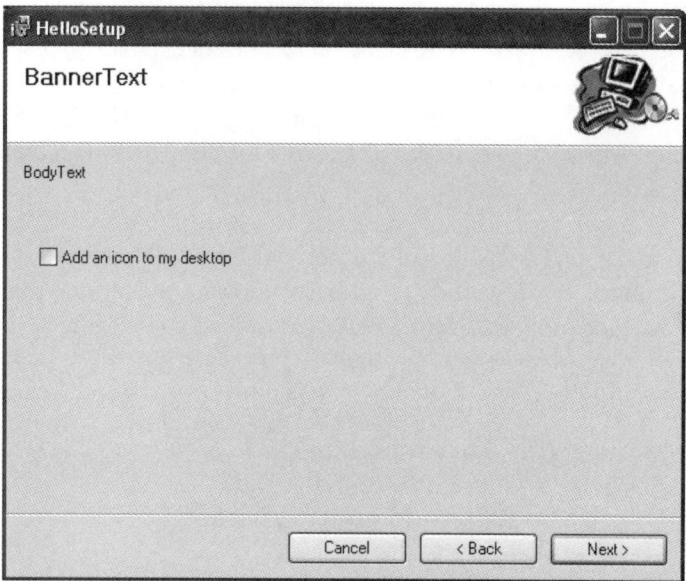

Figure 11-11. Choosing whether to install a desktop icon

Creating Installation Packages for ASP.NET

You can also create setup projects for Web applications that simplify their deployment to the web server. The presence of the runtime is assumed in Web projects.

Launching from Internet Explorer

You can launch managed applications from Internet Explorer 5 or higher. This is different from applets. The applications do not appear inside the page, nor do they interact with the page that they were launched from. Follow these steps:

1. Create a new Windows Application project called **BrowserLaunchExample**. Add Label, TextBox, and Button controls to the form and arrange them as shown in Figure 11-12. Modify their respective Text properties to match those shown in the figure.

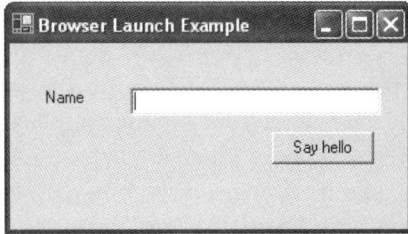

Figure 11-12. The WinForms application

2. Pressing the `Button` should display a message box, so double-click it and modify the button click handler as follows:

```
private void button1_Click(object sender, System.EventArgs e)
{
    MessageBox.Show( this, "Hello " + textBox1.Text );
}
```

3. Build and run the application to make sure it works correctly.

4. Now create a new ASP.NET Web Application project called **BrowserLauncher**.

5. Using Windows Explorer, copy BrowserLaunchExample.exe from the output directory of its project (BrowserLaunchExample\bin\Debug) into the directory containing BrowserLauncher. This is normally located at C:\Inetpub\wwwroot\BrowserLauncher. Take care not to place it in the bin subdirectory or things will not work correctly.

6. Now, switch back to Visual Studio .NET and add a hyperlink to the WebForm1 page. Change the `Text` property to **Run the program** and make the `NavigateUrl` property **BrowserLaunchExample.exe**. You will have to type this in because you cannot select the file in the dialog box.

7. Run the BrowserLauncher ASP.NET project. When the Web page appears, click the hyperlink. The WinForms application will run. Even when you close the browser, the application does not close until you choose to exit it.

Dealing with Security Issues

Applications launched this way are subject to quite different security than applications launched locally. The rights a downloaded application is granted depends on the zone from which it originates. These are the same security zones used by Internet Explorer. A last minute change just before .NET 1.0 was released tightened up those rules so that, by default, such applications cannot be launched when they originate from the Internet zone.

Applications downloaded from the intranet zone can run, but not modify anything on your machine other than isolated storage (details of which follow).

You can grant additional permissions to a specific assembly using the .NET Framework Configuration tool, which is in the Control Panel's administrative tools.

Using Isolated Storage

Even if you allow downloaded programs to execute, you do not want to allow them to write to anywhere on your hard drive. However, it is often useful for them to be able to remember settings. To accommodate limited access to local storage, .NET has *isolated storage.*

Isolated storage is not restricted to downloaded code but is useful for such applications. Request an isolated store for the user, assembly, and domain it originates from unless you have a good reason to request it just by user and assembly. An isolated store is not a file, it is a directory. You can create files and subdirectories to suit your needs, but you should be aware that the available space is limited by a quota. The local administrator can configure the quota, so you cannot assume a default size.

Now modify the example to save the name entered in the TextBox into a file in isolated storage:

1. First, add using statements for System.IO and
    System.IO.IsolatedStorage.

2. Then modify the button click handler to save the name as follows:

```
private void button1_Click(object sender, System.EventArgs e)
{
    using ( IsolatedStorageFile ifs
                = IsolatedStorageFile.GetUserStoreForDomain() )
    {
        using ( IsolatedStorageFileStream isfs
                = new IsolatedStorageFileStream( "ble.txt",
                                                 FileMode.Create,
                                                 ifs ) )
```

```
            {
                using ( StreamWriter sw = new StreamWriter( isfs ) )
                {
                    sw.WriteLine( textBox1.Text );
                }
            }
        }
    }
    MessageBox.Show( this, "Hello " + textBox1.Text );
}
```

GetUserStoreForDomain obtains a store isolated by user, assembly, and domain. You can use other methods to obtain stores isolated by other criteria. The IsolatedStorageFileStream provides access to a file within the store. Notice that the name of the file is relative to the root of the store.

3. Next, modify the form's constructor to read back the value to prime the TextBox with the last value used:

```
public Form1()
{
    InitializeComponent();

    try
    {
        using ( IsolatedStorageFile ifs
                    = IsolatedStorageFile.GetUserStoreForDomain() )
        {
            using ( IsolatedStorageFileStream isfs
                    = new IsolatedStorageFileStream( "ble.txt",
                                                      FileMode.Open,
                                                      ifs ) )
            {
                using ( StreamReader sr = new StreamReader( isfs ))
                {
                    textBox1.Text = sr.ReadLine();
                }
            }
        }
    }
    catch
    {
        // tolerate when the file does not exist yet
    }
}
```

4. Obtain the store and file in the same way as before, but in this case you cannot expect that the file already exists. Rather than looking to see if the file exists, tolerate the exception.

5. Use the `storeadm` tool to list and clear your isolated storage stores. Unfortunately, it does not let you see the contents of the stores or remove them selectively. You could create such tools using the classes in `System.IO.IsolatedStorage`.

Installing into the Global Assembly Cache

The Global Assembly Cache (GAC) is a special location on each machine that provides a common place to store assemblies used by multiple applications. If you have a component used by multiple applications and want to avoid each application storing its own copy, install one into the GAC.

Assemblies installed into the GAC must be strong named and are usually version controlled. The GAC can contain multiple versions of an assembly to support applications bound to those versions.

Managed COM+ server (out of process) applications must be installed into the GAC so that the system can locate them.

The GAC is located at %SYSTEMROOT%\assembly. When you browse to that folder with Windows Explorer, a special extension is used, as shown in Figure 11-13.

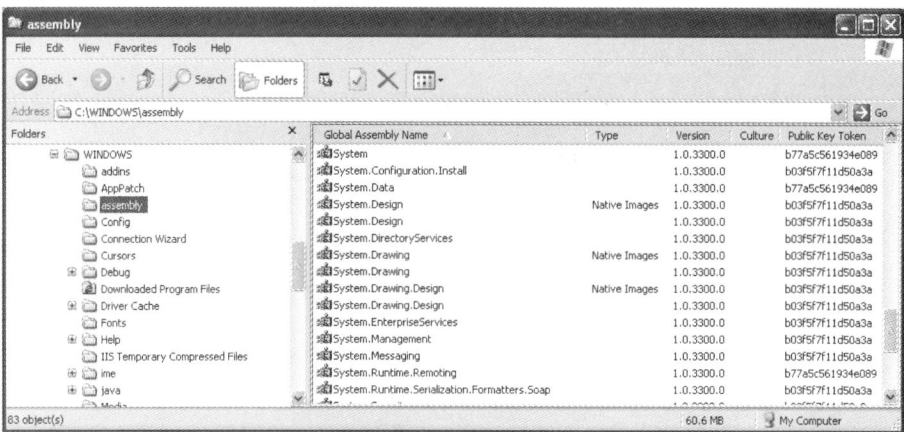

Figure 11-13. The GAC as shown in Windows Explorer

You can install a file into the GAC in several ways. To demonstrate this, follow these steps:

1. Create a new Class Library project called **MyGacComponentExample**.

2. Delete the default Class1.cs file and add a component called **MyGacComponent**.

3. Add a Message property like you did in the previous chapter. You must strong name any component to be installed into the GAC, so add an .snk file to the AssemblyKeyFile attribute in AssemblyInfo.cs.

4. Finally, build the component and you are ready to try the different installation methods.

Using the Windows Explorer Extension

For testing purposes, the easiest way to install an assembly into the GAC is to drag it into the GAC viewer in Windows Explorer. Figure 11-14 shows the assembly after dropping it into the folder.

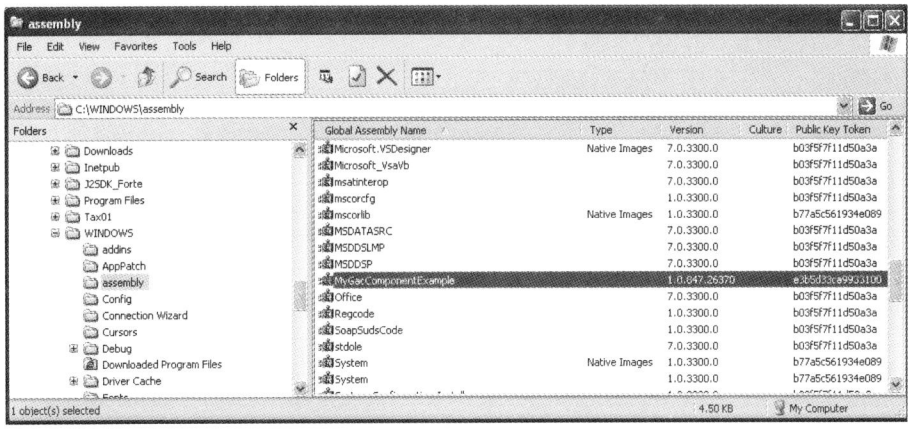

Figure 11-14. The component after dropping it into the GAC using Windows Explorer

Uninstalling the component is as straightforward as deleting any other file in Windows Explorer. Highlight the assembly and hit the Delete button.

Using the `gacutil` `tool`

The command-line solution for installing assemblies is the `gacutil` tool. The assembly is installed using the `/i` option:

```
gacutil /i MyGacComponentExample.dll
```

To uninstall the assembly, use the `/u` option and omit the .dll suffix:

```
gacutil /u MyGacComponentExample
```

Using the Windows Installer

Adding assemblies to the GAC as part of running an installation package is straightforward. Follow these steps:

1. Create a new Setup Wizard project called **MyGacComponentSetup**. Go through the wizard and when prompted, select the Primary Output from MyGacComponentExample option.

2. Once the project has been created, add a new special folder to the project. Right-click File System on Target Machine and then select Add Special Folder ➤ Global Assembly Cache Folder, as shown in Figure 11-15.

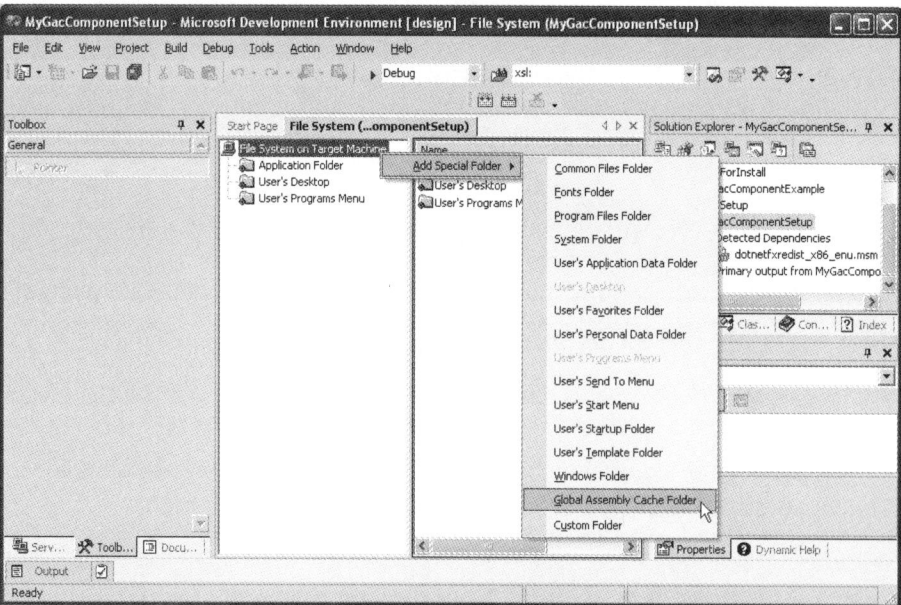

Figure 11-15. Adding a GAC folder to the setup project

3. Once the folder has been created, move the destination for the component's assembly into it. Open the Application Folder and drag the Primary Output from MyGacComponentExample item into the Global Assembly Cache Folder.

4. You can now build the project and install it. Once the installation is complete, you can verify that the assembly is in the GAC using Windows Explorer. Uninstalling the setup project removes the assembly from the GAC.

Setting Dynamic Properties

When you build an application to be installed by end users, you are expected to provide dialog boxes to allow them to configure settings for the application. When you build an enterprise application, you are expected to provide a configuration file that administrators can use to configure settings that end users should not modify. These settings contain information such as database connection strings, message queue names, mail servers, logging locations, and other deployment-specific information.

In Java you would turn to resource files to fill this requirement. In .NET you use application configuration files. You have already used these in earlier chapters to configure system settings such as assembly versioning and remoting.

Predictably, Visual Studio .NET facilitates this process. It does so through what are termed *dynamic properties*. These are ordinary component properties that obtain their value from configuration files.

Using Dynamic Properties in Visual Studio .NET

To use dynamic properties in Visual Studio .NET, follow these steps:

1. Create a new Windows Application project called **HelloConfProp**.

2. Drag a Label control onto the form. At this point you would normally set the Text property; but for this example you want Text to be a dynamic property. Select the Label and scroll its property sheet until you find the section labeled (DynamicProperties), as shown in Figure 11-16.

3. Now click in the value area of the row labeled (Advanced) and an ellipsis button should appear, as shown in Figure 11-17.

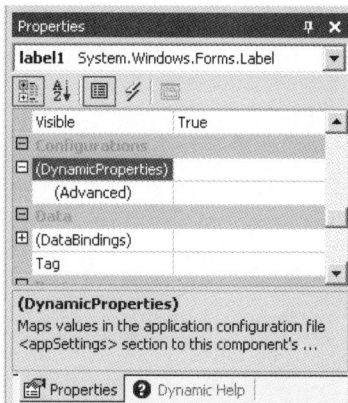

Figure 11-16. The dynamic properties section of the property sheet for label1

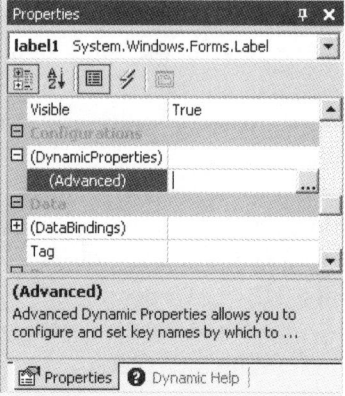

Figure 11-17. Making the ellipsis button appear

4. Click the button and the Dynamic Properties dialog box appears, as shown in Figure 11-18.

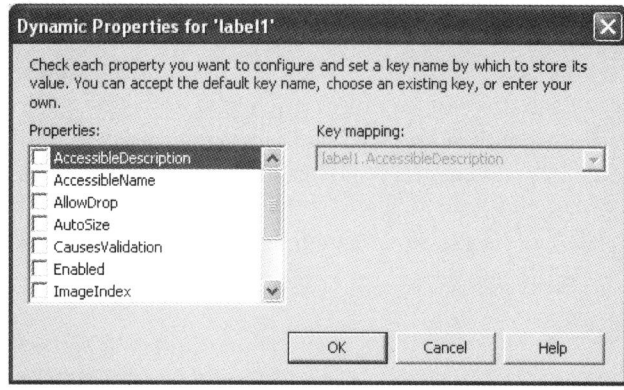

Figure 11-18. The Dynamic Properties dialog box

5. This dialog box lists all the properties of `label1` that you can set using dynamic properties. Scroll down to the Text property and check it, as shown in Figure 11-19.

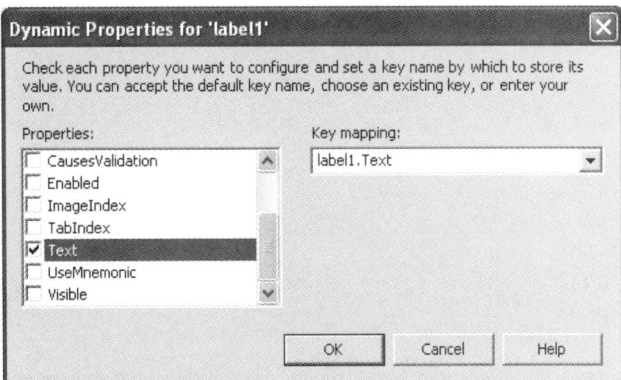

Figure 11-19. The Dynamic Properties dialog box with the Text *property checked*

6. Once you check the Text property, the key textbox becomes active. This allows you to specify the key that will be used in the configuration file. If you have several dynamic properties that need to have the same value, specify the same key for all of them. The default of `label1.Text` is fine for this example, so click OK. The property sheet now displays the Text property in the dynamic properties section, as shown in Figure 11-20.

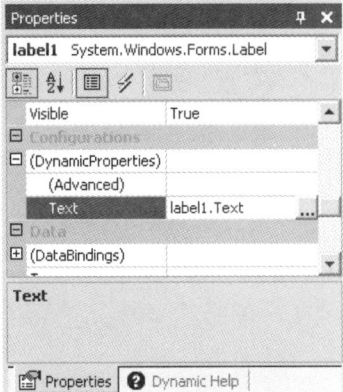

Figure 11-20. The Text *property as one of the dynamic properties*

7. Scroll the property sheet to find the Text property in its usual place under the Appearance section. As you can see in Figure 11-21, the name has a special icon next to it to denote that the property is dynamic.

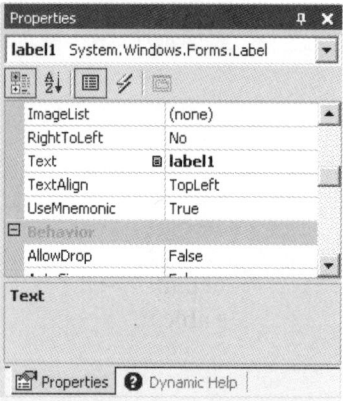

Figure 11-21. The Text *property after making it dynamic*

8. When you clicked OK on the Dynamic Properties dialog box, you may have noticed that a new file was added to the project. If not, take a look at the Solution Explorer now. You should see a new file called app.config, as shown in Figure 11-22.

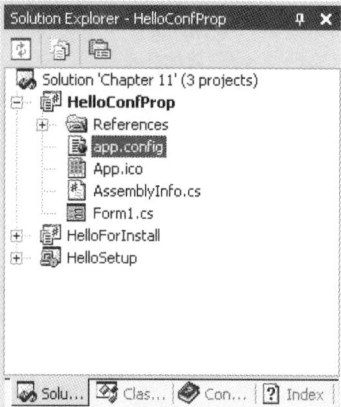

Figure 11-22. The new app.config file in the Solution Explorer

9. Open the app.config file and look at its contents:

```
<?xml version="1.0" encoding="Windows-1252"?>
<configuration>
  <appSettings>
    <!-- User application and configured property settings go here.
      -->
    <!-- Example: <add key="settingName" value="settingValue"/> -->
    <add key="label1.Text" value="label1" />
  </appSettings>
</configuration>
```

As you can see, the key-value pairs are stored in the appSettings section. The administrator would be able to change these without much difficulty.

10. Now take a look at the code that was inserted into Form1.cs to read the value. Open the code view of Form1.cs and expand the Windows Form Designer Generated Code region. The relevant code is in InitializeComponent:

```
private void InitializeComponent()
{
    System.Configuration.AppSettingsReader configurationAppSettings
        = new System.Configuration.AppSettingsReader();
    this.label1 = new System.Windows.Forms.Label();
    this.SuspendLayout();
    //
    // label1
    //
    this.label1.Location = new System.Drawing.Point(96, 122);
    this.label1.Name = "label1";
    this.label1.TabIndex = 0;
    this.label1.Text
        = ((string)(configurationAppSettings.GetValue(
                        "label1.Text",
                        typeof(string))));
```

The first statement in InitializeComponent creates an AppSettingsReader instance, configurationAppSettings, which extracts the key-value pairs from the configuration file. The statement that initializes the Text property then uses configurationAppSettings to obtain the value associated with label1.Text.

11. While you are developing the application, Visual Studio .NET keeps the configuration file, designer, and property panel synchronized whenever you change the default value. Go ahead and experiment with changing the value to see this in action.

12. Build the application. The app.config file is copied to the output directory and renamed to HelloConfProp.exe.config. When you run the application the value from the configuration file is displayed in the Label.

Comparing Dynamic Properties to Java Property Resource Bundles

Java's property resource bundles are often used to provide the functionality of dynamic properties. Although not XML based, they provide the ability to retrieve values from key-value pairs stored in a file.

The biggest difference from Java is that you could have multiple resource files scattered throughout a single JAR file, whereas in .NET you can only have a single application configuration file. It is important to recognize that Java property resource bundles are not just used for configuration purposes. They are also used in the same way as Windows resource files to store text strings to facilitate localization.

Integrating Installation Components

You can use installation components to reproduce aspects of the development system configuration during installation, based on the properties of other components. A good example of this is the EventLogInstaller component, which uses the configured value of the EventLog component's Log and Source properties to create that event log and event source.

Using Predefined Installation Components

There are five installation components provided by the framework:

- EventLogInstaller

- PerformanceCounterInstaller

- MessageQueueInstaller

- ServiceInstaller

- ServiceProcessInstaller

EventLogInstaller has already been mentioned. PerformanceCounterInstaller uses properties of the PerformanceCounter component to ensure custom performance counters are created. MessageQueueInstaller will be covered in Chapter 12, "Communicating via Message Queuing," and both ServiceInstaller and ServiceProcessInstaller will be covered in Chapter 14, "Developing Windows Services."

Using an Installation Component

As an example, create a simple application that updates a custom performance counter:

1. Start by creating a new Windows Application project called **PerfCounterExample**. Drag a Button onto the form and change its Text property to read **Update Counter**.

2. Now create the performance counter for development purposes. Open the Server Explorer. You will see a node called Performance Counters. Right-click the node and select Create New Category . . . , as shown in Figure 11-23.

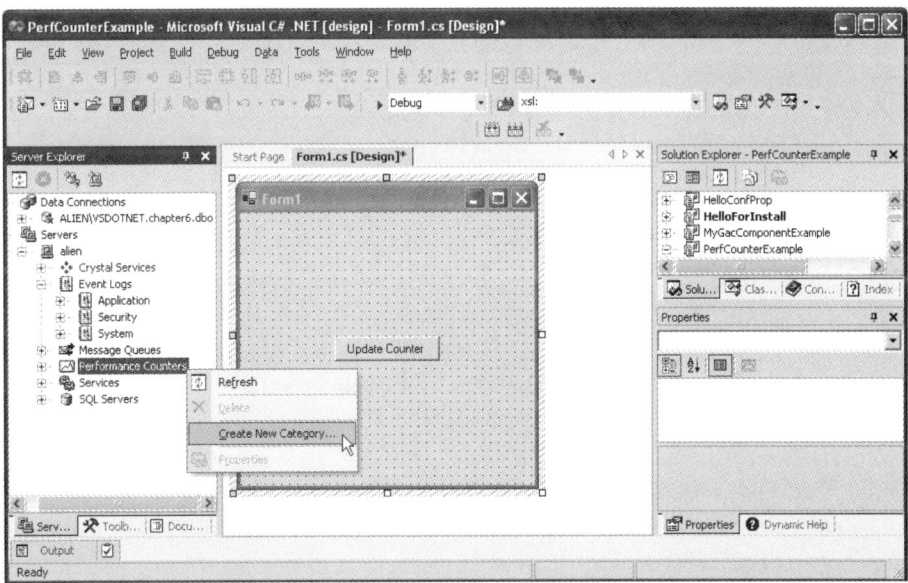

Figure 11-23. Creating a new performance counter category

3. When the dialog box opens, enter a name of **PerfCounterExample** and click New. Then enter a counter name of **ExampleCounter** and the dialog box should appear as in Figure 11-24. Click OK to create the counter and category.

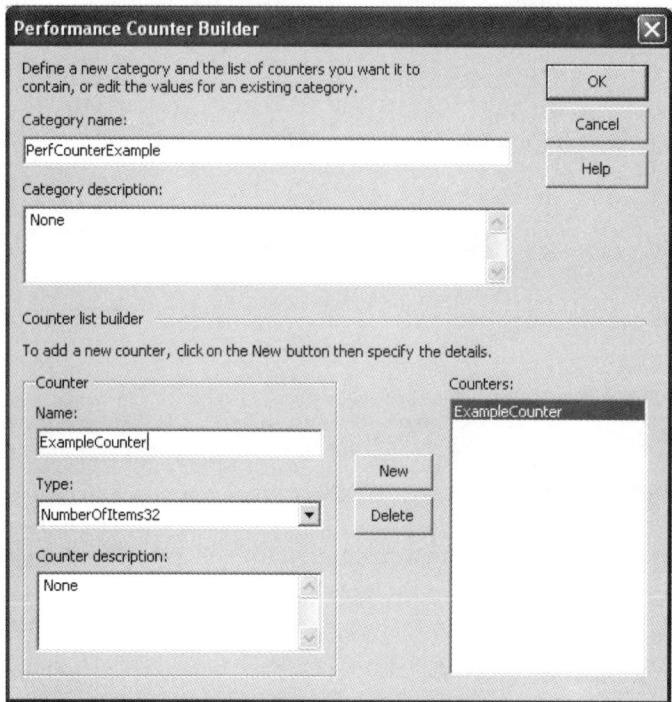

Figure 11-24. The Performance Counter Builder dialog box

4. Now expand the Performance Counters node and then the PerfCounterExample category. Drag the ExampleCounter node to the form as in Figure 11-25.

5. This will create an instance of the `PerformanceCounter` component with its properties preset for the counter. The only change necessary is to change the `ReadOnly` property to **false**.

6. Now double-click the `Button` and add the following to increment the counter each time the `Button` is pressed:

```
private void button1_Click(object sender, System.EventArgs e)
{
    performanceCounter1.Increment();
}
```

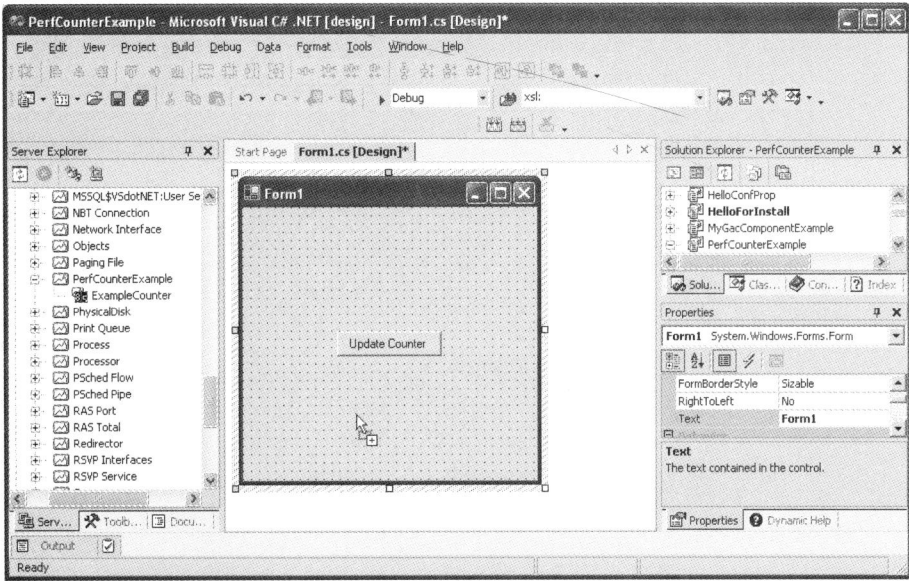

Figure 11-25. Dragging the performance counter to the form

7. When you run the application, every time you click the Button the counter will be incremented. Figure 11-26 shows this reflected in the Performance Monitor tool, perfmon.

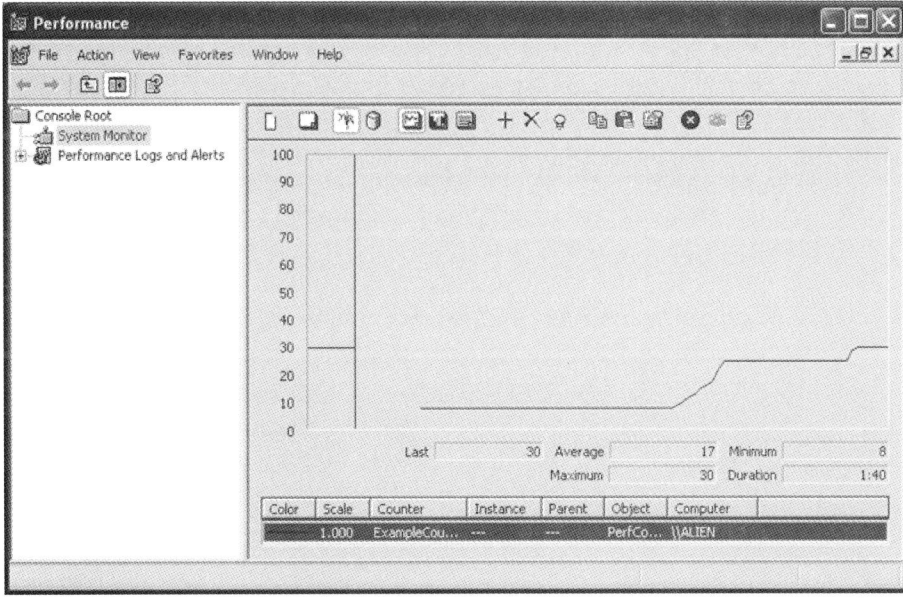

Figure 11-26. The counter changing in perfmon

8. Now for the reason you are writing this: Switch back to the design view and select the performance counter component. On the properties view for the component is an Add Installer link, as you can see in Figure 11-27. Click the link.

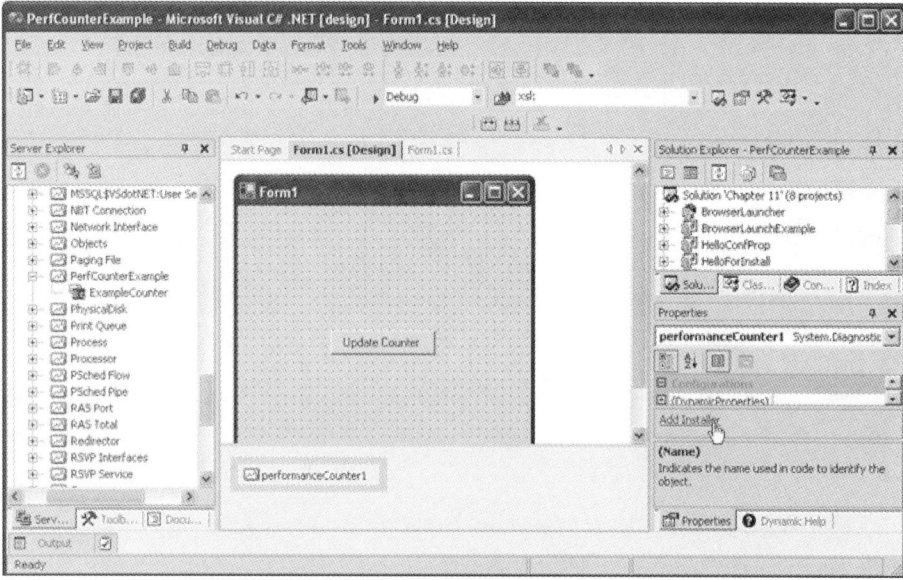

Figure 11-27. The Add Installer link on the Properties panel

9. This creates a new file called ProjectInstaller.cs, which opens in design mode containing the `PerformanceCounterInstaller` instance. Rebuild the project.

10. Now create a setup project for PerfCounterExample in the same solution. Name it **PerfCounterExampleSetup** and use the Setup Wizard. Follow the preceding example if necessary.

11. You want the installation component to be run as a custom action during setup. To do this, right-click the project and select View ➤ Custom Actions. In the custom action panel, right-click the Custom Action node and select Add Custom Action . . . , as shown in Figure 11-28.

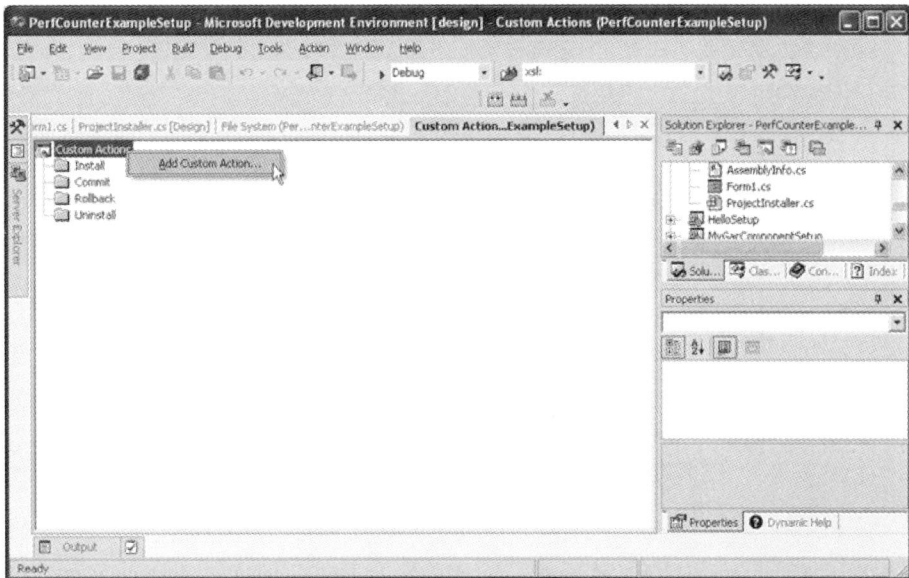

Figure 11-28. Adding a custom action

12. In the dialog box, double-click the Application Folder, as shown in Figure 11-29.

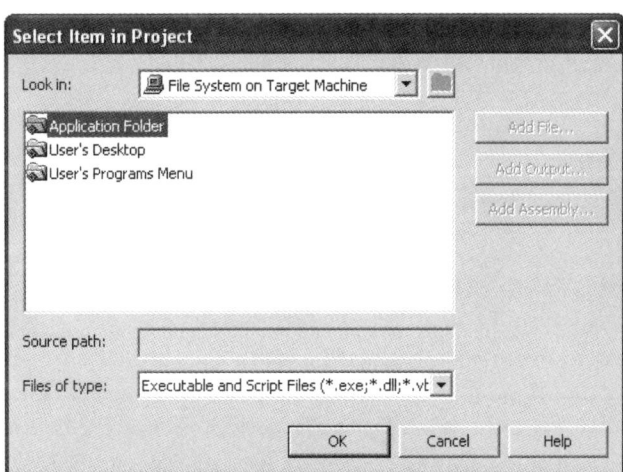

Figure 11-29. Selecting the Application Folder

13. Then double-click the Primary Output from PerfCounterExample, as shown in Figure 11-30.

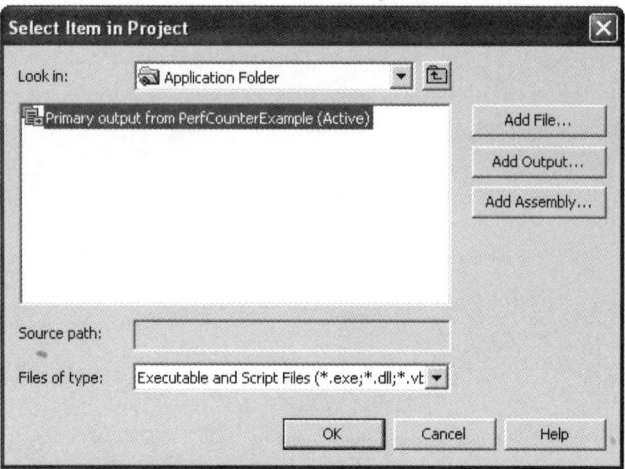

Figure 11-30. Selecting the project output

14. The Custom Actions panel now shows the PerfCounterExample assembly being used for all four steps. This will invoke the installation component. Build the setup project.

15. Before you install the setup project, delete the performance counter category PerfCounterExample, as shown in Figure 11-31.

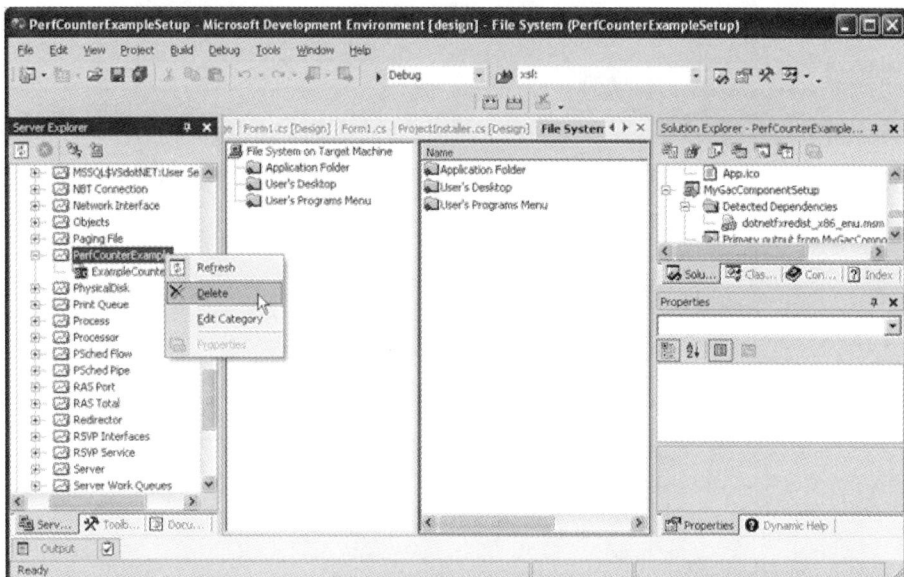

Figure 11-31. Deleting the performance counter category

16. Now when you install the setup project, the performance counter and category will be re-created as part of the installation process. When you uninstall the application, they will be removed.

Summary

This is one area where things are quite different from Java. Fortunately, using Visual Studio .NET makes creating installation packages for your projects relatively straightforward, and not just for WinForms applications. Delivering WinForms applications over the intranet through the browser has some interesting parallels with applets, but it differs significantly.

CHAPTER 12

Communicating via Message Queuing

MESSAGE QUEUING IS AN EXAMPLE of *Message-Oriented Middleware* (MOM). There are two basic types of MOM: point to point (PTP) and publish and subscribe (pub/sub). Message Queuing is an example of the former.

Message Queuing was originally known as MSMQ and many people continue to use the name to distinguish Microsoft's product from the category of point-to-point MOM products that are based on message queues. Even Microsoft itself cannot make up its mind with much material referring to the latest version of Message Queuing released in Windows XP as MSMQ 3.0.

Message Queuing is available on many versions of Windows, even Windows CE. All Windows 2000 versions and Windows XP Professional can operate as Message Queuing servers.

One of the features of Message Queuing is that clients can disconnect from the network and continue to queue messages. When they rejoin the network, those messages are transferred to the appropriate queues. This can enable Message Queuing applications for field workers or allow continued operation in the event of network failures.

Prior to the release of MSMQ 3.0 with Windows XP, Message Queuing was strictly a point-to-point system. MSMQ 3.0 adds the ability to send a message to multiple destinations using either an explicit list of queues or a multicast address. These are important changes that permit new application architectures, but as they are configuration options, nothing changes from the programmer's perspective.

Configuring Message Queuing

Message Queuing has several categories of queues. The most important distinction is between public and private queues:

- **Public queues** are advertised in Active Directory. You do not know which machine is the server, and the queue could be moved without any change to client applications.

- **Private queues** are owned by a machine. References to these queues must include the machine name. If the queue moves, applications that use it need to be reconfigured to reflect the change. If you are not part of a domain, you can only use private queues.

Queue operations can participate in a transaction, but to do so the queue must be created as a transactional queue. This has performance implications as all send and receive operations on such queues must be enclosed in a transaction.

Queues are normally administered using the Computer Management tool located in the Administrative Tools folder of Control Panel. The Visual Studio .NET Server Explorer allows developers to perform some of those functions from the Server Explorer inside the IDE.

Creating a Queue Using Computer Management

To create a queue using the Computer Management tool, follow these steps:

1. Open Computer Management and navigate to the Message Queuing node, as shown in Figure 12-1.

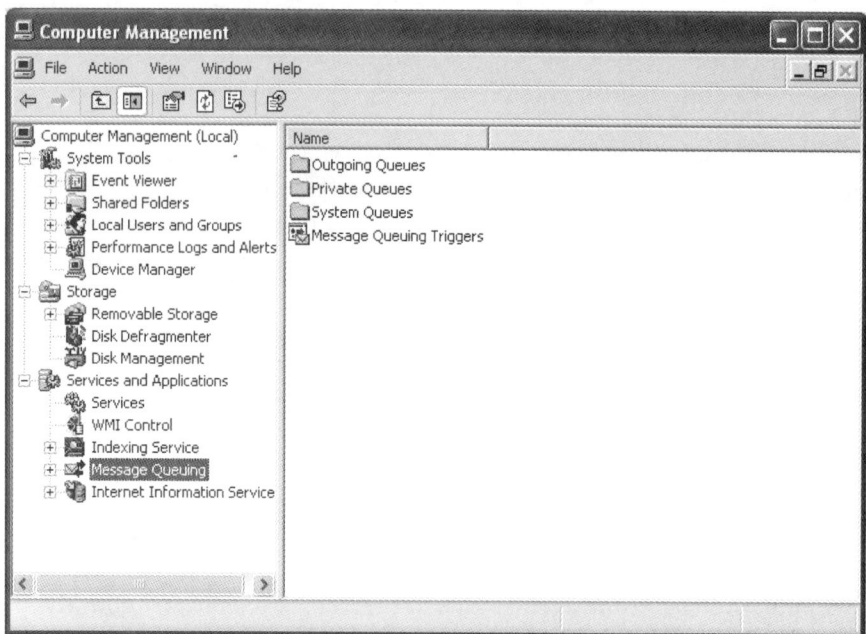

Figure 12-1. Message queuing in the Computer Management tool

2. Now expand the node. Create public queues under Public Queues and private queues under Private Queues. For this example, right-click Private Queues and select New ➤ Private Queue, as shown in Figure 12-2.

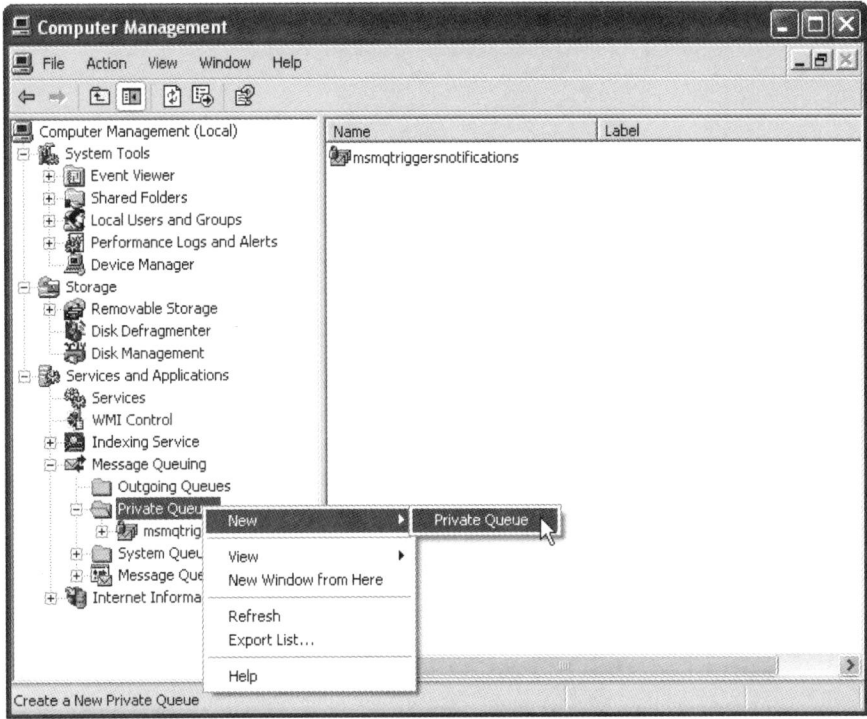

Figure 12-2. Creating a queue in the Computer Management tool

3. You will be prompted to enter a name for the queue as in Figure 12-3. Enter **myfirstqueue** as shown.

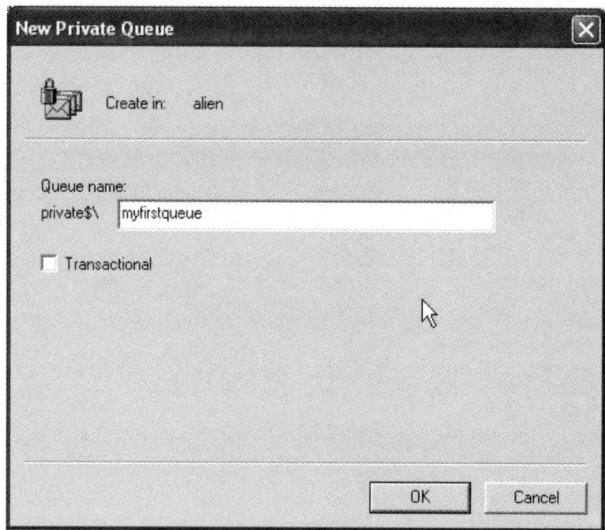

Figure 12-3. Entering the queue name in the Computer Management tool

Creating a Queue Using Server Explorer

Create a queue in Server Explorer in a similar way:

1. Navigate to the Message Queues node of the server and expand it. Right-click Private Queues and select Create Queue . . . , as shown in Figure 12-4.

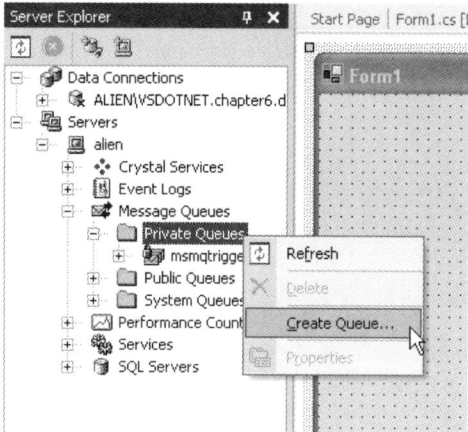

Figure 12-4. Creating the queue using the Server Explorer

2. You will be prompted to enter a name for the queue as in Figure 12-5. This time enter **mysecondqueue**.

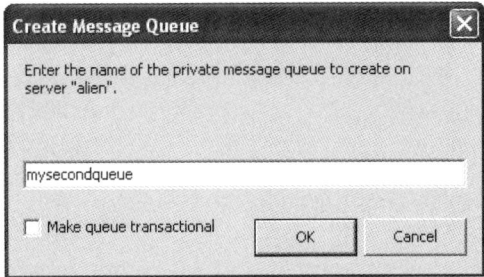

Figure 12-5. Entering the queue name in the Computer Management tool

Comparing the Tools

The big difference between using these tools comes when you want to look at the queue properties. In Computer Management, you can configure a queue to use a multicast address or manipulate queue security. Using Server Explorer, you can see properties of the queue that cannot be obtained using Computer Management. Both tools will let you look at the messages in the queue.

Creating a Message-Queuing API

Because not everyone reading this book will have an Active Directory server I will refrain from using public queues in the examples. The difference between public and private queues is primarily a matter of convenience and the only thing that changes in the code is the queue name.

Creating the Queue

Use either the Computer Management tool or Visual Studio .NET Server Explorer to create a new private queue named **example**.

Creating the Producer

Create a new Windows Application project called **ProducerExample** to write messages to the queue. Add a Label, TextBox, and Button, as shown in Figure 12-6.

Figure 12-6. The producer form

Now add the message-queuing code:

1. The first step is to create a MessageQueue component and configure it to refer to the queue created in the previous section. Open the Components panel of the Toolbox and drag a MessageQueue component onto the form. Set the Path property of the MessageQueue component to refer to the private queue. Clicking in the value area exposes an ellipsis button, as shown in Figure 12-7.

Figure 12-7. The Path *property of the* MessageQueue *component*

2. Unfortunately clicking the button attempts to contact the message queuing network. If you are not part of a domain, you will get an error. Enter the path **.\Private$\example** by hand as you are using a private queue.

3. Now, send a message when the button on the form is pressed. Double-click the button on the form to add a button click handler. Change it to read as follows:

```
private void button1_Click(object sender, System.EventArgs e)
{
    System.Messaging.Message msg
        = new System.Messaging.Message( textBox1.Text );
    messageQueue1.Send( msg );
}
```

The fully qualified name of System.Messaging.Message is used to disambiguate it from System.Windows.Forms.Message.

4. Run the program. Enter some text in the TextBox and click the button. Each time you press the button, a message is written to the example queue. You can see the messages in either Server Explorer or Computer Management.

Creating the Consumer

Now for the other half of the equation:

1. Create a new Windows Application project called **ConsumerExample** to read messages from the queue. Drag a ListBox onto the form and change its Dock property to **Fill**.

2. Instead of adding a MessageQueue component and configuring it, take the shortcut of dragging the Example private queue node from the Server Explorer onto the form. This action creates a MessageQueue instance configured for the queue called messageQueue1.

3. To read the messages from the queue, use the .NET asynchronous model instead of starting a separate thread. This leverages the thread pool to run a handler when a message is received.

4. Double-click the form to create a load handler. This is where you call BeginReceive to initiate the first receive from the queue as follows:

```
private void Form1_Load(object sender, System.EventArgs e)
{
    messageQueue1.BeginReceive();
}
```

5. Next, double-click the messageQueue1 component in the designer to create a ReceiveCompleted handler and register it with the ReceiveCompleted delegate of messageQueue1. This will be called when a message is received from the queue. Add a using statement for System.Messaging and enter the following code:

```
private delegate int AddListboxItemDelegate( object obj);
private void messageQueue1_ReceiveCompleted( object sender,
                        System.Messaging.ReceiveCompletedEventArgs e )
{
    MessageQueue mq = (MessageQueue)sender;
    System.Messaging.Message msg = mq.EndReceive( e.AsyncResult );
    msg.Formatter = new XmlMessageFormatter(
                        new String[] { "System.String, mscorlib", } );

    AddListboxItemDelegate ali
        = new AddListboxItemDelegate( listBox1.Items.Add );
    listBox1.BeginInvoke( ali,
                        new object[] { (string)msg.Body, } );

    mq.BeginReceive();
}
```

6. Retrieve the message by calling EndReceive on the MessageQueue component. Before you can extract the body, provide a formatter that understands how to deserialize the message. Even though you are using the default XML formatter, you have to explicitly add it with a list of the types you are expecting in the message. Notice that the types are specified using their assembly qualified names. Extract the body of the message using the Body property of the message. As the handler runs on a thread from the thread pool, update the ListBox using BeginInvoke.

7. Because the initial call to BeginReceive only initiates receiving a single message, call BeginReceive before the handler exits to set up for the next message.

Transactions

You can combine operations on message queues into transactions, just as you can combine operations on databases. You can also include message queuing in a COM+ distributed transaction. These two types of transactions require different changes in your code.

To participate in a transaction of any sort, a queue must be created as transactional. Operations on nontransactional queues cannot be part of a transaction and will cause an exception to be thrown if you attempt to use them in a transaction.

CAUTION *The asynchronous* `BeginReceive` *method does not support transactions and therefore cannot be used with transactional queues.*

Internal Message-Queuing Transactions

Internal transactions apply only to message-queuing operations. They may, however, involve multiple queues. Internal transactions must be explicitly coded. There is no equivalent to COM+ transactional attributes.

Create two new private transactional queues called **txq1** and **txq2**. Do this using Server Explorer or Computer Management. Just remember to check the box that makes the queue transactional.

Next create a new Console Application called **InternalTransactionProducer** to write messages onto txq1. Add a reference to System.Messaging.dll and then modify Class1.cs as shown in Listing 12-1.

Listing 12-1. Writing to a Transactional Message Queue Using Internal Transactions

```
using System;
using System.Messaging;

namespace InternalTransactionProducer
{
    class Class1
    {
        [STAThread]
        static void Main(string[] args)
        {
            MessageQueue txq1
                = new MessageQueue( @".\Private$\txq1" );

            for ( int i =1; i <= 20; i++ )
```

```
                    {
                        Message msgOut = new Message();
                        msgOut.Body = "Message " + i;
                        txq1.Send( msgOut,
                                    MessageQueueTransactionType.Single );
                    }
                }
            }
        }
```

As you cannot use the designer with a console application, you need to explicitly create the MessageQueue instance. Because the queue is transactional all operations must be performed as part of a transaction. As each Send is independent, you can use the shortcut of specifying MessageQueueTransactionType.Single to have a transaction created automatically.

Now create an application to copy the messages from txq1 to txq2. Transactions will ensure that in the event of a failure, no messages are lost. Create a new Console Application project called **InternalTransactionExample**. Again, add a reference to System.Messaging.dll, and then modify Class1.cs as shown in Listing 12-2.

Listing 12-2. Writing Messages from One Transacional Queue to Another
```
using System;
using System.Messaging;

namespace InternalTransactionExample
{
    class Class1
    {
        [STAThread]
        static void Main(string[] args)
        {
            MessageQueue txq1
                = new MessageQueue( @".\Private$\txq1" );
            MessageQueue txq2
                = new MessageQueue( @".\Private$\txq2" );

            while ( true )
            {
                using ( MessageQueueTransaction mqtx
                            = new MessageQueueTransaction() )
                {
```

```
                    try
                    {
                        mqtx.Begin();
                        Message msgIn = txq1.Receive( mqtx );
                        msgIn.Formatter = new XmlMessageFormatter(
                            new String[]
                                { "System.String, mscorlib", }
                        );
                        Message msgOut = new Message();
                        msgOut.Body = (string)msgIn.Body;
                        txq2.Send( msgOut, mqtx );
                        mqtx.Commit();
                    }
                    catch
                    {
                        mqtx.Abort();
                    }
                }
            }
        }
    }
}
```

In this case, the transaction needs to span operations on both queues, so you must create a MessageQueueTransaction instance. Construct a try . . . catch block to ensure the Begin, Commit, and Abort methods are called appropriately. The Receive and Send methods must explicitly reference the transaction.

The last step is to read the messages from the txq2 queue. Create a third Console Application called **InternalTransactionConsumer**. The code for this should read as shown in Listing 12-3.

Listing 12-3. Reading from a Transactional Message Queue

```
using System;
using System.Messaging;

namespace InternalTransactionConsumer
{
    class Class1
    {
        [STAThread]
        static void Main(string[] args)
        {
            MessageQueue txq2
                = new MessageQueue( @".\Private$\txq2" );
```

```
            while ( true )
            {
                Message msgIn = txq2.Receive(
                            MessageQueueTransactionType.Single );
                msgIn.Formatter = new XmlMessageFormatter(
                    new String[] { "System.String, mscorlib", }
                );
                System.Console.WriteLine( "Received: {0}",
                                    (string)msgIn.Body );
            }
        }
    }
}
```

Because the receive operation is independent of other operations, an automatic transaction can be specified using MessageQueueTransactionType.Single as in the producer.

When you run these applications in sequence, you can see all the messages displayed by the consumer. Now make the transactions prove they are working. Modify InternalTransactionExample so that 50 percent of the transactions are aborted. Add the following line after the MessageQueue creation:

```
Random r = new Random();
```

Then insert the following in place of the line that issues the commit:

```
if ( r.NextDouble() > 0.5 )
{
    System.Console.WriteLine( "Aborting message: {0}",
                            (string)msgIn.Body );
    mqtx.Abort();
}
else
{
    mqtx.Commit();
}
```

Now when you run the applications in sequence, despite the aborts, all the messages are still displayed by the consumer.

Distributed Transactions Involving Message Queuing

Message queuing can be part of a COM+ distributed transaction. Naturally, the code that processes the messages must be part of a ServicedComponent. To demonstrate this, create a new Class Library project called **ComPlusConsumerExample** that will take the messages from txq1 and write them to a database table.

First use Server Explorer to create a database called **Chapter12**. Then create a table to hold the information in the messages called **messdrop,** as shown in Figure 12-8.

dbo.messdrop ...NET.Chapter12)			
Column Name	Data Type	Length	Allow Nulls
id	uniqueidentifier	16	
msgtext	nvarchar	50	

Figure 12-8. The table to which the message values will be written

Now return to the project, rename Class1.cs to **ComPlusConsumer.cs,** and change its contents to Listing 12-4.

Listing 12-4. Using Message Queuing in a COM+ Distributed Transaction

```
using System;
using System.Data;
using System.Data.SqlClient;
using System.Data.SqlTypes;
using System.EnterpriseServices;
using System.Messaging;

namespace ComPlusConsumerExample
{
    [ Transaction ]
    public class ComPlusConsumer : ServicedComponent
    {
        public ComPlusConsumer()
        {
        }

        protected TimeSpan timeout = new TimeSpan( 0, 0 , 1 );

        protected string cstr = @"Server=.\VSdotNET;"
            + @"Database=Chapter12;"
            + @"Integrated Security=SSPI";
```

```
[ AutoComplete ]
public bool ProcessQueue()
{
    bool rc = true;
    string mess = null;

    using ( MessageQueue txq1
                = new MessageQueue( @".\Private$\txq1" ) )
    {
        try
        {
            using ( Message msgIn = txq1.Receive( timeout,
                    MessageQueueTransactionType.Automatic ) )
            {
                msgIn.Formatter
                    = new XmlMessageFormatter(
                            new String[]
                            { "System.String, mscorlib", }
                            );
                mess = (string)msgIn.Body;
            }

            using ( SqlConnection conn
                            = new SqlConnection( cstr ) )
            {
                conn.Open();

                SqlCommand cmd = new SqlCommand(
"insert into messdrop ( id, msgtext ) values ( @id, @msgtext )",
                                                conn );
                SqlParameter id
                    = cmd.Parameters.Add( "@id",
                            SqlDbType.UniqueIdentifier );
                SqlParameter msgtext
                    = cmd.Parameters.Add( "@msgtext",
                                SqlDbType.NVarChar, 50 );

                id.Value = Guid.NewGuid();
                msgtext.Value = (string)msgIn.Body;

                cmd.ExecuteNonQuery();
            }
        }
```

```
                catch( MessageQueueException mqe )
                {
                    // receive timed out - queue is empty
                    rc = false;
                }
            }

            return rc;
        }
    }
}
```

ProcessQueue attempts to read a message from the transactional queue txq1. To participate in a COM+ transaction, specify MessageQueueTransactionType.Automatic on the Receive method as shown. ProcessQueue also uses a form of Receive that allows a timeout to be specified. If a message is received, ProcessQueue writes it to the messdrop table in the database and returns true. If the Receive times out, it throws a MessageQueueException. ProcessQueue catches the exception, and it returns false.

Add references to System.EnterpriseServices and System.Messaging. Modify Assembly.cs to name the COM+ application **MQConsumer** and strong name the assembly.

To test the component, create a new Console Application project called **ComPlusConsumerDemo**. Add references to System.EnterpriseServices and the ComPlusConsumerExample project. Modify Class1.cs as shown in Listing 12-5. This invokes ProcessQueue repeatedly until it returns false to indicate the queue is empty.

Listing 12-5. Test Harness for the Transactional Queue Consumer

```
using System;
using ComPlusConsumerExample;

namespace ComPlusConsumerDemo
{
    class Class1
    {
        [STAThread]
        static void Main(string[] args)
        {
            using ( ComPlusConsumer cpc = new ComPlusConsumer() )
            {
                int i = 0;
```

```
                        for ( ; cpc.ProcessQueue(); i++ );
                        System.Console.WriteLine( "Processed {0} messages",
                                                        i );

                }
            }
        }
    }
```

First run `InternalTransactionProducer` to place some messages in the txq1 queue. Then run `ComPlusConsumerDemo` and the messages should disappear from the queue and appear in the messdrop table in the database.

To prove the transactions are working, modify `ComPlusConsumerExample` so that 50 percent of the transactions are aborted. Add the following variable to the `ComPlusConsumer` class:

```
Random r = new Random();
```

Then insert the following, prior to the line containing the return from `ProcessQueue`:

```
if ( rc && ( r.NextDouble() > 0.5 ) )
{
    throw new Exception( "randomly aborting: " + mess );
}
```

Now in `ComPlusConsumerDemo`, replace the for loop with the following:

```
bool b = true;
while ( b )
{
    try
    {
        b = cpc.ProcessQueue();
        if ( b )
        {
            i++;
        }
    }
    catch( Exception exc )
    {
        b = true;
        System.Console.WriteLine( exc.Message );
    }
}
```

Again, run `InternalTransactionProducer` to prime txq1. Now when you run `ComPlusConsumerDemo`, you will see some of the updates being aborted, but all the records will eventually be written to the database.

Identifying Queues

Up to this point, all queues have been identified by their path name such as .\Private$\SomeQueue. These are the human-friendly names normally used to identify a queue.

Format names are an alternative name that can be used to identify queues programmatically. You can see the format name of a queue in the Properties panel when you select the queue in Server Explorer. Computer Management does not display format names. If you want to allow disconnected operation, you must identify queues by their format name.

Use format names in your programs by specifying **FormatName:** followed by the format name in the `Path` property for a `MessageQueue` component. For example, you could specify the path to the example queue used earlier in this chapter as follows:

```
messageQueue1.Path
    = @"FormatName:DIRECT=OS:alien\private$\example";
```

Format names are also essential when using the new delivery mechanisms in MSMQ 3.0. A queue configured for HTTP access can be specified using a format name similar to the following:

```
messageQueue1.Path
    = @"FormatName:DIRECT=http://localhost/msmq/Private$/example";
```

A set of multicast queues can be sent to using the following format name:

```
messageQueue1.Path
    = @"FormatName:MULTICAST=230.230.230.230:8230";
```

You can specify a list of queues using a multielement format name by specifying a comma-separated list as follows:

```
messageQueue1.Path = @"FormatName: " +
                @"DIRECT=OS:alien\private$\ex1," +
                @"DIRECT=OS:alien\private$\ex2";
```

Comparing Message Queuing to JMS

Java Message Service (JMS) was designed to provide a vendor-independent MOM interface for Java programmers. It has API sets for both publish/subscribe and point-to-point variants of MOM.

The support for MOM in .NET is specific to Microsoft's Message Queuing product. There has been no discernable effort in the Windows world to provide a vendor-agnostic interface for MOM similar to those that exist for databases.

As Message Queuing is a point-to-point technology, it only makes sense to compare System.Messaging with the point-to-point API in JMS. System.Messaging makes no attempt to support different implementations, so it does not have the concept of factories such as JMS. Create the MessageQueue instance and you have the key object; there are no separate connection, session, sender, and receiver objects to worry about. You can send and receive messages directly from the MessageQueue object.

System.Messaging supports three message formats: XML, binary, and ActiveX. The examples in this chapter all use the default XML formatter for serialization. JMS supports several formats, including text that can be used for XML.

If you use another vendor's MOM product, you must use their proprietary API. Contact your vendor to see if they have a managed API or if you need to use COM interop.

Using the Message Queuing Installation Component

The MessageQueueInstaller component is an installation component that uses information from the MessageQueue component to ensure that the required queue exists when the assembly is installed. Follow these steps to use it:

1. Create a new Windows Application project called **MQInstallExample**. Add a Label, TextBox, and Button to the form, as shown in Figure 12-9.

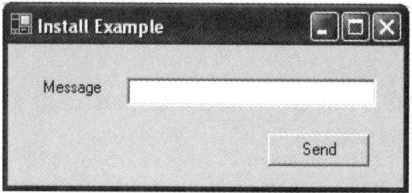

Figure 12-9. The simple form for the installation example

2. Create a new private queue called **InstallExample** on the local machine. Drag the queue to the form to create a configured MessageQueue component. Double-click the button to create a button click handler and modify it to send the contents of the TextBox as a message to the queue as follows:

```
private void button1_Click(object sender, System.EventArgs e)
{
    using ( System.Messaging.Message msg
                = new System.Messaging.Message( textBox1.Text ) )
    {
        messageQueue1.Send( msg );
    }
}
```

3. Return to the designer and select the messageQueue1 component. Click the Add Installer link displayed on the Properties panel. Build the project and verify that it adds messages to the queue.

4. Now create a setup project for MQInstallExample called **MQInstallExampleSetup** using the Setup Wizard. Configure the setup project to install the primary output of the MQInstallExample project and to use it as a custom action. Refer to Chapter 11, "Packaging and Installing Applications," for details if necessary.

Before installing the setup project delete the queue. Once the install is complete the queue will have been re-created. It will also be removed when the project is uninstalled.

Summary

Those of you who have used the JMS point-to-point interface should have little difficulty adapting to Message Queuing. Others should consider using this technology where it is appropriate. Because Message Queuing is included in all NT-based operating systems (excluding Windows XP Home Edition), there is no incremental software cost.

Using Active Directory Service Interface

ACTIVE DIRECTORY is Microsoft's directory service for domains. It replaces the older domain controller concept. As such, it combines both the directory and the control functionality. This chapter is not particularly concerned about Active Directory per se, but focuses more on the Active Directory Service Interface (ADSI) that allows you to manipulate data stored in Active Directory.

ADSI has similarities to Java Naming and Directory Service (JNDI) in that it defines a mechanism for accessing a directory and a provider model to permit different directory services to be used.

The .NET Framework has its managed interface to ADSI in the System.DirectoryServices namespace. The most important class in the namespace is DirectoryEntry.

Reading Directory Entries

The equivalent to HelloWorld for ADSI is to list the users in the system. To demonstrate ADSI, you do not need to be part of an Active Directory domain. You can access information on a workgroup computer using ADSI and the WinNT provider. In this example you will list the users on the local system.

A DirectoryEntry represents a node in the directory tree. Access the schema of the node through the SchemaClassName property. Access the properties collection of the node using the Properties property of DirectoryEntry. Follow these steps:

1. Create a new Windows Application project called **ListUsers**. Place a ListBox on the form and set its Dock property to **Fill**. Now add a DirectoryEntry component from the Components panel of the Toolbox and set its Path property. In my case I am not part of a domain, so I specified the workgroup MSHOME and machine alien, as shown in Figure 13-1. You will need to replace these elements with your workgroup or domain and your machine name, respectively.

Figure 13-1. Specifying the path for the local machine

2. To list the users, double-click the form to add a form load handler. Add a using statement for System.DirectoryServices and then change the handler as follows:

```
private void Form1_Load(object sender, System.EventArgs e)
{
    foreach( DirectoryEntry entry in directoryEntry1.Children )
    {
        if ( entry.SchemaClassName == "User" )
        {
            listBox1.Items.Add( entry.Name );
        }
    }
}
```

3. Iterate through the child nodes of the computer using the Children collection. As there are many different objects in this collection, examine the SchemaClassName property and discard any that are not users. Display the names of the users in the ListBox control. Run the program and you should see a list of users as in Figure 13-2.

4. The Name property on DirectoryEntry is a convenient shortcut. To display the full name of the user, use the following line, which demonstrates accessing a property from the directory node:

```
listBox1.Items.Add( entry.Properties[ "FullName" ].Value );
```

Figure 13-2. The list of users from the local machine

Adding and Modifying Directory Entries

ADSI is not restricted to reading data. An administrator can add users to the system using ADSI. Follow these steps:

1.   Create a new Windows Application project called **AddUser**. Create a form that looks like the one shown in Figure 13-3.

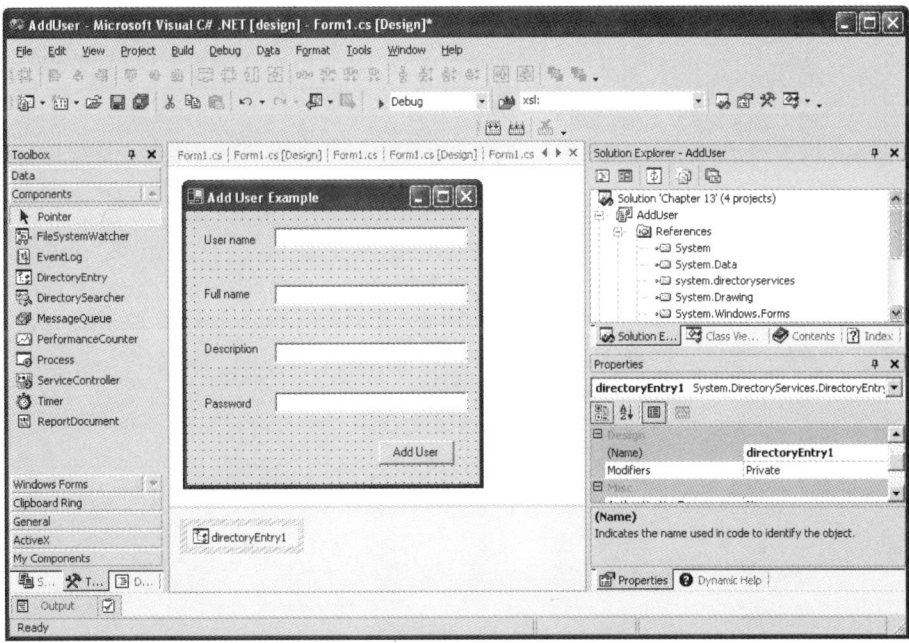

Figure 13-3. The form for adding users

2. To keep the password textbox from displaying the password, set its `PasswordChar` property as shown in Figure 13-4.

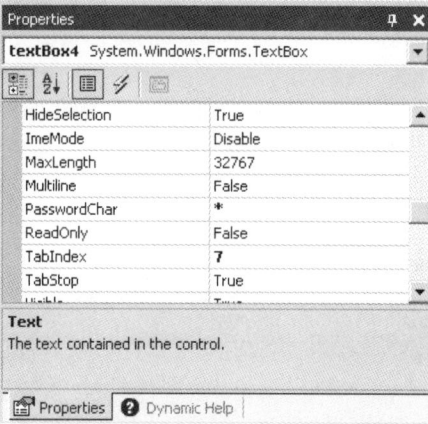

Figure 13-4. Setting the `PasswordChar` property to hide the password

3. Add two `DirectoryEntry` components from the Components panel of the Toolbox. Modify the `Path` property of the first one to your local machine. In my case this is **WinNT://MSHOME/alien**. Modify the second to the `Path` for a group to which you want the users added. I chose **WinNT://MSHOME/alien/Users**.

4. Now, double-click the Add User button to create a button click handler. Add a using statement for `System.DirectoryServices` and then modify the button click handler as shown in Listing 13-1.

Listing 13-1. Adding a New User to the System Using ADSI

```
private void button1_Click(object sender, System.EventArgs e)
{
    try
    {
    DirectoryEntry newUser
        = directoryEntry1.Children.Add( textBox1.Text,
                                        "User" );
    newUser.Properties[ "FullName" ].Add( textBox2.Text );
    newUser.Properties[ "Description" ].Add( textBox3.Text );
    newUser.Invoke( "SetPassword",
                    new object[] { textBox4.Text, } );
    newUser.Properties[ "PasswordExpired" ].Add( 1 );
    newUser.CommitChanges();
```

```
                directoryEntry2.Invoke( "Add",
                                    new Object[] { newUser.Path, } );
                directoryEntry2.CommitChanges();
                MessageBox.Show( this, textBox1.Text + " added" );
        }
        catch( Exception exc )
        {
                MessageBox.Show( this, exc.ToString() );
        }
    }
}
```

5. Start the handler by adding a new child entry to the machine node. Specify a schema of **User** and use the name entered on the form. Set the FullName and Description properties using the appropriate values from the form. Then invoke a method on the User object called **SetPassword**, passing the desired password from the form. Following the normal practice, set the PasswordExpired property so that the user must change their password. To create the user, the changes must be committed by calling CommitChanges.

6. Once you have created the user, you can add it to the group specified in the second DirectoryEntry added to the form. Do this by invoking the Add method of the group object, passing the path to the user object. Again call CommitChanges and the process is complete.

7. Run the example and add a new user as shown in Figure 13-5. Verify the user was added correctly using the Control Panel's Computer Management tool.

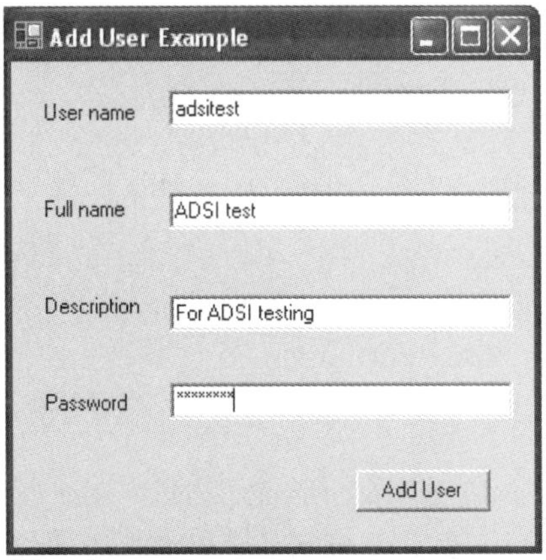

Figure 13-5. The Add User application in action

Using Providers

You do not have to install ADSI providers as separate packages the way you do with some JNDI providers. You install them either as part of the operating system or by the product installation. You identify the provider you want to use when you enter the Path property of the DirectoryEntry. The part of the path preceding the colon identifies the provider following the familiar URL convention.

WinNT

You can use the WinNT provider to access information in Active Directory or on Windows workgroup systems. This is the provider used in the preceding examples.

LDAP

You can access Active Directory using the ADSI LDAP provider in addition to the WinNT provider. If you are familiar with Lightweight Directory Access Protocol (LDAP) from using JNDI, this may be a preferable choice. You cannot use LDAP to access system information in a workgroup. You can also use the LDAP provider to access information on some LDAP servers other than Active Directory.

The LDAP provider supports using LDAP search expressions to retrieve nodes using the DirectorySearcher class.

NDS *and* NWCOMPAT

There are two Netware providers. NDS supports Netware Directory Services, and NWCOMPAT supports older Netware 3 systems. This is a similar distinction to that seen in JNDI Netware providers.

IIS

The most notable nondirectory provider is IIS. Internet Information Services (IIS) exposes its configuration information, known as the *metabase*, through ADSI.

To demonstrate using the IIS provider, follow these steps:

1. Create a new Windows Application project called **ListVirtualRoots**. Follow the same pattern as for listing users, but set the Path of the DirectoryEntry instance to **IIS://localhost/W3SVC/1/ROOT**, which specifies the root object of the default Web site on your local machine.

2. Now double-click the form to create a form load handler. Add the using statement for System.DirectoryServices as before. This time in the form load handler, iterate through the children looking for instances of the schema class IIsWebVirtualDir. Instead of simply displaying the name, display the file system path associated with the virtual root:

```
private void Form1_Load(object sender, System.EventArgs e)
{
    foreach( DirectoryEntry entry in directoryEntry1.Children )
    {
        if ( entry.SchemaClassName == "IIsWebVirtualDir" )
        {
            listBox1.Items.Add( entry.Properties[ "Path" ].Value );
        }
    }
}
```

You could create a virtual root, or some other IIS object, using System.DirectoryServices in a similar fashion to creating a user.

Comparing ADSI to JNDI

ADSI bears a strong resemblance to Java Naming and Directory Interface (JNDI). However, the service providers focus on the directory services space. There are no equivalents to JNDI's CORBA naming, RMI registry, or DNS providers in ADSI. There is nothing like the JNDI file system provider. For a system administrator, the ADSI IIS provider facilitates Web site management.

The .NET DirectoryEntry has similarities to the JNDI DirContext. Both provide a façade for accessing arbitrary objects in the directory tree. DirectoryEntry exploits .NET properties to simplify the interface, particularly the Children and Properties collections. One key difference is that updates in System.DirectoryServices must be explicitly committed by calling CommitChanges.

Summary

ADSI is a powerful administrative tool and not just for Active Directory. System.DirectoryServices makes it available to .NET developers. Java developers who have used JNDI should find many of the concepts familiar.

CHAPTER 14

Developing Windows Services

Windows Services, also commonly known as NT Services, are processes that run in the background without a user interface. Examples of these are database servers, the message queuing system, Internet Information Services (IIS), and many network servers. If you are more familiar with Unix than Windows, these are the equivalents of daemon processes.

Prior to .NET, writing services was almost exclusively the domain of C++ programmers and considered somewhat of a black art. That has been changed by .NET. The System.ServiceProcess namespace provides classes that facilitate service development, and Visual Studio .NET has a project template for creating Windows Services.

Creating a Windows Service

Writing a service is not as simple as creating an application that has no user interface (UI) and never writes to the console. Windows Services must follow a specific programming model. To create one, follow these steps:

1. Create a new Windows Service project called **FirstWindowsServiceExample**. You will see your service component in the designer as a blank canvas. Change the ServiceName property to **MyFirstService**. Now switch to code view. The important methods are OnStart and OnStop.

2. OnStart is called when your service is started, and it should be used to initiate whatever processing your service performs. It cannot be used to perform the processing because if it does not return in approximately 30 seconds, the Service Control Manager (SCM) will consider that your service has failed.

3. OnStop is called when your service is stopped. It should terminate the processing initiated by the OnStart method.

4. For the purpose of this example, have these methods write a message to the event log as follows:

```
protected override void OnStart(string[] args)
{
    EventLog.WriteEntry( "Hello from MyFirstService" );
}

protected override void OnStop()
{
    EventLog.WriteEntry( "Goodbye from MyFirstService" );
}
```

5. Now build the application.

6. Testing your service is more complicated than with other application types. The service must run under the SCM and as a result cannot be launched by the debugger. You must install your service before you can test it. Switch to the view of your service in the designer. In the Properties panel you will see an Add Installer link, as shown in Figure 14-1.

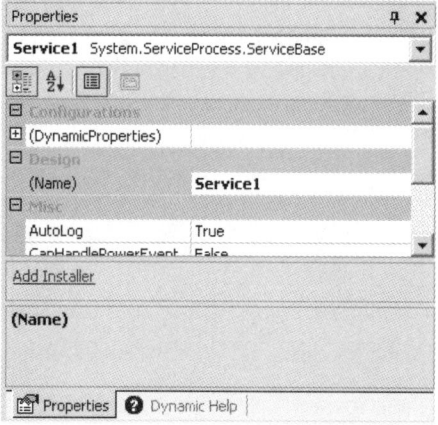

Figure 14-1. The Properties panel for the service showing the Add Installer link

7. Click this link to add two installation components, a `ServiceInstaller` and a `ServiceProcessInstaller`. The former installs the service and the latter the service process. It is possible to have multiple services share a single process, hence the separation.

8. You could create a setup project to install your service for testing, but it is easier to use the `installutil` tool during development. Open the Visual Studio .NET command prompt and change the directory to the output directory of the service project. Use `installutil` as follows:

```
installutil FirstWindowsServiceExample.exe
```

9. You will be prompted to enter the user id and password for the user the service will impersonate. This dialog box is shown Figure 14-2.

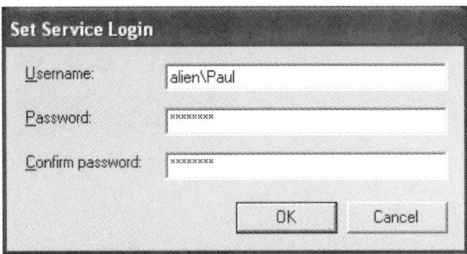

Figure 14-2. User and password prompt during service install

CAUTION   *The user must be qualified with the machine or domain name as shown in Figure 14-2, or the install will fail.*

10. Once the service is installed, you can open the Control Panel's Computer Management tool to start it. Open the Services and Applications node and then the Services node. Scroll the list of services until you find MyFirstService, as shown in Figure 14-3.

11. Right-click the service and select Properties to open the Properties dialog box, as shown in Figure 14-4. Click the Start button to start the service, wait 30 seconds, and then click Stop.

12. The only evidence that your service is actually running are the entries it makes in the event log. In Computer Management, expand the Event Viewer node and then the Application node. You will see four entries from MyFirstService, as shown in Figure 14-5.

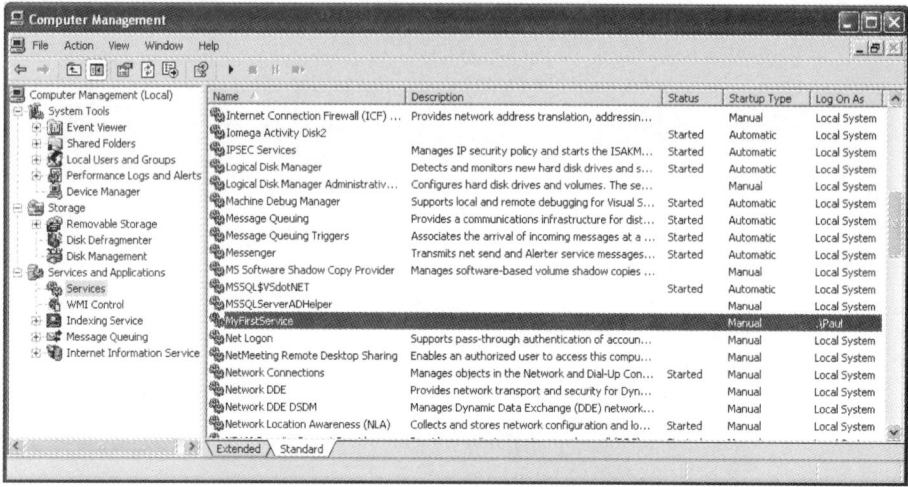

Figure 14-3. MyFirstService in the Computer Management tool

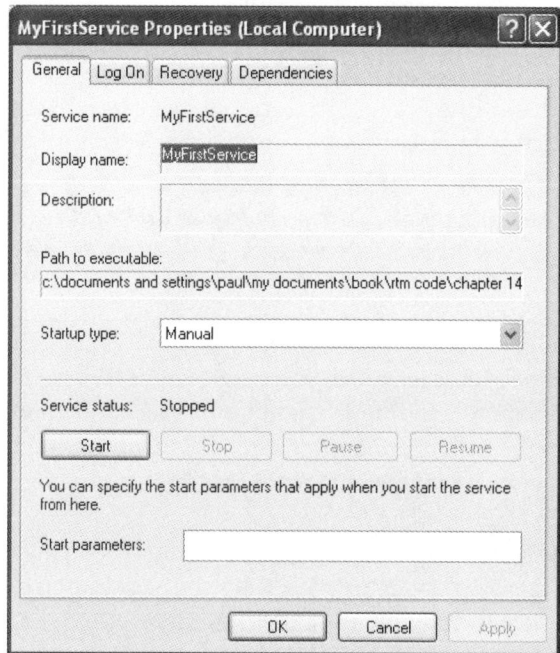

Figure 14-4. The Properties dialog box for MyFirstService

13. Double-click the entries to view them. Two of the entries are the hello and goodbye messages you coded into OnStart and OnStop. The other two are messages added automatically by ServiceBase, one each for the start and stop events. You can also look at the events in Server Explorer.

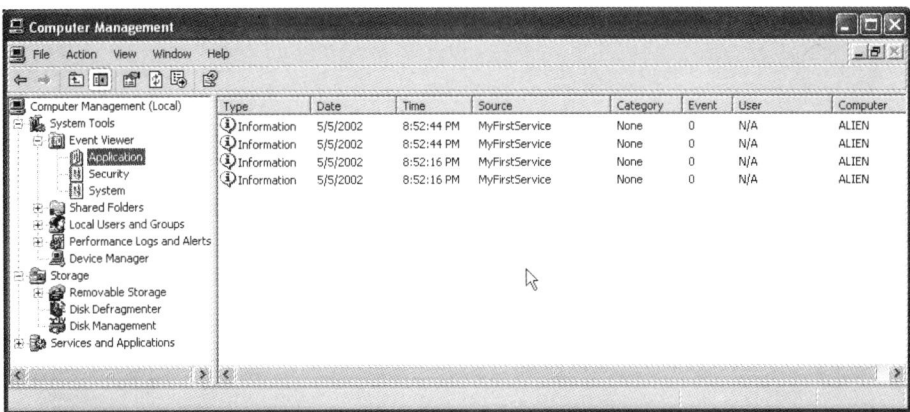

Figure 14-5. Entries in the event log from MyFirstService

As you can see in Figure 14-6, the Server Explorer groups messages by their source. It also displays the first few words of the message.

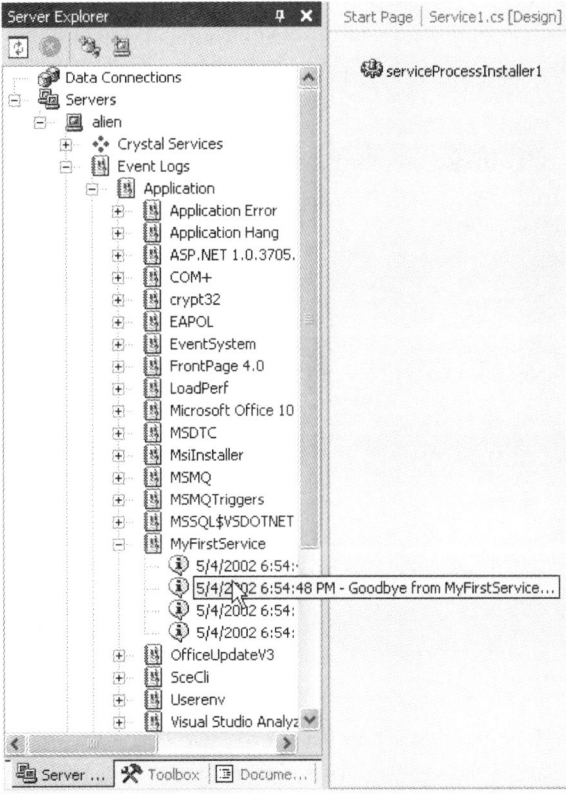

Figure 14-6. Events in Server Explorer

14. When you have finished testing your service, you can remove it by invoking installutil as follows, but do not do that just yet:

```
installutil /u FirstWindowsServiceExample.exe
```

Debugging

To debug your service you need to start your service and then attach your debugger. This means you are going to have difficulty debugging your OnStart method. Some people insert a temporary sleep into their OnStart to buy time to attach the debugger. An added complication is that your OnStart must return within 30 seconds or the SCM decides there is a problem and terminates your service.

Attaching to the Service

To attach to the service, follow these steps:

1. Start your service from Computer Management or the Server Explorer. In Visual Studio .NET, select Debug ➢ Processes . . . , as shown in Figure 14-7.

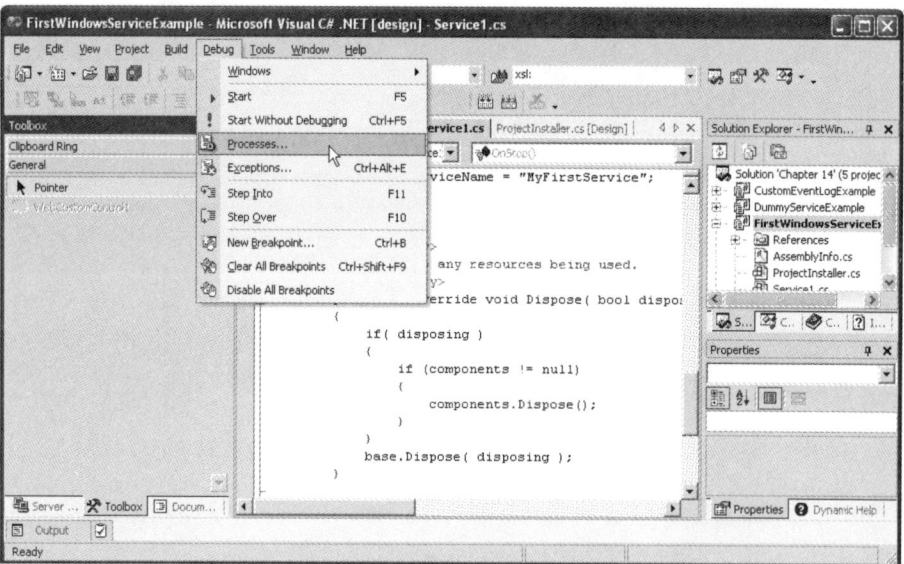

Figure 14-7. Selecting to debug an external process

2. Scroll the list to find the service, as shown in Figure 14-8.

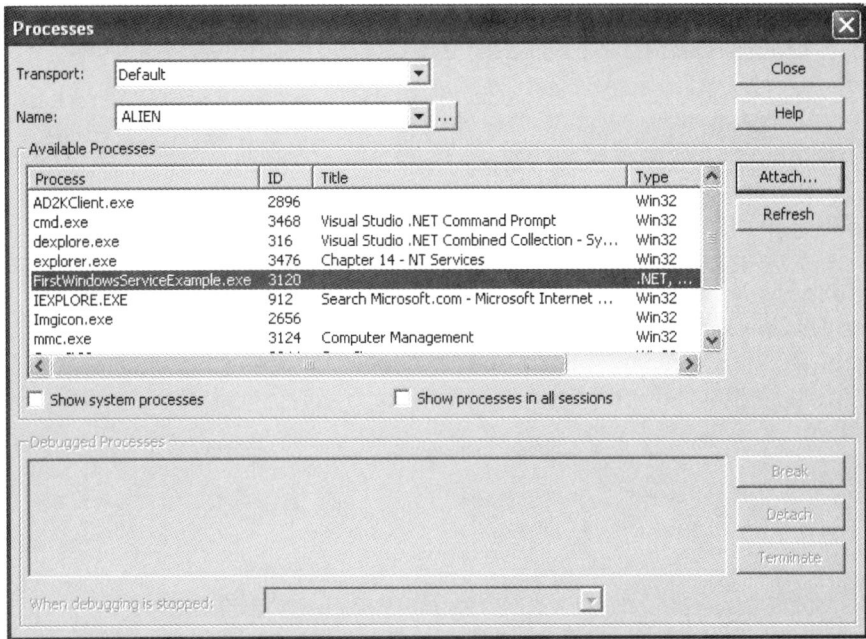

Figure 14-8. Selecting the service process to attach the debugger

3.   Click Attach and you will be prompted to select the type of program you want to debug, as shown in Figure 14-9.

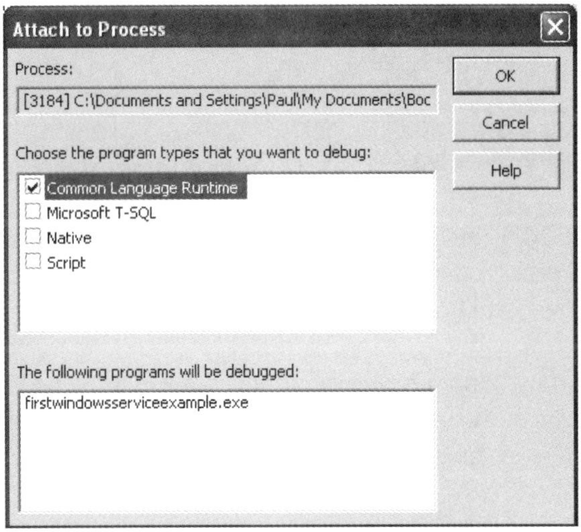

Figure 14-9. Indicating the type of code you want to debug

4.   Ensure that Common Language Runtime is checked as shown and click OK.

5. Once the process is attached, the Processes dialog box will change, as shown in Figure 14-10. Then press Break to interrupt the process.

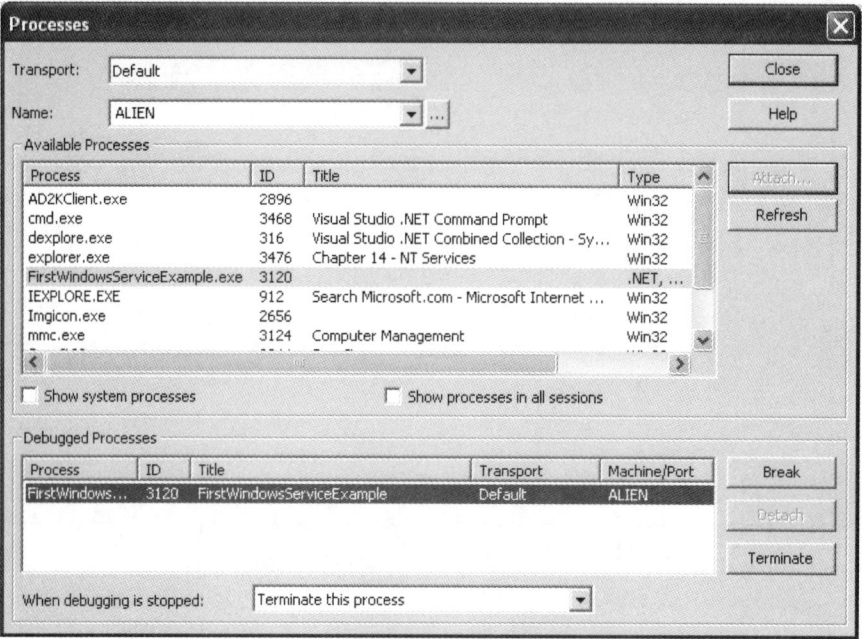

Figure 14-10. Debugger attached to the service process

6. Now set breakpoints and debug as normal. In this case, you can only debug the OnStop method.

Using a Dummy Service to Facilitate Debugging

The Visual Studio .NET documentation suggests you temporarily add a second service to your process to facilitate debugging your OnStart method, but unfortunately it does not explain how this is done. Follow these steps:

1. Create a new Windows Service project called **DummyServiceExample**. Change the name of the service from Service1 to **MyRealService**. Add a single line to the OnStart method as follows:

```
protected override void OnStart(string[] args)
{
    int x = 1;
}
```

2. Add a second service to the project by right-clicking the project and selecting Add ➤ Add New Item . . . ➤ Windows Service. Name the new service **DebugDummy**. Modify the line in `Main` that initializes `ServicesToRun` to read as follows:

```
ServicesToRun = new System.ServiceProcess.ServiceBase[] {
        new Service1(),
        new DebugDummy()
    };
```

3. Now add installation components for both services by clicking the Add Installer links for each one in turn. This results in a single `ServiceProcessInstaller` instance and two `ServiceInstaller` instances. Build the project.

4. Install the project using `installutil`. This will install both services. You can now start the DebugDummy service, which creates the service process. Now attach to the process prior to starting MyRealService and set breakpoints in its `OnStart` method. When you start MyRealService you can debug the `OnStart` method. However, you are still subject to the 30-second limit for processing a command.

Using SCM Command Handlers

The Windows Software Development Kit (SDK) documentation indicates these command handlers must return in about 30 seconds with the exception of `OnShutdown`, which has approximately 20 seconds to complete.

Starting and Stopping

You have already written `OnStart` and `OnStop` methods in the preceding example. You should use `OnStart` to initiate the processing the service performs.

There are two common models for services. If the service is to perform ongoing processing, start a thread in `OnStart` to perform the work. In `OnStop`, signal the thread to exit and join it before returning. The other model is to register event handlers in `OnStart` that perform the work asynchronously. An example of this is processing a non-transactional message queue.

`OnStart` receives a parameter list similar to a console program. The user can specify parameters in the Properties dialog box of Computer Management if required. This can be useful to enable diagnostic behavior in production settings.

If you are familiar with Windows Services, you are probably aware that it is possible to respond to a stop command indicating that the service is stopping but needs more time to complete the process. Unfortunately, the `System.ServiceProcess` classes do not support this action. If this behavior is essential, create your own service wrapper classes using Platform Invoke.

Pausing and Continuing

Pause and continue exist so that you can permit a service process to be suspended without releasing all of its resources. To support this, set your service's `CanPauseAndContinue` property to `true` and implement the `OnPause` and `OnContinue` methods. `OnPause` should suspend any processing being performed by your service and `OnContinue` should restore normal operation.

Shutting Down

If your service must clean up resources when the system is shutting down, set its `CanShutdown` property to `true` and implement `OnShutdown`. You have approximately 20 seconds to complete any processing in `OnShutdown` before the system proceeds to shut down anyway.

Powering Events

Some services need to react to power management events, particularly suspend and resume events. You can set `CanHandlePowerEvent` to `true` and implement `OnPowerEvent` if you need such behavior. `OnPowerEvent` receives a parameter indicating the actual power event to allow you to handle only the pertinent events.

Customizing Commands

`OnCustomCommand` allows your service to respond to commands beyond those issued by the SCM. These can be issued by an instance of `ServiceController`, which allows you to control a service programmatically. `OnCustomCommand` accepts an integer between 128 and 256 to represent the custom command.

Writing to Event Logs

Windows Services cannot display a user interface or write to a console. The only way to record any messages for human consumption is by writing to the event log.

By default your service contains an EventLog property that facilitates writing to the Application event log. It also records each SCM command (start, stop, pause, and so on) that is handled by your service. This behavior is controlled by the AutoLog property of the service, which by default is set to true. You might choose to record to a different log or even create your own log. In either case, you need to set AutoLog to false.

Creating Custom Event Logs

To create a custom event log, follow these steps:

1. Create a new Windows Service application called **CustomEventLogExample**. Change the service component's ServiceName property to **CustomEventService**. Now change the AutoLog property to **false** and drag over an EventLog component from the Toolbox. Specify the Source property on the EventLog component as **CustomEventService2** and the Log property as **MyCustomLog**.

 **CAUTION** *Do not use* CustomEventService *as the source name. The name of the service is registered as a source for the Application log when the service is installed.*

2. Modify the OnStart and OnStop methods to make entries in the event log as follows:

```
protected override void OnStart(string[] args)
{
    eventLog1.WriteEntry( "Hello",
                    EventLogEntryType.Information );
}

protected override void OnStop()
{
    eventLog1.WriteEntry( "Goodbye",
                    EventLogEntryType.Warning );
}
```

3. The second parameter specifies the type of event being raised. If this is not specified, the event is treated as an informational event. Stopping

the service might be undesirable under normal conditions, so specify that the event type is a warning.

4. Add installation components for the service, and install it using `installutil`. When you start the service and the "Hello" event is written, the new event log is created. You will need to restart the Computer Management tool to see the log, as the list of logs cannot be refreshed. The Server Explorer does not have this limitation.

Unfortunately, you cannot replace the `EventLog` instance in the service's `EventLog` property, which would allow you to change the log location and still get the benefit of the automatic command logging.

Using the `EventLogInstaller` Installation Component

Even though logs and sources are implicitly created when they are used, they do not get cleaned up. The `EventLogInstaller` component can be used to install and uninstall event sources with your application.

Select your `EventLog` component in the designer and click the Add Installer link to create an installation component configured from your `EventLog` component. The source will be added by `installutil` when you install your service. If you create a setup project, add the `EventLogInstaller` as a custom action.

Using Performance Counters

Performance counters provide a mechanism for monitoring your applications in production. They are particularly useful for Windows Services because you have no user interface to help judge if the application is behaving correctly. Monitor performance counters using the System Monitor tool. This is more commonly known as *perfmon*.

In Chapter 11, "Packaging and Installing Applications," you created a performance counter to demonstrate installation components. This time the focus will be on the performance counter itself:

1. Open the Server Explorer and right-click the Performance Counters node. Select Create New Category . . . and enter **MyPerfCounters** for the category name. Use the New button to create two counters named **Absolute** and **ServiceRate** of types NumberOfItems32 and RateOfCountsPerSecond32, respectively.

2. Create a new Windows Service project called **PerfCounterExample**. Drag the counters you just created onto the designer from the Server Explorer. This will create two configured `PerformanceCounter` components. By default these are created with a `ReadOnly` property set to `true`. You need to update these counters, so change the `ReadOnly` property of both components to **false**.

3. Now you need to simulate some process to demonstrate the counters in action. Replace the default `OnStart` and `OnStop` methods with the code in Listing 14-1.

Listing 14-1. Updating Performance Counters in a Windows Service

```
protected Thread m_worker = null;
protected int m_timeToStop = 0;
protected Random m_rand = new Random();

protected override void OnStart(string[] args)
{
    m_worker = new Thread( new ThreadStart( this.DoWork ) );
    m_worker.Start();
}

protected override void OnStop()
{
    Interlocked.Increment( ref m_timeToStop );
    m_worker.Join();
}

protected void DoWork()
{
    while ( m_timeToStop == 0 )
    {
        int sleepTime = (int)(m_rand.NextDouble() * 100.0);
        Thread.Sleep( sleepTime );
        performanceCounter1.Increment();
        performanceCounter2.Increment();
    }
}
```

4. This creates a new thread in `OnStart` that sleeps for a random time before updating the counters. Add installation components and use `installutil` to install the service as described earlier. Then start the service using Computer Management or the Server Explorer.

5. Launch `perfmon` from Start ➤ Control Panel ➤ Performance and Maintenance ➤ Administrative Tools ➤ Performance. When `perfmon` starts it will load a default set of counters and should look like Figure 14-11.

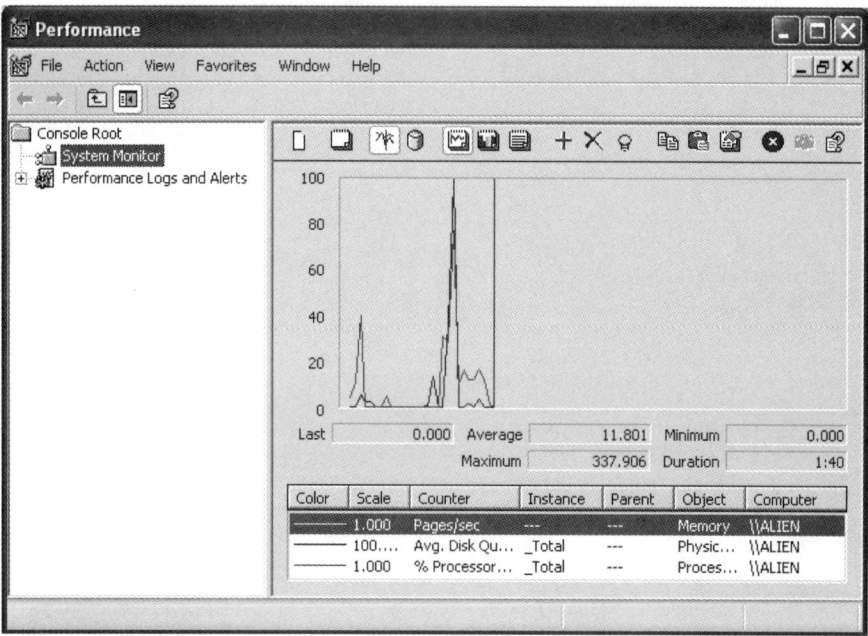

Figure 14-11. The System Monitor or `perfmon` *tool*

6. Remove the counters from the display by clicking the X button until there are no more counters displayed. Then click the plus (+) button to add your counters. When the Add Counters dialog box appears, select the MyPerfCounters category from the Performance Object combo box and then select the All Counters radio button, as shown in Figure 14-12.

7. Press Add and then Close. Your counters are now displayed in perfmon. Because the "absolute" counter continuously increases, you need to change its scale factor to make the display useful. Press the Properties button, as shown in Figure 14-13.

8. Select the Data tab and then the absolute counter. Modify the Scale combo box to 0.001 so that the chart displays thousands of your mythical operations performed. Your `perfmon` display will now look similar to Figure 14-14, which shows that your service is running with a through-put of around 18 operations per second.

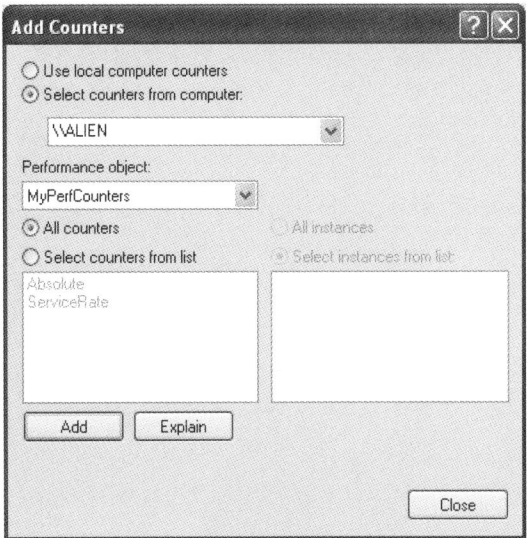

Figure 14-12. Adding your custom counters to the display in perfmon

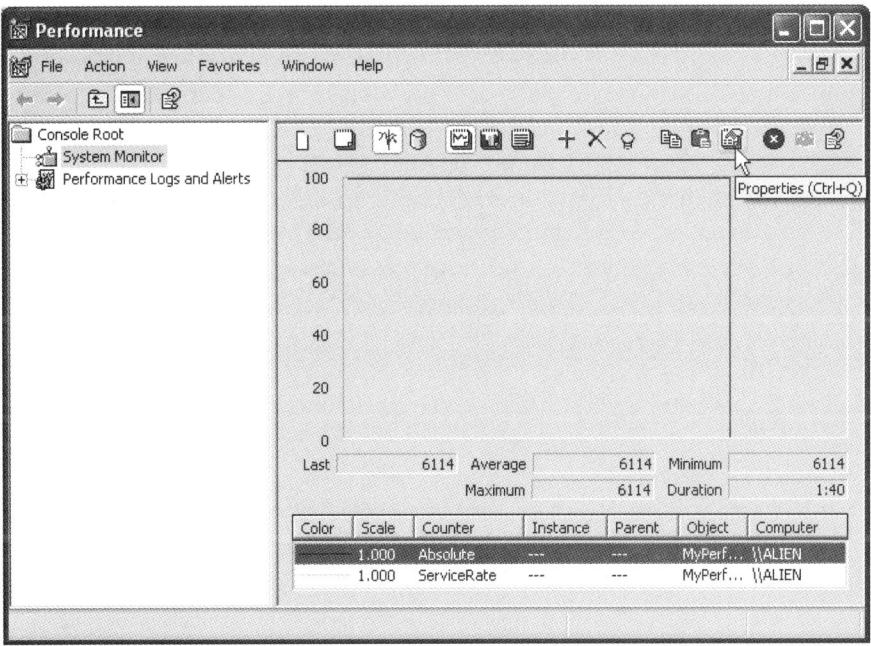

Figure 14-13. The Properties button in perfmon*'s toolbar*

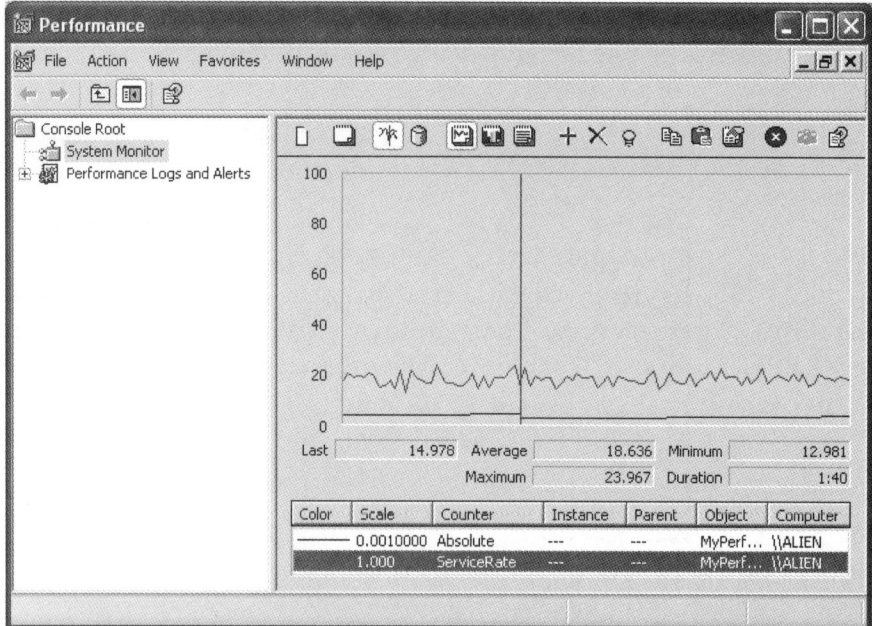

Figure 14-14. Your custom counters displayed by perfmon

You can start and stop your service to see what happens to the display when your service has problems.

When you are ready to distribute your service, you can add installation components to ensure that the appropriate counters are created when your application is installed. Select the PerformanceCounter instance in the designer and click the Add Installer link on the Properties panel to create a configured PerformanceCounterInstaller in the project.

Creating Setup Projects for Windows Services

You have already seen how to add the installation components for Windows Services to your application. Ensure they are invoked as custom actions when you create a setup project. Before you create a setup project, you probably want to review some of the settings on your service.

Startup Mode

Up to this point you have been explicitly starting and stopping your services. When you place them into production, you often want the service to start when the machine boots, as most services do. Use the ServiceInstaller component to control this. The StartType property defaults to Manual. Change the value to Automatic to make the service start up when the machine boots.

Account

As you installed each service, you were prompted to enter a user ID and password for the service to use when it ran. You are unlikely to want this in production. The ServiceProcessorController component allows you to choose one of four values for its Account property to control this. The default of User is what you have used so far. The other options of LocalSystem, LocalService, and NetworkService are more typical for production use. They differ in the level of privilege they provide on the local system and how they authenticate over the network.

LocalSystem is the most restrictive of these, acting as a nonprivileged user locally and an anonymous user to the network. Uninstall FirstWindowsServiceExample, modify it to use LocalSystem, and then install it again. This time you are not prompted to enter a user ID and password. This level of privilege is quite sufficient to write event log messages.

Summary

Although Windows Services perform the same function as Unix daemons, they require quite a different programming model. Creating Windows Services using .NET is easier than with previous technologies, and Visual Studio .NET facilitates many aspects of the process. Debugging is not as straightforward as with other applications but is not difficult once you have tried it a few times. Windows Services are an important facet of developing enterprise applications on Windows.

CHAPTER 15

Getting Outside the Box

Aｌｔｈｏｕｇｈ ｔｈｅ ｃｌａｓｓ ｌｉｂｒａｒｙ provided by the .NET Framework is quite extensive, it cannot cover all possibilities. At some point you will need to use functions from an unmanaged library. In Java, you use Java Native Interface (JNI) to interoperate with code outside the Java Virtual Machine (JVM). In .NET, use a facility called *Platform Invoke* (PInvoke). Sometimes the problem is reversed. To incorporate the ability to run managed code into a server process, you need to be able to host the Common Language Runtime (CLR).

 **CAUTION**   *Although the rest of the book strives to avoid requiring any knowledge of C or C++, the problems addressed in this chapter inherently require some familiarity with one of these languages.*

Using Platform Invoke

Platform Invoke, or *PInvoke*, is the feature of the .NET Framework that enables you to call functions in unmanaged DLLs without the need to write unmanaged code, such as you would when using JNI.

I have not been able to locate a managed version of the Win32 LockWorkStation function. If you need to lock the user's workstation programmatically, call this function through PInvoke. Follow these steps:

1. Create a new Windows Application project called **LockWorkStationExample**. Place a single Button on the form and change its Text property to **Lock**. Double-click the Button to add a button click handler, which should read as follows:

    ```
    private void button1_Click(object sender, System.EventArgs e)
    {
        LockWorkStation();
    }
    ```

2. Now you need to have the call to `LockWorkStation` invoke the Win32 API version. Add a `using` statement for `System.Runtime.InteropServices` and then add the following declaration before the button click handler:

```
[ DllImport( "user32.dll" ) ]
private static extern bool LockWorkStation();
```

This specifies that the call to `LockWorkStation` is actually a call to the unmanaged function of the same name, which can be found in user32.dll.

3. Now build and run the application. There is no need to use a tool such as javah to generate a C++ skeleton from the C# file nor is there a need to write any unmanaged code to marshal parameters between C# objects and C/C++ types.

Creating the Managed Signature

Typically, you only have a C/C++ signature for the method to be called, and you need to determine how to declare it in your C# class.

The first part is the `DllImport` attribute. You must always specify the DLL that contains the function and in many cases that is sufficient. For Win32 API, DLL is normally specified in the Platform Software Development Kit (SDK) documentation. To use a different name for the function, specify the unmanaged name using the `EntryPoint` property. Other properties of `DllImport` control how character sets are marshaled between managed and unmanaged code and the calling convention used.

Marshalling is the process of moving parameter data between two environments—in this case, managed and unmanaged code. For the simple types, this is often trivial. For strings there are a lot of possibilities. In the unmanaged world there are many representations for strings. There is the C-style null terminated string and then the `BSTR` used by COM and Visual Basic that has a length at the start followed by the data. Another dimension is if the string should remain as Unicode or be converted to an 8-bit character set. Obviously things get even more interesting when structures are involved. These conversions may need to happen when the function is called and again when it returns.

The rules for marshalling types between managed and unmanaged code affect how you translate the unmanaged function signature into a managed method signature. If the parameters and return type have direct equivalents in C#, it is straightforward to create the remainder of the signature. Sometimes the true type of a parameter can require some research, as the C/C++ preprocessor is often used to define aliases to defend against portability issues. In the preceding example, the C/C++ signature of `LockWorkStation` is this:

```
BOOL LockWorkStation(VOID);
```

It is reasonable to expect that PInvoke can map the C/C++ `BOOL` to a C# `bool`, but types such as `HRESULT`, `HDC`, and `HLOCAL` are less intuitive. PInvoke methods always start with `static extern`, so the preceding becomes this:

```
private static extern bool LockWorkStation();
```

You can find a table of the default mappings for the simple C/C++ types and many of the aliases such as `BOOL` and `LPWSTR` in the .NET Framework SDK documentation.

Understanding Parameter Marshalling

Sometimes the default marshalling rules for the simple types do not match what you need. Fortunately, PInvoke can usually determine the correct mapping without your assistance. To explicitly control how a parameter is marshaled, use the `MarshallAs` attribute. `MarshallAs` takes an `UnmanagedType` value to specify how the parameter should be marshaled for unmanaged code.

Strings provide an example of how this can be useful. PInvoke can marshal strings in a variety of formats. If you want a C-style null terminated Unicode string, specify `[ MarshallAs( UnmanagedType.LPWStr ) ]` on the parameter.

When PInvoke has to copy a parameter in the process of marshalling it, you may need to specify which directions marshalling should occur. Use the `In` and `Out` attributes on the parameter to achieve this.

NOTE *Do not confuse the* `Out` *attribute with the* `out` *modifier.*

Use `StringBuilder` in place of `string` when providing a character buffer that will be modified by the unmanaged function. Set the initial size of the `StringBuilder` to the size of the buffer you need to provide. Listing 15-1 demonstrates how to do this.

Listing 15-1. Using a `StringBuilder` *Object to Represent an Unmanaged Character Buffer*

```csharp
using System;
using System.Runtime.InteropServices;
using System.Text;

namespace GetComputerNameExample
{
    class Class1
    {

        [ DllImport( "kernel32.dll" ) ]
        static extern bool GetComputerName(
            StringBuilder name,
            ref ulong size );

        [STAThread]
        static void Main(string[] args)
        {
            ulong size = 256;
            StringBuilder name = new StringBuilder( (int)size );
            bool success = GetComputerName( name, ref size );
            System.Console.WriteLine( name.ToString() );
        }
    }
}
```

Mapping Structures

To interoperate with unmanaged code you often need to pass structures as parameters. Creating equivalent structures in managed code is not just a matter of declaring the same elements with equivalent types. Unknown to you, the run-time may reorder the elements of a structure for efficiency. When using PInvoke, use attributes to specify that the structure be arranged exactly as required.

Use the `StructLayout` attribute specifying a member of `LayoutKind` enumeration to define how the arrangement of the structure is determined. The default is `Automatic`, which should never be used when interacting with unmanaged code. The natural choice is `Sequential`, which specifies that you want the fields in the order you define them. This is a good choice when the desired structure follows the natural alignment of the element types.

For precise control over the structure, use the Explicit option and precede each field with a FieldOffset attribute. FieldOffset specifies where the field starts, in terms of its byte offset from the beginning of the structure.

Listing 15-2 retrieves information about a monitor attached to the system. You see a demonstration of using Explicit and Sequential structures. You can also see how you can use Marshal.SizeOf to obtain the size of a structure when needed.

Listing 15-2. Marshalling Structures

```
using System;
using System.Runtime.InteropServices;

namespace GetMonitorInfoExample
{
    [ StructLayout( LayoutKind.Explicit ) ]
    struct Point
    {
        [ FieldOffset( 0 ) ]
        public int x;
        [ FieldOffset( 4 ) ]
        public int y;
    }

    [ StructLayout( LayoutKind.Sequential ) ]
    struct Rect
    {
        public int left;
        public int top;
        public int right;
        public int bottom;
    }

    [ StructLayout( LayoutKind.Sequential ) ]
    struct MonitorInfo
    {
        public uint size;
        public Rect monitor;
        public Rect work;
        public uint flags;
    }

    class Class1
    {
```

```
[ DllImport( "user32.dll" ) ]
static extern IntPtr MonitorFromPoint( Point p,
    ulong flags );
[ DllImport( "user32.dll" ) ]
static extern bool GetMonitorInfo( IntPtr hmon,
    ref MonitorInfo mi );

[STAThread]
static void Main(string[] args)
{
    Point p = new Point();
    p.x = 1;
    p.y = 1;
    IntPtr hmon = MonitorFromPoint( p, 1 );

    MonitorInfo mi = new MonitorInfo();
    mi.size = (uint)Marshal.SizeOf( mi );
    bool success = GetMonitorInfo( hmon, ref mi );

    // do something with the information
}
}
}
```

Understanding Callback Functions

Sometimes when you call an unmanaged API you provide a pointer to a function that will be used as a callback. Callbacks are usually invoked when an event occurs or data becomes available. They are also used when enumerating collections. PInvoke enables you to specify a delegate for callback parameters. You must ensure that the delegate is not garbage collected before the unmanaged code has finished using it.

Listing 15-3 builds on the example from Listing 15-2. The Win32 EnumDisplayMonitors call takes a callback, which is called once for each monitor attached to the system. The MonitorEnumDelegate passes the callback method through PInvoke.

Listing 15-3. Using a Delegate in Place of an Unmanaged Callback Function
```
using System;
using System.Runtime.InteropServices;
```

```
namespace EnumDisplayMonitorsExample
{
    [ StructLayout( LayoutKind.Sequential ) ]
    struct Rect
    {
        public int left;
        public int top;
        public int right;
        public int bottom;
    }

     [ StructLayout( LayoutKind.Sequential ) ]
    struct MonitorInfo
    {
        public uint size;
        public Rect monitor;
        public Rect work;
        public uint flags;
    }

    class Class1
    {
        delegate bool MonitorEnumDelegate( IntPtr hMonitor,
            IntPtr hdcMonitor,
            ref Rect lprcMonitor,
            IntPtr dwData );

        [ DllImport( "user32.dll" ) ]
        static extern bool EnumDisplayMonitors( IntPtr hdc,
            IntPtr lprcClip,
            MonitorEnumDelegate lpfnEnum,
            IntPtr dwData );

        [ DllImport( "user32.dll" ) ]
        static extern bool GetMonitorInfo( IntPtr hmon,
            ref MonitorInfo mi );

        static bool MonitorEnum( IntPtr hMonitor,
            IntPtr hdcMonitor,
            ref Rect lprcMonitor,
            IntPtr dwData )
        {
```

```
            MonitorInfo mi = new MonitorInfo();
            mi.size = (uint)Marshal.SizeOf( mi );
            bool success = GetMonitorInfo( hMonitor, ref mi );

            // do something with the information

            return true;
        }

        [STAThread]
        static void Main(string[] args)
        {
            MonitorEnumDelegate med
                = new MonitorEnumDelegate( MonitorEnum );
            EnumDisplayMonitors( IntPtr.Zero,
                                 IntPtr.Zero,
                                 med,
                                 IntPtr.Zero );
        }
    }
}
```

Writing Unsafe Code

Unsafe code is a C# language feature that allows you to manipulate memory locations directly in a manner similar to C or C++. The name comes from the fact that because the code uses pointers and not references, the loader is unable to verify that the code will not corrupt memory.

As such code has the ability to manipulate any location inside the process, it can potentially defeat any security enforcement by the CLR. Unsafe code must be fully trusted in order to execute.

Given these concerns, why would you use unsafe code? Sometimes you need to manipulate structures returned by unmanaged code that contains pointers. Sometimes the parameters to unmanaged code functions are pointers that cannot be mapped to references. In these cases, resort to unsafe code.

The Pitfalls of Pointers

If you have never programmed in C, C++, or another language that used pointers, you are probably wondering what the problem is. Pointers and references are quite similar concepts. However, references have rules that prevent you from falling into many of the traps inherent with pointers.

References must be initialized. A reference always refers to an object, whereas a pointer does not have this requirement. You could never accidentally take a code path that resulted in a reference not pointing to a valid location; but this is a common error with pointers.

Array element references are bounds checked. You cannot refer to a nonexistent element of an array without the runtime throwing an exception. No such checks occur for pointers. If the memory location is valid, you can use a pointer to access elements past the end of the array as if they were part of it. This typically results in you reading bad data or corrupting some other structure in your program.

Looking at an Unsafe Example

To see an example of unsafe code, follow these steps:

1. Create a new Windows Application project called **UnsafeHelloExample**. Methods that contain unsafe code must be declared with an unsafe modifier. The documentation often uses the term *unsafe scope* or *unsafe context* to refer to the body of such a method. Add this modifier to the Main method as follows:

   ```
   static unsafe void Main(string[] args)
   ```

2. You want Main to pass a pointer to the characters in a string to a method called SayHello. Declare a pointer to a type by appending an asterisk like this:

   ```
   char* p;
   ```

   Notice that you did not need to initialize the pointer the way you would with a reference.

 **CAUTION**   *Those familiar with C or C++ might get tripped up because the asterisk binds with the type and not the variable. The line* char *p, q; *creates two* char* *variables—not a* char* *and a* char.

3. Use the address-of operator (&) to assign a value to a pointer. In this case, you want the address of the first character in the string. Use the following:

```
string s = "Hello from unsafe code";
p = &( s.ToCharArray()[ 0 ] );
```

4. You may be surprised to learn that the garbage collector can move objects around in memory. When it does this it adjusts all the references to point at the correct location. However, it has no knowledge of pointers. If the pointer refers to a local value type variable, those are allocated on the stack so there is no problem. In this case, the character array is not on the stack. You need to tell the garbage collector not to move objects you are using with pointers so that the address remains stable. Do this using the `fixed` statement. You combine the allocation and assignment to a pointer inside the `fixed` statement. So replace the preceding lines with these:

```
string s = "Hello from unsafe code";
fixed ( char* p = &( s.ToCharArray()[ 0 ] ) )
{
    ...
}
```

5. Now create the `SayHello` method to actually output the string. Declare it as this:

```
static unsafe void SayHello( char* p, int len )
```

An `unsafe` method can have pointer parameters. This implies that you have to call it from another `unsafe` method.

6. To output the character, you need to access the character to which the pointer refers. Do this by using the dereference operator (*), like so:

```
System.Console.Write( *p );
```

7. That takes care of the first character in the array. You now need to walk the array of characters. Do this by changing the pointer to refer to each of the characters in the array inside a loop. You can perform arithmetic on pointers to make them refer to different locations. The most useful is the increment operator (++). It adds the size of the underlying type to the pointer's value, which makes it ideal for walking arrays. There are also −,

+=, and -= operators, which work in a similar fashion. Wrap the `Write` in a loop as follows:

```
for ( int i = 0; i < len; i++, p++ )
{
    System.Console.Write( *p );
}
```

8. To build an application with unsafe code, you must pass the `/unsafe` flag to the compiler. In Visual Studio .NET, modify the project properties to allow unsafe code. Select Project ➤ Properties and when the properties dialog box opens, select the Configuration Properties folder and then the Build panel. Change the Allow Unsafe Code Blocks property to **true**, as shown in Figure 15-1.

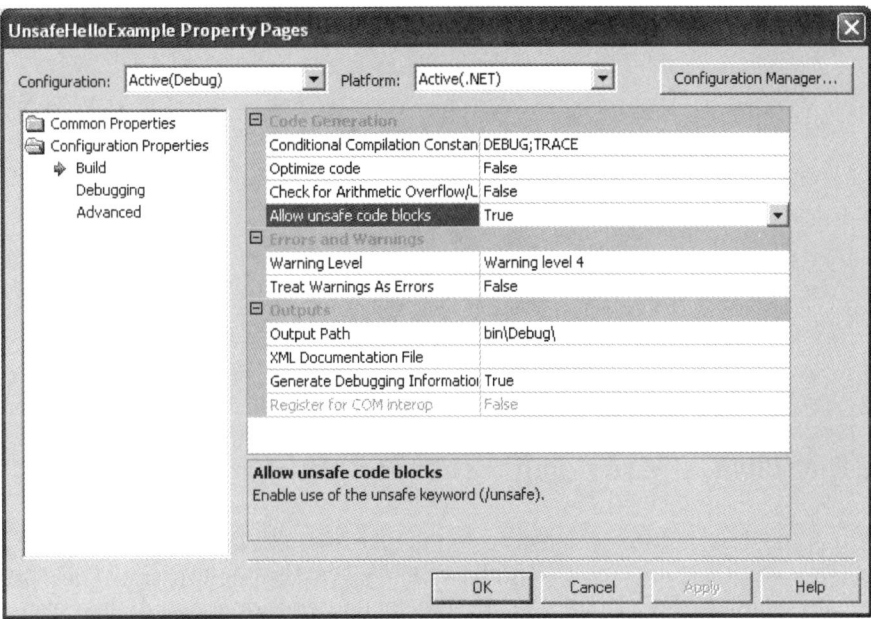

Figure 15-1. Modifying the project's properties to allow unsafe code

Listing 15-4 contains the complete example.

Listing 15-4. HelloWorld Using Unsafe Code

```
using System;

namespace UnsafeHelloExample
{
    class UnsafeHello
    {
        static unsafe void SayHello( char* p, int len )
        {
            for ( int i = 0; i < len; i++, p++ )
            {
                System.Console.Write( *p );
            }
            System.Console.WriteLine();
        }

         [STAThread]
        static unsafe void Main(string[] args)
        {
            string s = "Hello from unsafe code";
            fixed ( char* p = &( s.ToCharArray()[ 0 ] ) )
            {
                SayHello ( p, s.Length );
            }
        }
    }
}
```

Using Unsafe Code and Platform Invoke

Most of the time, pointer parameters to PInvoke methods can be mapped to a reference in C#. Occasionally, you need to use a real pointer. You must declare PInvoke methods that have pointer parameters using the `unsafe` modifier. They can only be called by other unsafe methods.

An example of this is the `NetWkstaGetInfo` function that returns a pointer to a structure, which it allocates. This structure must be released explicitly by a call to `NetApiBufferFree`. Listing 15-5 demonstrates this.

Listing 15-5. Using Unsafe Code with Platform Invoke

```
using System;
using System.Runtime.InteropServices;
using System.Text;
```

```
namespace NWGetInfoExample
{
    class NWGetInfo
    {
        [ StructLayout( LayoutKind.Sequential ) ]
        struct WkstaInfo102
        {
            public uint platform_id;
            public IntPtr computername;
            public IntPtr langroup;
            public uint ver_major;
            public uint ver_minor;
            public IntPtr lanroot;
            public uint logged_on_users;
        }

        [ DllImport( "Netapi32.dll" ) ]
        static extern unsafe int NetWkstaGetInfo(
            IntPtr servername,
            int level,
            byte** bufptr );

        [ DllImport( "Netapi32.dll" ) ]
        static extern unsafe int NetApiBufferFree( byte* bufptr );

        [STAThread]
        static unsafe void Main(string[] args)
        {
            byte* bp = null;
            int rc = NetWkstaGetInfo( IntPtr.Zero, 102, &bp );

            WkstaInfo102* wip = (WkstaInfo102*)bp;
            System.Console.WriteLine(
                "System {0} has {1} users logged on",
                Marshal.PtrToStringAuto( wip->computername ),
                wip->logged_on_users );

            rc = NetApiBufferFree( bp );
        }
    }
}
```

Understanding Stack Allocation

In an unsafe method you can obtain a block of memory from the stack by using the stackalloc initializer as follows:

```
char* name = stackalloc char[ 256 ];
```

Stack allocation has the advantage that the block does not need to be garbage collected, as it is freed when the block goes out of scope. Being on the stack, it also does not need to be fixed. Listing 15-6 demonstrates using stackalloc with PInvoke.

Listing 15-6. Using stackalloc

```
using System;
using System.Runtime.InteropServices;

namespace StackAllocationExample
{
    class StackAllocator
    {
        [ DllImport( "kernel32.dll" ) ]
        static extern unsafe bool GetComputerNameW( char* name,
            ref ulong size );

        [STAThread]
        static unsafe void Main(string[] args)
        {
            ulong size = 256;
            char* name = stackalloc char[ (int)size ];

            bool success = GetComputerNameW( name, ref size );

            for ( uint i = 0; i < size; i++, name++ )
            {
                System.Console.Write( *name );
            }
            System.Console.WriteLine();
        }
    }
}
```

> **NOTE** *The* stackalloc *initializer is not valid inside a* catch *or* finally *block.*

Hosting the .NET Runtime

Hosting the JVM or the CLR by definition requires you to resort to native code. To load the JVM into a process and run a method, perform the following steps:

1. Create the JVM by calling JNI_CreateJavaVM.

2. Load a class into the JVM by calling the FindClass method.

3. Invoke a static method on the class to start execution. Use the GetStaticMethodID and CallStaticVoidMethod methods to do this.

The steps for the CLR are similar:

1. Load the CLR by calling CorBindToRuntimeEx.

2. Obtain a reference to the default AppDomain by calling the GetDefaultDomain method.

3. To run the Main method, call ExecuteAssembly. Otherwise, use Load and then reflection through COM interop to locate the desired method and run it.

The following example loads the CLR and runs the HelloWorld program from Chapter 1, "Introducing C#":

1. Create a new Visual C++ project called **CLRHostExample** selecting the Win32 Project template, as shown in Figure 15-2.

2. Click OK. This opens the Win32 Application Wizard dialog box shown in Figure 15-3.

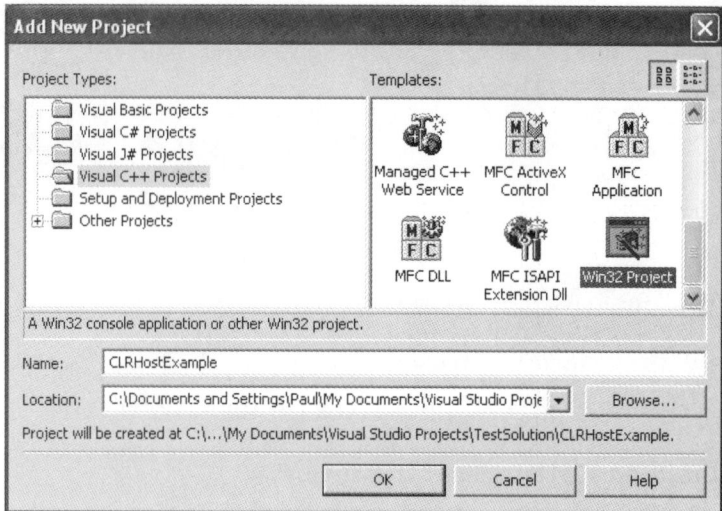

Figure 15-2. Selecting the Win32 Project type from Visual C++ Projects

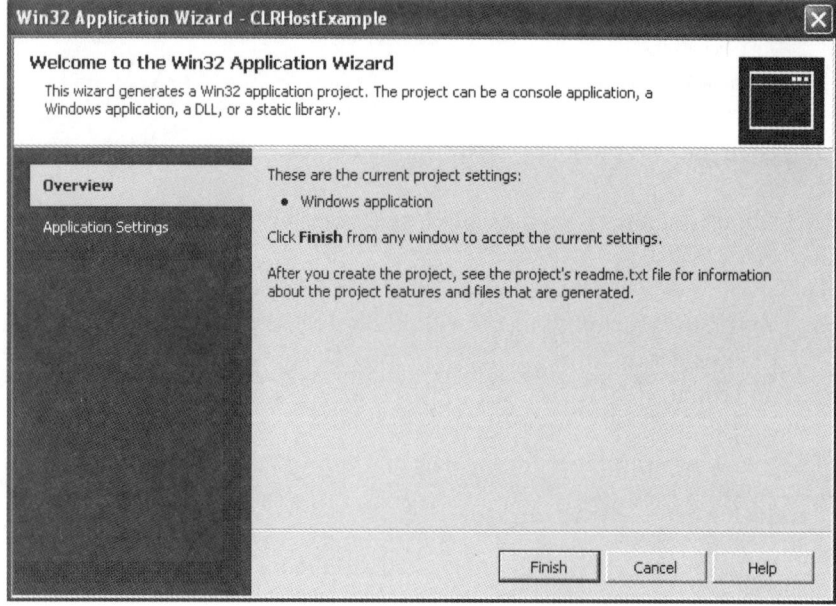

Figure 15-3. The Win32 Application Wizard dialog box

3. Select the Application Settings tab and change the Application Type option to Console Application, as shown in Figure 15-4. Then click Finish. This creates the project.

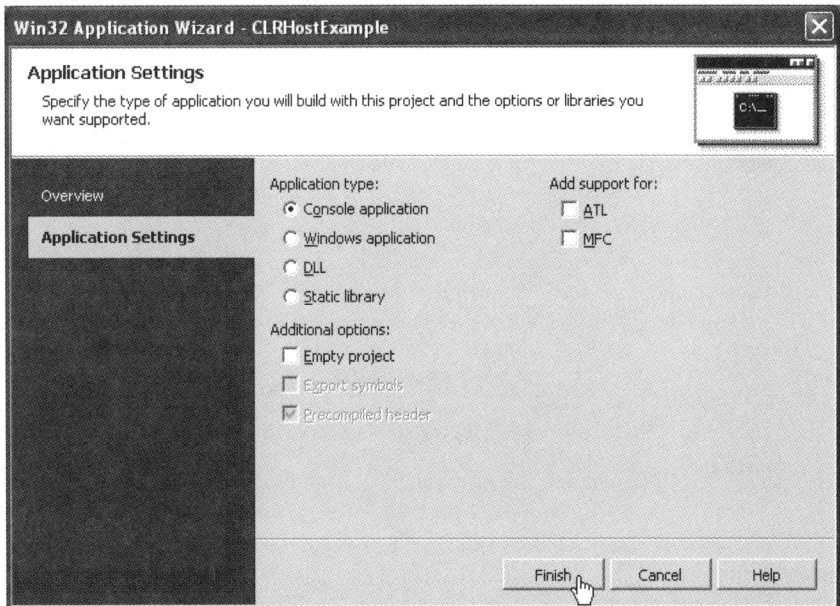

Figure 15-4. Changing the Application Type option to Console Application

4. Open CLRHostExample.cpp and enter the code shown in Listing 15-7.

Listing 15-7. Hosting the CLR in Unmanaged C++

```
#include "stdafx.h"

#include "mscoree.h"


#import <mscorlib.tlb> raw_interfaces_only \
    high_property_prefixes("_get","_put","_putref")
using namespace mscorlib;

int _tmain(int argc, _TCHAR* argv[])
{
    ICorRuntimeHost *pCor = NULL;
    IUnknown *pUnk = NULL;
    _AppDomain *pDomain = NULL;
    long retVal;

    HRESULT hr = CorBindToRuntimeEx( L"v1.0.3705",
        L"wks",
        STARTUP_LOADER_OPTIMIZATION_SINGLE_DOMAIN,
```

```
            CLSID_CorRuntimeHost,
            IID_ICorRuntimeHost,
            (PVOID*)&pCor );

    hr = pCor->Start();

    hr = pCor->GetDefaultDomain( &pUnk );

    hr = pUnk->QueryInterface( __uuidof( _AppDomain ),
            (PVOID*)&pDomain );

    hr = pDomain->ExecuteAssembly_2(
            _bstr_t( "C:\\path to my chapter 1\\HelloWorld.exe" ),
            &retVal );

    pDomain->Release();
    pUnk->Release();

    return 0;
}
```

5. Modify the call to `ExecuteAssembly_2` to refer to your HelloWorld example from Chapter 1. "Introducing C#."

6. Right-click the project and select Properties to open the properties dialog box. Open the C/C++ folder and then select the General node.

7. Enter the path to the .NET Framework SDK's include directory in the entry labeled Additional Include Directories. On my system, this is in the default location of **C:\Program Files\Microsoft Visual Studio .NET\FrameworkSDK\include**, but you should verify that this is correct for you.

8. Now select the Linker folder and then its General node. Enter the path to the .NET Framework SDK's library directory in the entry labeled Additional Library Directories. For me this is **C:\Program Files\Microsoft Visual Studio .NET\FrameworkSDK\Lib**, but your system may differ.

9. Select the Input node of the Linker folder. Enter **mscoree.lib** in the Additional Dependencies field. Click OK.

10. You can now build and run the application. You should see the familiar message in the console window.

A *Closer* Look at CorBindToRuntimeEx

The signature of CorBindToRuntimeEx is as follows:

```
STDAPI CorBindToRuntimeEx(LPCWSTR pwszVersion,
    LPCWSTR pwszBuildFlavor,
    DWORD startupFlags,
    REFCLSID rclsid,
    REFIID riid,
    LPVOID FAR *ppv);
```

The first parameter specifies the build of the runtime you want to use. The preceding example passed "v1.0.3705", which specifies the .NET Framework Version 1 release. You can also specify NULL for the latest build installed on the system.

There are two versions of the CLR installed on each system: the workstation and server versions. The server version of the CLR is optimized for multiprocessor server processes and the workstation version for interactive applications. The only way to get the server version is by writing an unmanaged loader and passing "svr" as the second parameter to CorBindToRuntimeEx. Use "wks" to request the workstation version. Fortunately, you do not have to determine if the system is capable of running the server CLR. If you ask for the server CLR and the request cannot be honored, the workstation CLR is silently substituted.

The third parameter is a set of flags that mostly enable you to control how code is loaded into the appdomains within the CLR. The notable exception is the value STARTUP_LOADER_SAFEMODE, which allows you to require the exact build you specified regardless of binding policy.

The fourth and fifth parameters are always coded as shown in the example, specifying the COM coclass and interface ID for the runtime.

The final parameter is the pointer to the location where the address of the runtime instance will be placed (in other words, the real return value). As always, the actual return value is a HRESULT.

CAUTION *The code in the example does not test the* HRESULT *values for errors to keep the example clear and focused on the task of launching code in the runtime. Always test the return values for errors in production code.*

Running Code in an AppDomain

Once the runtime has been loaded into the process, you need to load an assembly into it. You do not load code directly into the .NET runtime, you load it into an appdomain within the runtime. Although you can create appdomains at this point, fortunately a default instance is created when you load the runtime.

Obtain a reference to the default AppDomain by calling GetDefaultDomain. The AppDomain is marshaled using COM, so you have to use QueryInterface and Release correctly.

The easiest way to run managed code in your appdomain is to call ExecuteAssembly. This will invoke the same Main method that would be run if you executed your assembly directly from the shell. The other option is to load in a class or assembly and then use COM interop to invoke a method from your unmanaged code.

In some cases you may want to load a class from unmanaged code, which then uses managed code to create further appdomains and load in the code to do the real work. Even if you are comfortable working in C++, you should consider this option as C# is a more productive language to use.

Summary

C# provides excellent support for interoperability with unmanaged code. PInvoke avoids the need to resort to C or C++ as you would have done with JNI. Hosting the CLR is slightly more difficult than hosting the JVM because of appdomains. If Microsoft could provide a simple build-time flag to indicate you want the server runtime, many people would never need to learn how to host the CLR.

CHAPTER 16

Migrating to .NET

You have read all the preceding chapters and have decided that .NET is part of your future. The question is, "How do I get there from here?" That is the purpose of this chapter. You need to know what your options are.

To some extent it depends on where *there* is. For some it will be to develop your next project using .NET, and for others it will be to switch technologies on existing projects.

It also depends on where *here* is. Options are available to users of Microsoft's Visual J++ product that are not available to others.

JUMPing to .NET

Shortly after Microsoft announced .NET, it announced the JUMP to .NET program for users of its Visual J++ product. JUMP stands for Java User Migration Path. There are two products that have come out of that effort that are in beta at this time, Java Language Conversion Assistant (JLCA) and Visual J#.

Java Language Conversion Assistant

JLCA is an add-in to Visual Studio .NET that converts Visual J++ projects into C# projects. It does not provide any way to specify its input other than as a Visual J++ project file. As a result, it will be of little use to other developers, even if they have Java 1.1 code to migrate.

The beta version only converts statements using classes from the JDK 1.1.4 and com.ms libraries that were present in Visual J++. You need to complete the conversion process by hand for any other class libraries you use. As a beta, it is incomplete and does not convert the full set of classes.

The read-me file for JLCA hints that it may be enhanced to process other files including Java Server Pages (JSP). At that time, it may offer a chance to process non-Visual J++ Java code.

Visual J#

Visual J# is the successor to Microsoft's Visual J++. Visual J# targets the Common Language Runtime (CLR), not the Java Virtual Machine (JVM). Microsoft goes to great lengths to point out that it is not endorsed by Sun. Visual J# supports many of the Java class libraries from JDK 1.1.4 as well as the .NET classes.

Visual J# includes an upgrade wizard that can import a Visual J++ project and convert it to a Visual J# project. As with JLCA, it does not support individual Java files. It only supports entire projects, so it is of no use to developers moving from other platforms.

Visual J# is not just a migration tool; it is a full language in Visual Studio .NET that has a full set of templates and supports building applications in the designer. Most of the applications you have built in the course of reading this book can be built in J# by following similar steps. To demonstrate this, build the WinForms HelloWorld application using J# instead of C#.

NOTE   *You will need to install Visual J# to do this. At the time of writing, Beta 2 was available for free download from MSDN.*

Follow these steps:

1. Create a new project, but instead of selecting from the C# projects, select Windows Application from the Visual J# Projects folder, as shown in Figure 16-1. This will create a WinForms project that looks almost identical to the one created in Chapter 4, "Using WinForms." The fact that the source files have a .jsl suffix will be the only immediate difference.

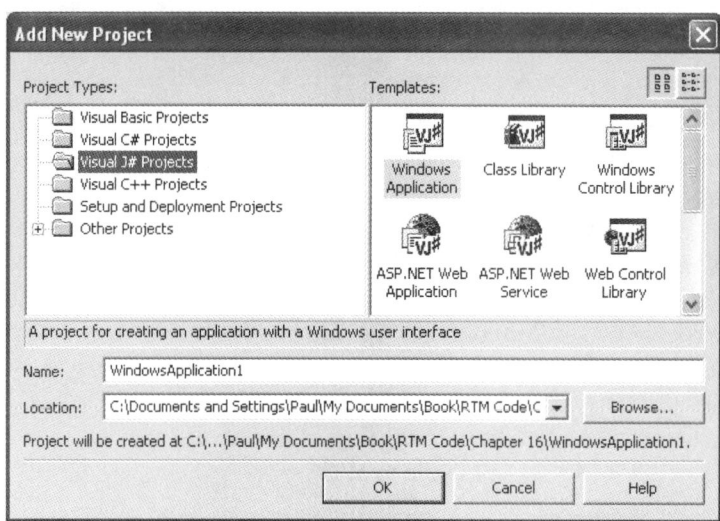

Figure 16-1. Selecting a project template from the Visual J# Projects folder

2. Create the user interface in the designer exactly as you would for a C# project. Make it resemble Figure 16-2.

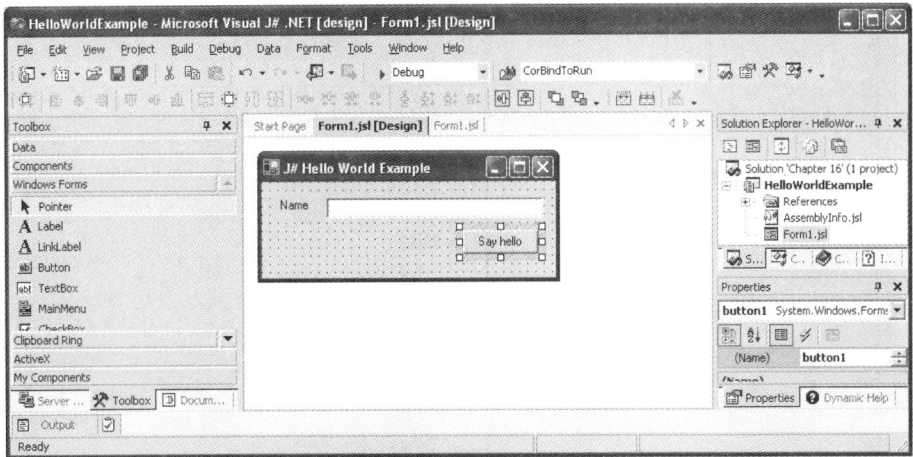

Figure 16-2. The WinForms interface for HelloWorld in J#

3. Now double-click the Button to create the button click handler that looks much like the C# handler. Complete it as follows:

```
private void button1_Click (System.Object sender,
                                System.EventArgs e)
{
    MessageBox.Show( this,
                    "Hello " + textBox1.get_Text() + " from J#" );
}
```

The only thing that indicates it is J# and not C# is that the Text property is accessed using the get_Text method.

4. Now build the application and run it like any other .NET application. The only restriction is that to run Visual J# applications you must install the Visual J# Redistributable Package. You can add this as a merge module to a deployment project.

Visual J# includes a notable feature: the JbImp tool. You can use it to convert Java byte codes from a class or JAR file to Microsoft Intermediate Language (MSIL) in a .NET assembly. The intent is to allow you to continue to use classes for which you do not have the source. The classes must not include any byte codes from

JDKs above the 1.1.4 release and should not use methods from beyond JDK 1.1.4. There are other restrictions, including no support for RMI or JNI.

Some of you are probably asking, "Why would I use C# when I could use J#?" Consider the following points:

- At the time of writing, Visual J# is still a beta product, whereas C# is released and a core language in the .NET initiative.

- Visual J# does not fully support some features of .NET, including delegates, events, value types, and enumerations.

- Who knows how Sun will react when Visual J# is released? Given the history of Microsoft, Sun, and Java, you have to be cautious.

- You will be able to find new C# developers more easily than people with J# skills.

Some, who are not even existing Visual J++ users, may try to mitigate their risk by using Visual J# as a stepping stone. Even in its Beta 2 form, you can build large Java projects successfully under J#. Evaluate your own situation and choose the option that seems right for you.

Exploring Migration Strategies for the Rest of Us

If you do not use Visual J++, you come back to answering what *there* means to you. Are you planning to just do new development in .NET, convert an existing project, or continue development of an existing project using C# instead of Java?

Creating New Projects in .NET

This is the easiest path. Your new development will be in C# and .NET, and you are not going to attempt to convert anything you already have. Your biggest challenge is getting your team trained in .NET development.

If you are coming from a non-Windows background, the learning curve will be steeper. Develop some prototypes before taking on a project. If you can add an experienced Windows developer who wants to learn C# and .NET, you will make fewer mistakes. You are also setting up your team to help one another. Your Java team will have an easier time with C# and can help the Windows person; nobody is "the guru."

Do not cut corners and try to save money by not using Visual Studio .NET and relying on the Software Development Kit (SDK) alone. This is a false economy.

Many of the productivity gains in .NET development come from Visual Studio .NET. If your developers cost you $50 an hour, saving 20 hours of development time will pay for a copy of Visual Studio .NET Professional.

Converting Existing Projects

With Microsoft already in this space, albeit with a tool that only targets Visual J++, nobody else has announced the intention to offer a conversion tool. If you really want to do this, you are going to have to write the conversion utility yourself or have your developers convert everything by hand.

In either case you need to get your staff trained in C# and .NET development. Converting a small application would be a great training exercise.

You will not just be trading languages; you will be trading the underlying technologies. Make sure you understand their different characteristics, such as the different garbage collection schemes in Remote Method Invocation (RMI) and .NET remoting. A straight translation may not perform anything like the original.

Switching to .NET for New Development in Existing Projects

This is the most likely scenario and also the most complex. First, find a point where you can interface your existing Java project with .NET.

For many people this point will be the database. It does not have to be SQL Server. ADO.NET has the OleDB managed data provider, which supports mainstream databases such as Oracle. It also has the ODBC managed data provider that can access any database with an ODBC driver. This includes databases on non-Windows platforms including PostgreSQL and MySQL, which are popular choices on Linux.

The other popular technology you can exploit is Web Services. ASP.NET Web Services can communicate with many Java toolkits, including Sun's Web Services Developer Pack (WSDP), so whether you want to consume an existing service or introduce new services, you have a good point of interoperability. Remember that many toolkits default to encoding parameters using Section 5 encoding rules, whereas ASP.NET Web Services default to Literal XML encoding. Many older toolkits support only Section 5 encoding. Specifying a compatible encoding scheme, possibly using the `SoapRpcService` attribute, can be critical to successful interoperability with other Simple Object Access Protocol (SOAP) toolkits. If you use another middleware product, such as a Message-Oriented Middleware (MOM) product, which has both Java and Windows interfaces, that may be another opportunity. It does not have to include a managed interface as you can exploit COM interop or PInvoke as appropriate.

Common Object Request Broker Architecture (CORBA) is often used to provide interoperability between Java and applications written in other languages. The absence of a CORBA product that supports managed code is notable. You have to resort to COM-CORBA bridge products such as Iona's COMET to take this route.

Summary

Migrating to a new platform is always fraught with risk. A carefully thought out plan can help manage that risk. The more opportunity you have to prototype and become familiar with C# and .NET, the better off you will be when it comes time to start a real project.

However you decide to make the trip, I hope you enjoy the journey as much as I did, and I hope that by writing this book, I was able to help.

Index

Apress Titles

ISBN	PRICE	AUTHOR	TITLE
1-893115-73-9	$34.95	Abbott	Voice Enabling Web Applications: VoiceXML and Beyond
1-893115-01-1	$39.95	Appleman	Dan Appleman's Win32 API Puzzle Book and Tutorial for Visual Basic Programmers
1-893115-23-2	$29.95	Appleman	How Computer Programming Works
1-893115-97-6	$39.95	Appleman	Moving to VB .NET: Strategies, Concepts, and Code
1-59059-023-6	$39.95	Baker	Adobe Acrobat 5: The Professional User's Guide
1-59059-039-2	$49.95	Barnaby	Distributed .NET Programming
1-893115-09-7	$29.95	Baum	Dave Baum's Definitive Guide to LEGO MINDSTORMS
1-893115-84-4	$29.95	Baum, Gasperi, Hempel, and Villa	Extreme MINDSTORMS: An Advanced Guide to LEGO MINDSTORMS
1-893115-82-8	$59.95	Ben-Gan/Moreau	Advanced Transact-SQL for SQL Server 2000
1-893115-91-7	$39.95	Birmingham/Perry	Software Development on a Leash
1-893115-48-8	$29.95	Bischof	The .NET Languages: A Quick Translation Guide
1-59059-053-8	$44.95	Bock/Stromquist/ Fischer/Smith	.NET Security
1-893115-67-4	$49.95	Borge	Managing Enterprise Systems with the Windows Script Host
1-59059-019-8	$49.95	Cagle	SVG Programming: The Graphical Web
1-893115-28-3	$44.95	Challa/Laksberg	Essential Guide to Managed Extensions for C++
1-893115-39-9	$44.95	Chand	A Programmer's Guide to ADO.NET in C#
1-59059-015-5	$39.95	Clark	An Introduction to Object Oriented Programming with Visual Basic .NET
1-893115-44-5	$29.95	Cook	Robot Building for Beginners
1-893115-99-2	$39.95	Cornell/Morrison	Programming VB .NET: A Guide for Experienced Programmers
1-893115-72-0	$39.95	Curtin	Developing Trust: Online Privacy and Security
1-59059-014-7	$44.95	Drol	Object-Oriented Macromedia Flash MX
1-59059-008-2	$29.95	Duncan	The Career Programmer: Guerilla Tactics for an Imperfect World
1-893115-71-2	$39.95	Ferguson	Mobile .NET
1-893115-90-9	$49.95	Finsel	The Handbook for Reluctant Database Administrators
1-59059-024-4	$49.95	Fraser	Real World ASP.NET: Building a Content Management System
1-893115-42-9	$44.95	Foo/Lee	XML Programming Using the Microsoft XML Parser
1-893115-55-0	$34.95	Frenz	Visual Basic and Visual Basic .NET for Scientists and Engineers
1-59059-038-4	$49.95	Gibbons	Java Development to .NET Development
1-893115-85-2	$34.95	Gilmore	A Programmer's Introduction to PHP 4.0
1-893115-36-4	$34.95	Goodwill	Apache Jakarta-Tomcat
1-893115-17-8	$59.95	Gross	A Programmer's Introduction to Windows DNA
1-893115-62-3	$39.95	Gunnerson	A Programmer's Introduction to C#, Second Edition
1-59059-009-0	$49.95	Harris/Macdonald	Moving to ASP.NET: Web Development with VB .NET
1-893115-30-5	$49.95	Harkins/Reid	SQL: Access to SQL Server
1-893115-10-0	$34.95	Holub	Taming Java Threads
1-893115-04-6	$34.95	Hyman/Vaddadi	Mike and Phani's Essential C++ Techniques
1-893115-96-8	$59.95	Jorelid	J2EE FrontEnd Technologies: A Programmer's Guide to Servlets, JavaServer Pages, and Enterprise JavaBeans
1-893115-49-6	$39.95	Kilburn	Palm Programming in Basic
1-893115-50-X	$34.95	Knudsen	Wireless Java: Developing with Java 2, Micro Edition
1-893115-79-8	$49.95	Kofler	Definitive Guide to Excel VBA

ISBN	PRICE	AUTHOR	TITLE
1-893115-57-7	$39.95	Kofler	MySQL
1-893115-87-9	$39.95	Kurata	Doing Web Development: Client-Side Techniques
1-893115-75-5	$44.95	Kurniawan	Internet Programming with VB
1-893115-38-0	$24.95	Lafler	Power AOL: A Survival Guide
1-893115-46-1	$36.95	Lathrop	Linux in Small Business: A Practical User's Guide
1-893115-19-4	$49.95	Macdonald	Serious ADO: Universal Data Access with Visual Basic
1-893115-06-2	$39.95	Marquis/Smith	A Visual Basic 6.0 Programmer's Toolkit
1-893115-22-4	$27.95	McCarter	David McCarter's VB Tips and Techniques
1-59059-021-X	$34.95	Moore	Karl Moore's Visual Basic .NET: The Tutorials
1-893115-76-3	$49.95	Morrison	C++ For VB Programmers
1-59059-003-1	$39.95	Nakhimovsky/Meyers	XML Programming: Web Applications and Web Services with JSP and ASP
1-893115-80-1	$39.95	Newmarch	A Programmer's Guide to Jini Technology
1-893115-58-5	$49.95	Oellermann	Architecting Web Services
1-59059-020-1	$44.95	Patzer	JSP Examples and Best Practices
1-893115-81-X	$39.95	Pike	SQL Server: Common Problems, Tested Solutions
1-59059-017-1	$34.95	Rainwater	Herding Cats: A Primer for Programmers Who Lead Programmers
1-59059-025-2	$49.95	Rammer	Advanced .NET Remoting
1-893115-20-8	$34.95	Rischpater	Wireless Web Development
1-893115-93-3	$34.95	Rischpater	Wireless Web Development with PHP and WAP
1-893115-89-5	$59.95	Shemitz	Kylix: The Professional Developer's Guide and Reference
1-893115-40-2	$39.95	Sill	The qmail Handbook
1-893115-24-0	$49.95	Sinclair	From Access to SQL Server
1-893115-94-1	$29.95	Spolsky	User Interface Design for Programmers
1-893115-53-4	$44.95	Sweeney	Visual Basic for Testers
1-59059-002-3	$44.95	Symmonds	Internationalization and Localization Using Microsoft .NET
1-59059-010-4	$54.95	Thomsen	Database Programming with C#
1-893115-29-1	$44.95	Thomsen	Database Programming with Visual Basic .NET
1-893115-65-8	$39.95	Tiffany	Pocket PC Database Development with eMbedded Visual Basic
1-59059-027-9	$59.95	Torkelson/Petersen/Torkelson	Programming the Web with Visual Basic .NET
1-893115-59-3	$59.95	Troelsen	C# and the .NET Platform
1-59059-011-2	$59.95	Troelsen	COM and .NET Interoperability
1-893115-26-7	$59.95	Troelsen	Visual Basic .NET and the .NET Platform
1-893115-54-2	$49.95	Trueblood/Lovett	Data Mining and Statistical Analysis Using SQL
1-893115-68-2	$54.95	Vaughn	ADO.NET and ADO Examples and Best Practices for VB Programmers, Second Edition
1-59059-012-0	$49.95	Vaughn/Blackburn	ADO.NET Examples and Best Practices for C# Programmers
1-893115-83-6	$44.95	Wells	Code Centric: T-SQL Programming with Stored Procedures and Triggers
1-893115-95-X	$49.95	Welschenbach	Cryptography in C and C++
1-893115-05-4	$39.95	Williamson	Writing Cross-Browser Dynamic HTML
1-893115-78-X	$49.95	Zukowski	Definitive Guide to Swing for Java 2, Second Edition
1-893115-92-5	$49.95	Zukowski	Java Collections
1-893115-98-4	$54.95	Zukowski	Learn Java with JBuilder 6

Apress Titles Publishing SOON!

ISBN	AUTHOR	TITLE
1-59059-022-8	Alapati	Expert Oracle 9i Database Administration
1-59059-041-4	Bock	CIL Programming: Under the Hood of .NET
1-59059-000-7	Cornell	Programming C#
1-59059-033-3	Fraser	Managed C++ and .NET Development
1-59059-030-9	Habibi/Camerlengo/ Patterson	Java 1.4 and the Sun Certified Developer Exam
1-59059-006-6	Hetland	Instant Python with Ten Instant Projects
1-59059-044-9	MacDonald	.NET User Interfaces with VB .NET: Windows Forms and Custom Controls
1-59059-001-5	McMahon	A Programmer's Introduction to ASP.NET WebForms in Visual Basic .NET
1-893115-74-7	Millar	Enterprise Development: A Programmer's Handbook
1-893115-27-5	Morrill	Tuning and Customizing a Linux System
1-59059-028-7	Rischpater	Wireless Web Development, Second Edition
1-59059-026-0	Smith	Writing Add-Ins for .NET
1-893115-43-7	Stephenson	Standard VB: An Enterprise Developer's Reference for VB 6 and VB .NET
1-59059-035-X	Symmonds	GDI+ Programming in C# and VB .NET
1-59059-032-5	Thomsen	Database Programming with Visual Basic .NET, Second Edition
1-59059-007-4	Thomsen	Building Web Services with VB .NET
1-59059-018-X	Tregar	Writing Perl Modules for CPAN
1-59059-004-X	Valiaveedu	SQL Server 2000 and Business Intelligence in an XML/.NET World

Available at bookstores nationwide or from Springer Verlag New York, Inc. at 1-800-777-4643; fax 1-212-533-3503. Contact us for more information at sales@apress.com.

books for professionals by professionals™

About Apress

Apress, located in Berkeley, CA, is a fast-growing, innovative publishing company devoted to meeting the needs of existing and potential programming professionals. Simply put, the "A" in Apress stands for *"The Author's Press™"* and its books have *"The Expert's Voice™."* Apress' unique approach to publishing grew out of conversations between its founders Gary Cornell and Dan Appleman, authors of numerous best-selling, highly regarded books for programming professionals. In 1998 they set out to create a publishing company that emphasized quality above all else. Gary and Dan's vision has resulted in the publication of over 50 titles by leading software professionals, all of which have *The Expert's Voice™.*

Do You Have What It Takes to Write for Apress?

Apress is rapidly expanding its publishing program. If you can write and refuse to compromise on the quality of your work, if you believe in doing more than rehashing existing documentation, and if you're looking for opportunities and rewards that go far beyond those offered by traditional publishing houses, we want to hear from you!

Consider these innovations that we offer all of our authors:

- **Top royalties with *no* hidden switch statements**
  Authors typically only receive half of their normal royalty rate on foreign sales. In contrast, Apress' royalty rate remains the same for both foreign and domestic sales.

- **A mechanism for authors to obtain equity in Apress**
  Unlike the software industry, where stock options are essential to motivate and retain software professionals, the publishing industry has adhered to an outdated compensation model based on royalties alone. In the spirit of most software companies, Apress reserves a significant portion of its equity for authors.

- **Serious treatment of the technical review process**
  Each Apress book has a technical reviewing team whose remuneration depends in part on the success of the book since they too receive royalties.

Moreover, through a partnership with Springer-Verlag, New York, Inc., one of the world's major publishing houses, Apress has significant venture capital behind it. Thus, we have the resources to produce the highest quality books *and* market them aggressively.

If you fit the model of the Apress author who can write a book that gives the "professional what he or she needs to know™," then please contact one of our Editorial Directors, Gary Cornell (gary_cornell@apress.com), Dan Appleman (dan_appleman@apress.com), Peter Blackburn (peter_blackburn@apress.com), Jason Gilmore (jason_gilmore@apress.com), Karen Watterson (karen_watterson@apress.com), or John Zukowski (john_zukowski@apress.com) for more information.